Who Killed
Dripping Lewis?

The unsolved murder in Pontypool in 1939

By Monty Dart

CONTENTS

INTRODUCTION

Capital punishment in the UK, conducted by hanging was the ultimate solution for the crime of murder prior to November 1st 1965. The last hanging in Wales was that of 21 year old Vivian Teed on the 6th of May 1958, a case I researched for 'Capital Punishment in Britain' by Richard Clark[1]. Vivian Frederick Teed of Manor Road, Manselton, Swansea was charged with the murder of 73 year old William Williams who ran the sub Post Office and tobacconist's shop which was part of his home at 870 Carmarthen Road, Fforestfach in the suburbs of Swansea on the evening of Friday 15th November 1957.

The crime was discovered the following morning when post office employee, twenty one year old Margaret John couldn't open the door and on looking through the letter box and saw Mr Williams lying in the hall. She called the police who forced the door and discovered Mr Williams' badly beaten body, the skull fractured from multiple hammer blows. Examination of the crime scene revealed some size 6 bloody footprints in the hallway and also a woman's silk stocking under the body. Teed was quickly arrested. Nowadays, even if the death penalty still existed it would be doubtful if Teed would have suffered the final punishment of death.

The jury at his trial had difficulty coming to a decision, they returned to the jury room 3 times. One juror held out, stating his belief that Teed had 'diminished or impaired responsibility.' All but one doctor disagreed. Eventually Mr Justice Salmon donned the black cap and sentenced Teed under the Homicide Act of 1957, which had been created in March of that year just two months before the murder. Capital

---

[1] See www.capitalpunishmentuk.org

punishment represented 'an eye for an eye' justice. However there was no such punishment for the person or persons who murdered William Alfred Lewis – they have never been brought to justice despite a manhunt that crossed counties and countries.

William Alfred Lewis, also known locally as Dripping Lewis died aged 59, at his large detached home, Plasmont House, in Pontypool, Monmouthshire, South Wales. His ending is my beginning. I met him quite by chance, not in this world but in a thick file of Scotland Yard documents. I was researching Welsh murder cases that had ended in the perpetrator suffering the fate of his or her victim – death. A pronouncement by a Judge as *'Hanging by the rope until dead'* was their fate.

There are many versions in the folk-lore of Pontypool of how Dripping Lewis met his death. The tales of those arrested, of those acquitted and those who got away with it are part of Pontypool history. Many people in Pontypool think they know the identity of the murderer or murderers, names are still mentioned in connection with the murder. However, this book deals with the facts, nothing more, nothing less. It also recognises those suspected but subsequently cleared by diligent police investigation. Alibis might have been fully investigated and found infallible - but dirt sticks. Using contemporaneous reports and statements from the Scotland Yard file, this book is a snapshot in time, a few months in the life of pre-war Pontypool.

If your forebears lived in Pontypool in 1939 it is likely that they knew at least one person of the 400 who were interviewed by the police or one the additional 275 who had given a statement. Shop keepers, householders, pub landlords and their customers, gossip-mongers and rumour-spreaders all feature in this sad tale. So many people lived in property owned by Lewis and his sisters; he was a well-known man – albeit reclusive. People still talk about his murder today, remembering tales from their childhood or from family reminiscences. In the file are the clinical photographs taken by the photographer for the Monmouthshire Constabulary. A man lies diagonally on his bed, his head turned away from the camera and partially obscured by an uncased pillow. Splashes of blood can be seen on the bedclothes, which have been pulled off the bed and thrown back on again. The pink wallpaper has splashes of blood on it. There is blood on the bed, including perhaps the linear impression of the murder weapon, placed momentarily by the killer. Papers have been tossed upon the thin mat on the floor. What can be seen of the room on the police photographs certainly doesn't look like the bedroom of a wealthy property owner, pillar of the community.

In other rooms drawers have been ransacked, the contents strewn on the floor, the aftermath of a burglary which ended in the death of a quiet, unassuming, affable man. There is a photograph of three keys, found on the floor outside the bedroom door, what is the significance of the keys; did they hold a clue to the mystery?

The list of suspects in the murder of William Alfred Lewis reads like the cast of a West End farce. The Scotsman with an accordion and wooden leg, the two black men who sold rheumatism cures in Newport Market, a Vicar, a lady friend (or three). The names of local licensed premises and public houses - The Pineapple, The Unicorn, The Crown, The Castle, The Winning Horse amongst others, frequent this sad account.

Pontypool in 1939 suddenly had an influx of a large, itinerant male population. Men from all over the country had come to work at the ammunition factory; most of them lived in lodgings. The pub, a couple of beers and a game of darts was their only entertainment, especially for those who lived in rooms and couldn't relax at home with their own family of an evening. It was in the pubs that overheard remarks or incautious boasting resulted in an invitation to the police station to account for their words and actions. The meticulous work by the Pontypool Police, Scotland Yard and police forces throughout the country is revealed in the bulky file. Hundreds of statements were taken by the Scotland Yard detectives, who were chosen by their Chief for their knowledge of South Wales.

William Alfred Lewis was known locally as 'Dripping Lewis', or even 'Dripping Lewis the Pork Butcher'. It is generally acknowledged in the folklore of Pontypool that Mr Lewis was a butcher. Even on a map of old Pontypool shops, 1903 – 1912 which hangs in the office of Pontypool Museum (excellently compiled by local citizen George Booth), one shop on Crane Street is called 'Dripping Lewis Butcher', four doors along from the Market Arcade, with Mrs Baker's Cake Shop next-door to the butchers shop. Fowler's 'Lion House' was at the Cross, then Woods Chemist, with the White Lion next to it, Daniel's Grocers and William's butchers on the other side of the arcade.

In fact William Lewis was a draper; this is confirmed in the 1911 Census return, so no amount of argument can make him otherwise. He had a drapery business in Station Road, Cwm, Ebbw Vale until 1932 and when he retired from drapery he went back to the family home, Plasmont House to live with his spinster sister Sarah. Until that time he lived away only going back to the family home, Plasmont on a Sunday and returning to Cwm on Monday morning. So why the nickname

Dripping Lewis? Could it be that he was 'dripping with money'? Another theory which is the one I prefer was put to me by a Pontypool man born and bred. He said

> 'During the Depression of the 1920 many of the Pontypool citizens were able to feed their families because of the generosity of the Lewis family. Using their butcher's shops and slaughter-houses they distributed 'dripping' (the fat and solids rendered from cooking meat) to the poor. Bread and dripping was a cheap but nutritious meal.

William's brothers Thomas and Frederick are noted in the 1901 census as 'slaughter-house workers', in the case of Frederick *'of his own accord'* – which suggests that he either owned slaughter house premises or was a self-employed slaughterer, so there was a history of butchery in the family. Miriam Lewis (nee Lloyd) their mother also came from a family of butchers and slaughter-house owners, no doubt that is how she and Thomas her husband met. Half of Jubilee Buildings, owned by William Lewis was a meat market, as was a shop in Crane Street, once owned by his father and mother. However, despite the legend, William Alfred Lewis was definitely a draper.

MAY DAY 1939

May 1939 had an inauspicious start with the cancellation of the May Day Pageant. Pontypool had been busily preparing for the much awaited Pageant; it was going to be 'a blaze of music and colour'. With marching bands converging on the town from Varteg and Cwmbran it boasted a choir of over 1,200 voices chosen from the churches, Women's Institutes, operatic and dramatic societies and Trades Union members.

Town Criers had been advertising the Pageant in local towns for a number of weeks; it was to be the highlight of 1939.

FRIDAY, MAY 5, 1939   THE

Pontypool's May Day Pageant Washed Out

Article Heading in Pontypool Free Press

Unfortunately the rain started early in the morning and continued relentlessly. The performers and the audience gathered wherever they could find shelter. The Pontypool Free Press reported on Friday May 5th 1939 that cold, drizzling rain had been falling all day when Mr Norman Rutherford, the assistant pageant-master, arrived at Pontypool Park from Abertillery. Speaking through a microphone to the assembled throng of participants and spectators huddling under the grandstand he sorrowfully declared that the much awaited Pageant was totally washed-out Reluctantly, he agreed with the Pontypool Pageant Committee that

> 'It would be useless to continue with the programme. It means I would have to ask the spectators in the grandstand to stand in the rain, so that the choirs can take their place. I am very sorry as I have looked forward to the Pageant taking place. You have a fine setting, thank you so much for turning out so nobly.'

Despite the rain Mrs Obadiah Evans crowned the May Queen, Muriel Howells of Penyrheol, who was supported by her Court – Marjorie Newberry (Griffithstown), Marion Hill (Talywain) Betty Bowen (Griffithstown) and Molly Lovejoy (New Inn). Mrs Gladys Tudgay presided over the Opening

Ceremony, such as it was. Little Yvonne Jones presented sprays of flowers to the May Queen and Court and Mrs Tudgay. Mrs H. Harris (Griffithstown) presented buttonholes to the Officials. Mrs Sam Smith (New Inn) proposed a vote of thanks to the organisers which was seconded by Mrs H. Harris.

IF YOU WERE DISAPPOINTED ON MAY DAY, COME ALONG TO-MORROW TO SEE THE POSTPONED

PAGEANT of HISTORY

(which could not be held on Monday last) and which will take place

TO-MORROW (Sat.) at 6 o'clock
IN PONTYPOOL PARK

VARTEG BAND will start from VARTEG at 4.15, and PONTYPOOL MILITARY BAND from the Crown Bridge, SEBASTOPOL, at 5 o'clock.

In his response, Councillor Obadiah Evans, J.P. said to the audience

'Although the weather is bad it was nothing compared to the struggle of their forebears. They should commemorate and perpetuate the memory of the Chartists and they should not forget that the struggle was still going on'.

For those braving the rain the Pontypool Military Band picked up their sodden instruments and lead the community singing but many disappointed people went home, including the disheartened performers, some of whom were wearing costumes specially hired for the occasion from the famous stage and film costumiers Charles Fox Ltd of London. The May Day Pageant was successfully presented on the following weekend but May 1939 turned out to be a tragic month in the history of Pontypool. Little did the inhabitants know that there was a murderer in their midst and that there would be a fatal coach accident, these two incidents occurring within days of each other. Both incidents in one way or another would affect everyone in Pontypool.

HAS THE OLD MAN BEEN ABOUT YET?

When Thomas Brimble rushed breathless into Pontypool Police Station at 10.50 am on Wednesday 24th May 1939 he began a chain of events which involved a search throughout Britain and the Continent.

On the front desk was Police Constable James Thomas (No. 280). Brimble said he had discovered his employer, William Alfred Lewis dead in bed at Plasmont House, Conway Road. Constable Thomas quickly alerted Police Sergeant (No.51) Alfred Bowkett. Brimble's testimony was sufficiently alarming for Sergeant Bowkett to advise Detective Constable Victor Adams to go to the scene to see if

'Any suspicious circumstances surrounded the matter.'

Bowkett was unable to leave the Police Station himself as Petty Sessions was due to start at 11am and he was due in Court. However, his mind can't have been on Court matters and by 11.15 am he had received a message and left immediately to report to Superintendent. E. Casey. He also phoned the Chief Constable, Major Lucas - there had been a murder in Pontypool.

Pontypool Police Station

Pontypool in 1939 was a quiet Welsh market town 149 miles from London. It was once the greatest manufacturer of 'Japan Ware' a process of producing a lacquered surface upon metal, wood and papier-mâché.

Another invention, though not as decorative as the Japanware, was registered in 1893, a blacksmith, Joshua Jones of 2, Springfield Terrace, New Inn, invented an Inguinal Hernia Truss, a frightening device made of a steel band, covered in chamois leather, (Patent 10,848). He proudly pointed out its points of superiority over old trusses.

> 'No shifting when walking. Comfort to the wearer, with pressure only on necessary parts. Simple in construction and has been tested in severe case and proved highly satisfactory.' The final accolade, 'Approved of by my Medical Advisor.'

The town had a Free Library; a fire brigade consisting of 42 firemen, lights and gas were supplied by Pontypool Gas and

Water Company (est. 1850) there were numerous forges and iron mills within a short distance of the town for the manufacture of ironwork and tin plate. The Great Western Railway Company had two stations, one in Crane Street the other in Clarence Street. There were 4 reservoirs, having a capacity of 15 million gallons, including one at Cwmavon holding some 10 million gallons. A pumping plant had been erected at Cwmavon in 1894, to serve the higher parts of the district. It was also served by 8 springs, two at Cwmavon, two at Cwmyrafon, one at Nant-y-Mailor, one at Abersychan and two at The Folly. The Market building was first erected in 1846, and rebuilt in 1893/4 at a total cost of £27,000.

The town had suffered badly in the past; lack of work during the Depression had caused great deprivation to the Pontypool citizens. However the coming War was beginning to reverse this. An armament factory was being built at Glascoed and was providing work not only for the local population but men from all over Britain.

However, like every other town in Britain in May 1939, the threat of an imminent war spread uncertainty amongst the population. Gas masks were being issued; William Alfred Lewis had been fitted for his at 8.30 pm on May 22nd. As he left he said

'Let's hope I'll never have need of this.'

words that haunted Edmund Williams of 17, Brynderwen, the ARP Warden, who knew Lewis personally and was possibly one of the last (apart from the murderer) to speak to him as he fitted him with his gas mask.

The story beings on a warm day in May 1939 – with a statement made by Police Constable Thomas.

'On Wednesday, 24th of May, 1939 I was on duty at Pontypool at the station when Mr Brimble who was engaged in painting Plasmont House, Conway Road rushed into the station. He said that he had seen what appears to be the body of a man lying across the bed at the house. He had entered by the back door which was open and gone upstairs to the bedroom. He then discovered the body; he had not seen his (Lewis) injuries as a pillow was covering his face.'

So begins a story that seemed to have no end or has it, will you see the name of the murderer within these pages?

Thomas Brimble was the man who found the body. He was a builder who had worked for Mr Lewis since November 1938. He had recently agreed to decorate the exterior of Plasmont

Mr. Tom Brimble, Pontypool.

for £36 and was engaged on this at the time of the murder. In his statement, he talks of the last time he saw William Lewis.

'My name is Thomas Brimble of The Firs, Waterworks Lane, Abersychan. I last saw Mr Lewis alive on the 22nd May at about 5.00 pm. I left the house with Mr Lewis and Rev. Watkins (Lewis' brother-in-law) and went to George Street with them to see some properties. On Tuesday 23rd May about 7.30 am I was working at Plasmont all day until about 7.15 pm. During that time I saw nothing wrong with the house. I painted the outside of the window frames all around, with the exception of the northern side or Conway Road side of the house. The Conway Road was the side of the house where Mr Lewis slept. On Wednesday morning the 24th of May, at about 8.00 am I mixed my paints on the lawn. I was going to paint the walls of the house, then I thought I ought to have the windows open, so I knocked at the door but got no answer. I also knocked the door on Tuesday. I could gain access to the scullery at the rear of the house, and have been using that door as have other tradesmen and the postman. I saw that the scullery door was open and I remember it was opened on Tuesday. I went into the scullery and shouted upstairs for Mr Lewis but got no answer.'

On Tuesday 23rd. before he finished for the night, Brimble called on Mrs Barnett who lived in Plasmont Cottage (part of Plasmont House) He had borrowed a collar stud from her the previous day, because his collar was loose and now he was returning it. He asked if she had seen Mr Lewis, she hadn't; Brimble said it was very strange as Lewis was in the habit of seeing the workmen when they were about. In fact he would often help Brimble or his men when they were working at Plasmont. Mrs Barnett said something that puzzled Thomas Brimble

'I wonder if he has done something to himself?'

'There's no fear of anything like that is there?'

'I don't know, his brother hung himself and perhaps he is there now with his throat cut'[2]

and Brimble said jokingly 'Good Lord, if that's the case I'm going home!'

The next morning, Wednesday 24th May, Brimble called into Sandbrook and Dawes, Ironmongers, Crane Street,

---

[2] See Frederick Lewis

Pontypool and ordered some materials to be delivered to Plasmont. He then went to the house, put up his ladders (see photo) and started painting. The lorry with the materials arrived shortly afterwards. Brimble takes up the story again though from the stilted language it is obvious that his statement was written by a police officer. 'Mr Barnett came onto the lawn at about 9.30 am and said 'Has the old boy been about yet?' I said 'No, I haven't seen him alone. I must see him if possible because I want him to see the colour of the paints I've got and to open the windows. Mr Barnett and I stood in conversation for about 10 minutes in front of the bay window. I stood there for Mr Lewis to see me and come up to speak. I told Mr Barnett I would go to the back door and call Mr Lewis. I said that I thought Mr Lewis might have gone to Swansea and he said

'As he went on Monday, I don't think he would stay more than one day.'

I said 'I must find a way to open the windows because I painted them yesterday without being opened and I can't do that again today.'

Then I went to the back door. Mrs Barnett came down from Plasmont Cottage to the side door and said

'I'll come with you.'

and I said 'I see no necessity for that.'

Mr Barnett said to his wife 'You had better stay here. You don't know what he will find.', and stopped his wife entering the house. I turned to him and said

'What you mean?'

The front door of Plasmont – above a conservatory – Brimble's
ladder on the right

He said 'I don't know, you go on.'

I went into the back kitchen and I shouted

'Mr Lewis, are you at home?'

I got no reply. I returned to Mr Barnett who stayed
outside the back door and said

'It is quite evident that Mr Lewis is not about, he must
have gone away, I expect he left the back door open for
me to open the windows'.

Mr Barnett said 'That's strange, anyway.'

'With those words in my mind I went down the kitchen
steps and first entered the dining room. I was alone. In

the dining room I saw the coverings over the two chairs that Mr Lewis always used. This confirmed my opinion that he had gone away. I saw a sheet of paper on the table, I looked at this thinking he might have left me some written instructions. It was a list of names which I surmise were the persons he intended to call upon on Tuesday, to collect the rents, as I know it was his usual practice to make out a list the night before he made the calls. From the sitting room I went directly upstairs and I first entered the big sitting room over the front hall and dining room. I only glanced in this room. I then went into a bedroom that has a window overlooking George Street, only entering this room just inside the door. I then went across the landing to the other bedroom, opposite. There I saw the room in a state of terrible disorder. I went to the foot of the bed and saw Mr Lewis lying crossways on the bed, his legs hanging down over the side of the bed, his neck and one arm, the left, was visible. These were a bluey colour. There was a pillow over his head and I could instinctively see he was dead. There was a very bad smell.

I was only in a room for a minute or two. I then went downstairs, and to the back door where Mr and Mrs Barnett were waiting.' I said to Mrs Barnett

'Be a good woman and go into the house and be thankful you didn't come up there with me'. Mrs Barnett went away, I said to Mr Barnett

'Watch this back door, I'm going to the police'.

Brimble immediately ran to Pontypool Police Station and with Police Constable James Thomas ran back to Plasmont. He

entered the house asking Brimble to stand guard at the door and not let anyone unauthorised past him.

'The bedroom door was ajar. I lifted the pillow from Lewis' face, I could see there was a wound on the top of his head. The room was in disorder, drawers had been pulled out and put on the top of the dresser. I came to the conclusion there had been foul play. Then I went to a nearby phone and contacted Sergeant Bowkett at the Police Court'.

Detective Constable Adams arrived at Plasmont at 11 am. He went straight to the bedroom and found Lewis as Brimble had described, lying across the bed with a pillow over his head. He noted that the bedclothes were thrown in disarray over the body. There was a large pool of blood on the blanket which had dripped onto the bedroom floor. The wallpaper was also splashed with blood. The bedroom looked as if it had been ransacked, drawers pulled out from the wardrobe and dressing table. There were eight candlesticks on the dressing table, none had been disturbed. He described the small bedroom

'The space between the washstand and the bed was only 2ft and between the open drawer of the wardrobe and the bed only 1ft, which lessened the space for any struggle which might have taken place.'

In the bed and under the body Detective Adams found a gentleman's pocket watch, which was later to be identified as the property of the deceased. Outside the bedroom on the floor and near the grandfather clock he found 3 keys, two of which he discovered fitted the back door. Adams said that he took a look around the house for a possible weapon, or bloodstains in any other part of the house. Dr McAllen arrived, examined the body and pronounced life extinct and that rigor mortis had set in. Adams then helped to remove the body from the house to be conveyed to the mortuary. He took possession of a blanket, sheet, one bed tick, a part of the under tick, all of which were blood stained, plus the pillow that had covered Lewis' face. The next statement comes from Chief Inspector Rees.

'As a result of a telephone message received at this office *(Metropolitan Police at Scotland Yard)* at 12.45 pm on 24th May, 1939 from Chief Constable Lewis, Monmouth County Constabulary, asking for assistance to investigate a suspected case of murder at Pontypool, as directed, I - accompanied by Sergeant D.G. Davies, travelled by train leaving Paddington at 3.55 pm for

WELSH DETECTIVES

The four Scotland Yard officers who are investigating the crime have been specially chosen because of their knowledge of the Welsh language. The officers are :
Chief Detective-inspector Rees,
Chief Detective-inspector Cherrill,
Detective-sergeant Davies, and
Detective-sergeant Goodsall.

Newport, from which station we travelled by a police car to Pontypool. Superintendent Cherrill and Police Sergeant Godsell of the Finger Print Department travelled with us from London.'

The South Wales Argus said that the Scotland Yard Officers had been specially chosen because of their knowledge of the Welsh language. At the time the prevailing language in Pontypool was English and there is no evidence that any interviews were conducted in Welsh. It conjures up the vision of the four police officers chatting away to each other in Welsh, having found few in Pontypool to talk to in the native language. Inspector Rees, who was born in Cardiff, had spent more than half his working life in the Metropolitan police.

Rees had been involved in a number of interesting cases. In 1936 he was called in to assist Glamorgan police in the case of 64 year old Alice Bulley, a Porthcawl widow, who was found dead, under mysterious circumstances in her bath in July 1934. He was the officer in charge of the London inquires in the case of the Trunk Mystery in Brighton, the murder of Annie Kempson of Oxfordshire in 1931 (as result of which Henry Daniel Seymour was hanged, protesting his innocence to the last) and the tracing of a gang of East End fire-raisers.

Inspector Rees continued

'On arrival at Pontypool we were met by the Chief Constable Major W.R. Lucas, and other officers of his force. We proceeded to the scene of the crime which is known as Plasmont House, Conway Road, Pontypool and made a cursory examination of the premises, the body by that time having been removed. Superintendent Cherrill and Sergeant Godsell commenced their search of the house for finger impressions or other useful marks which might be of assistance in the investigation, while the Chief Constable accompanied Sergeant Davies and myself to Coed-y-Gric Mortuary, Griffithstown, to which the body had been taken.'

A crowd had gathered outside Plasmont and had been standing there some hours when the body was removed via the back door, to a waiting ambulance. An elderly lady recalled recently

'I was only a child at the time and I saw the body, covered by a sheet, except for his feet, they were sticking out from the end of the blanket – and he was wearing long black socks.'

The crime scene photographs confirm that indeed Lewis was wearing long black socks at the time of his death.

THE POST MORTEM

Dr J.M. Webster, Home Office Pathologist of the West Midlands Forensic Science Laboratory, Birmingham, had arrived at Plasmont at 4.20 pm on 24th. He was accompanied by Major Lucas the Chief Constable and various other police officers. He first examined the body in situ.

'The body lay diagonally across the bottom of the bed. The head being in the angle formed by the bottom of the bed and the wall, and the legs hanging free over the edge of the bed. The body was cold and was clad in woollen drawers, a flannel shirt and a woollen vest. Rigor mortis had passed from the eyes, jaw, neck, trunk and shoulder joints. It was partially present in both elbows and fully present in the hands and knees.'

The state of the body showed that Lewis had been dead some days. Blood splashes, close to the area of Lewis' head were observed on the wallpaper. Dr Webster examined these and remarked that they were

'Not arterial spurts but were of the nature of splashes such as might have been caused by the upward lift of a weapon from the head'.

The bedding was disarranged and a pillow partially covered the deceased face. The body was photographed and then conveyed to the mortuary, followed by Dr Webster and Dr McAllen.

Inspector Rees, Chief Constable Lucas and Sgt Davies went from Plasmont straight to Coed-y-Grig mortuary. Dr J.M. Webster, with his assistant Inspector Burgess had just concluded a post mortem examination of the deceased, which had commenced at 5.15 pm on Wednesday 24th May. Hair blood and scrapings from the nails were taken. The post mortem examination revealed that Lewis had been gripped by the throat, forcing his tongue to the right side, also by the upper left arm, and had received two blows on the left side of the head, level with the top and about 3 inches behind the ear. Each wound was about 1 inch in length and penetrated almost to the skull, being slightly curved in shape. Further examination showed 6 'very decided' bruised areas on the scalp. The two forefingers of the left hand were evenly bruised for their full length. His left shoulder and upper part of the left arm was found to be bruised.

'... such as could have been made with the four fingers of a hand' stated Dr Webster.

There was no fracture of the skull. The deceased's heart was somewhat diseased and he had some signs of old pleurisy in his lungs. In life he might have suffered a bit of an ache as a small stone was found in his gall bladder. Dr Webster noted that the deceased had not had a substantial meal for some hours before death, as the stomach was empty. In the small intestines he found some milky substance possibly consumed approximately 3 hours before death.

Dr Thomas McAllan, the police surgeon, of Hanbury Road, Pontypool who was present at the post mortem examination expressed the view that the deceased had not had a solid meal for at least 24 hours before death. In conclusion Dr Webster stated

'The cause of death is quite clear. This man died from shock and haemorrhage following upon multiple blows on the head. Immediately prior to death, this man had been gripped by the throat. I am of the opinion that this man was first of all forced backwards upon the bed and that he was hit in the position in which I found him. This in all probability accounts for the fact that there was no fracture of the skull, the head being in the awkward angle between the bottom of the bed and the wall, which would prevent the full force of the assailant's arm in wielding the weapon. The splashes on the wall, which are in an upward direction, were undoubtedly caused by the upward lift of the weapon. With regard to the type of instrument which caused these injuries, the suggestion that they may have been caused by a painter's scraper I regard as unlikely, though I cannot completely eliminate this possibility. My own opinion is that they are more likely to have been caused by something of the nature of a tire lever. From the bruised condition of the first two fingers of the left hand, I think it quite possibly that this may have been caused by a blow directed by the deceased against his assailant, and if so, it is extremely likely that the assailant bears the mark of some injury. With regard to the time of death, there is a decided anomaly present in this body, insomuch as whilst putrefaction is considerably advanced, rigor mortis had not completely passed off. Considering the two together, I am of the opinion, however, that this man died on Monday night (*22nd May*), but I would point out that the conditions of temperature on Tuesday and the fact that he was clad completely in woollen garments, is conductive to rapid decomposition and one occasionally sees this almost fulminating fact of decomposition taking place in twenty four hours.'

Chief Inspector Rees described Lewis

'Of small stature, about 5ft 4ins and under ten stone in weight, not a likely man to put up very much stout resistance and particularly in view of his suffering from hernia and heart disease.'

The local correspondent from South Wales Argus was on the scene within hours of the body being found

'At a late hour last night the police were still without a definite clue which would lead them to the murderer'.

Mr Lewis was described as a semi-recluse who 'owned 180 properties in Pontypool' and whose wealth was estimated at £50,000. The article further claimed that Lewis hoped to be married in the near future, his bride-to-be a local woman of his own age. Whilst no engagement had been announced a close personal friend had given this information to the Argus reporter.

THE FIRST INQUEST

The inquest was opened at noon on 25th May in the Board Room of Coed-y Gric. The Coroner was Mr D. J. Treasure, who had presided over the inquest of Lewis' brother Frederick Lewis in 1936. The Chief Constable of Monmouthshire and the Chief Detective Inspector Ivor Rees of Scotland Yard were among the police officers present and their first duty was to attend on the body of William Lewis in the mortuary. A jury of eight, with Mr G.G. Carr as foreman were sworn in and Mr Treasure said he did not think it necessary to tell the jury why they had been called to serve.

> 'They already knew that a body had been found' he said 'and it was their task to investigate the circumstances of the death.'

At this point he called on Lewis Alfred Pritchard of Cyncoed Road, Cardiff (nephew) to give evidence of identification. Treasure asked '

> When did you last see him alive?
> 'On Saturday May 13th at Plasmont.
> 'As far as you could see at that time, was he perfectly normal?' 'He was in very good spirits.'
> 'You went to speak to him on professional matters?' '
> 'Yes.'
> 'Your Uncle was a widower?'
> 'No, a bachelor.'
> 'How long had he lived in Pontypool?'
> 'About 8 years. He used to carry on a business at Cwm, Ebbw Vale, but he spent his weekends at Pontypool.'

The Coroner asked when Lewis had retired from his drapery business and the reply was 'about 1931'.

Dr McAllen the Pontypool Police Surgeon said that he and the Home Office Pathologist had undertaken the post-mortem and he gave evidence of the wounds found. He confirmed that the wounds were not self-inflicted. Lewis Pritchard asked a question about the wounds (the exact words are not recorded) but the Coroner intimated that the doctor had already said that they could not have been self-inflicted. The Coroner adjourned the inquest until Thursday 8th June.

THE FUNERAL

CRIME VICTIM'S FUNERAL.—Part of the crowd outside Crane-street Baptist Church, Pontypool, yesterday when Mr. W. A. Lewis was buried.

The funeral notice in the Pontypool Free Press was simple : LEWIS – At Plasmont, Pontypool, suddenly, on May 24th 1939, William Alfred, aged 59 years. Funeral Monday May 29th (Gentlemen only). Please meet at Crane Street Baptist Church for Service at 2.15 pm. It later reported:

'A small group of family mourners and a number of friends of the murdered man attended the funeral on Monday afternoon. The internment was at Penygarn Cemetery, and the obsequies were brief and simple to a degree.

There were of course, a large number of curious sightseers, mainly women. Some of them wore black, but bright holiday wear predominated. When the mourners had left the graveside many of the public remained behind to study the inscriptions on the wreaths.'

The coffin was conveyed from Coed-y-gric Institution, where the body had been taken after the discovery of the crime on Wednesday last, to Crane Street Baptist Church, Pontypool. There, a short service was conducted by the Rev E.W. Price Evans, pastor and Rev Richard Rees, of Tabernacle Baptist Church, Pontypool. Mrs Trenchard, at the organ played 'O Rest in the Lord' and other suitable voluntaries and the congregation sang the hymn, 'O Lord of Life, where'er they be.' The church was about half full. A large crowd assembled outside the church, and here again, women were in the majority.

Eight tenants acted as bearers – Messrs F. Dowell, W. J. Dowell, C. Amos, Albert Truman, D.Scott and W. Newman.[3]

THE SECOND INQUEST

'If the police inquiries take them to the far ends of the earth, a couple of months will give them ample time to pursue them.'

This rather confusing comment was made by Coroner, Mr D.J. Treasure when he reopened the inquest into the death of William Alfred Lewis on 8th June 1939. He acknowledged the evidence of Lewis Pritchard (nephew) presented at the first

---

[3] Details of other mourners and wreaths in Appendix

inquest and added that he believed Superintendent Edward Casey, wished for another adjournment.

'Do you require the adjournment for the purpose of pursuing the active enquiries upon which you and others are engaged'?

'Yes Sir.'

'Is it your opinion that if the inquest were continued today, it might stand to hamper you or fetter you in the efforts you are making?'

'Yes.'

The Coroner then announced

'In the circumstances, that is a very reasonable request, with which I intend to comply.' The only question is that of period. I think we shall give the holiday months of July and August a miss'.

With those words the inquest was again formally adjourned until September 20th 1939. By mid-day on Wednesday 24th Major Lucas, Superintendent Casey of Pontypool, Superintendent A. Gover of Abergavenny, Police Sergeant H. Maggs of Pontnewynydd and Police Sergeant Bowkett had visited Plasmont.
The South Wales Argus described Plasmont House as being guarded by policemen

'... Who kept out people who had no business on the premises.'

Sightseers were still gathered outside Plasmont, watching the comings and goings of the police and other officials. Superintendent Cherrill and Sergeant Godsell completed their examination of Plasmont House on the 25th of May, 1939, resulting in three finger marks being found on the wooden bedstead upon which the body was found. Plasmont originally consisted of 22 rooms and stood in its own grounds of approximately ¾ acre, and at that time had three entrances, one on the front in George Street, one almost directly into Conway Road and a side entrance leading to a backyard which gave admission to a semi-basement kitchen.

THE HOUSE OF DEATH.—Plasmont House, Pontypool, where Mr. W. A. Lewis, a well-known property owner, was found murdered.

PLASMONT HOUSE OF DEATH

For some years five rooms had been shut off from the main part of the house and a rented as a cottage to Mr and Mrs Barnett. These five rooms were known as Plasmont Cottage to differentiate them from Plasmont House.

There remained a dividing door, which had been papered over many years previously. Police Sergeant Bowkett looked at the outside of Plasmont and noted that a small window at the side of the house was opened and below it in the garden, an ornament, which was normally kept inside. Brimble had painted the windowsill and frame the previous day – before he knew Lewis was dead. The only print in the paint on this open window frame was that of a cat's paw. Detective Adams had searched the bedroom, which he described as

> 'In disorder, drawers had been pulled out and apparently ransacked.'

He discovered in the blood splashed bed the watch belonging to Lewis, it was under his body. A pair of blue trousers, with the braces attached was on the chair and a pair of boots underneath it. Outside the bedroom door, on the floor near the grandfather clock were three Yale keys, two of which, he discovered, fitted the back door. No sign of a weapon was found nor any bloodstains in any other part of the house. There was no sign of forced entry. Meanwhile, continuing inside the house Police Sergeant Bowkett saw a large patch of blood on the bedroom floor and commented on the fact that the contents of the bedroom drawers had been strewn all over the floor. He also mentioned that the space between the washstand and the bed was only 2ft (this bedroom was the smallest in the house) and between the opened drawer and the wardrobe just 1ft which lessened the space for any struggle which might have taken place.

He considered that it was impossible to tell from the disordered state of the bed whether it had been slept in or not. Having helped to remove the body he took effects from the bedroom – one blanket, one sheet, one eiderdown, one bed tick, a part of the under tick, all of which were blood stained.

He also took the pillow which had been on Lewis' face. The only furniture in the room was a washstand, a wardrobe, a dressing table and chair and the single bed. Under the bed was found a small 'hoard' of money in a tin. The amount wasn't released by the police – except to say that it was less than £100 in notes plus nine sovereigns. The following day The South Wales Argus stated

'Police Officers have been on an all-night vigil at Pontypool's house of mystery and death, Plasmont House, the lonely home of Mr William Alfred Lewis, 59-year-old bachelor, who, although he was reputed to be well-to-do, had, for several years led a most retiring life.

The door to Plasmont Cottage

Plasmont House, an old rambling house with about 10 bedrooms, stands in the shadow of Pontypool Catholic Church'. Major W. R. Lucas, Chief Constable was quoted as saying 'So far, we have not got a line on the problem.'

Police Sergeant William Davidson remained on duty at Plasmont. He received a message from Superintendent Casey to make a search for a brown mixture tweed suit. With the assistance of Police Sergeant William Guy (No. 214), a search was made of the murdered man's bedroom. In a wardrobe they found a jacket and waistcoat of a brown suit, it was folded and wrapped in brown paper. On the floor of the wardrobe were the suit trousers, Davidson handed them to Superintendent Gover, who was waiting to take the clothes to the Police Station.

THE SEARCH BEGINS

In a statement dated June 6th headed 'PONTYPOOL MURDER' to Superintendent Eugene Davies, Abertillery and Superintendent W. Casey, Pontypool, Detective Constable Ernest Booth wrote

'I have the honour to report to you particulars of enquiries I made on Friday 26th and Saturday 27th May 1939, at Pontypool respecting the above.

On Friday 26th May, 1939, accompanied by Detective Constables Atkins and Swift, I made a search of the house and grounds of Plasmont in an effort to find the instrument with which the murder was committed. We afterwards started on door-to-door enquiry in Conway Road, King Street and Broadway, Pontypool.

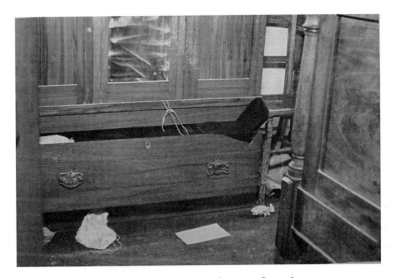

The bedroom where Lewis was found

On Saturday 27th May, accompanied by Detective Constables Atkins and Swift, I made door-to-door enquiry at Bushy Park, Fairfields Road, Queen Street, Edward Street, Helpstone Terrace, School Lane, Upper George Street, Prince Street and South View, with a view to obtaining information which may be useful.

During my enquiry I interviewed 88 persons and have each person's name in my pocket book.

On Friday 26th June 1939[4], acting on instructions from Supt. Gover and in company with D.C.'s Atkins and Swift, I made a search of the grounds at Plasmont. Shrubs and grass were cut to the ground in search for an object which might have caused the death. Later that day

---

[4] Some 36 days after the murder

we searched the rooms of the house and moved all furniture in a further search, without result.

I have the honour to be Sir, Your obedient Servant (Signed) Ernest Booth'

A similar letter was sent by Detective Constable Wood

'I travelled by road to Pontypool in the company of Detective Constable F. Barnstable.'

Wood and Barnstable went to the police station, where they reported to Inspector Casey. The two policemen received instructions to interview a number of persons

' to obtain statements from these persons relative to their Business Dealings with the late Mr Lewis' and I received a prescribed form as to the manner in which these statements were to be taken, and the information it was desired that they should obtain. These statements were then typewritten and submitted to the Pontypool police, immediately'.

One person he was instructed to interview, a Mrs Roberts of 11, Rockhill Road, had never met Mr Lewis and did not live in one of his rented houses. It was evident that that Detective Barnstable's searches were in vain but he was pleased to be involved in the enquiries.

Inspector Casey in his later report wrote that many days were spent searching the scene of the crime, surrounding grounds, the railway embankments running to the north side of Plasmont but nothing of note was found.

'From a bloodstain on the blanket on the bed and the nature of the wounds inflicted, there is but little doubt that the instrument used was an iron one'.

The police approached Lewis Pritchard, (nephew, son of Lewis' sister Miriam) to identify significant property found at Plasmont.

'One gold watch, yellow metal chain and coin, three white metal watches, one ring, set with white stone, two fountain pens, five thru'penny pieces, one yellow metal chain, seven pence bronze, four national savings certificates for £80 each, four National Savings Certificates for £40 each, nine golden sovereigns, nine five shilling pieces, a one shilling piece, a gold watch and chain, fifty six £1 Bank of England notes, thirty eight 10/- Bank of England notes, four pounds in large silver 11/5d in small change, one yellow metal watch chain, gold bracelet with two half sovereigns and one golden sovereign'.

The weekly rent collection averaged about £80, and that amount was found, wrapped in brown paper in a box in a bedroom on a floor above where Lewis was found. One of the bank notes found in the box had been issued by the Bank of England on 18th May 1939 and by the National Provincial Bank on 19th May to their branch in Pontypool. The police concluded therefore that the £80 consisted of notes collected during Lewis last rent round.

Originally the story released to the press was that £300 was missing. However, despite the fact that the safes were opened, the documents inside were dusty and the police decided that they had not been disturbed for some time. Personal documents and papers, leases and deeds of property were discovered and in one safe War Loan Stock and Savings Certificates to the value of £1,220 were found. It appeared that in fact the safes had not been raided. Though the house had been ransacked it seems that the burglar/s found nothing considered worth taking, despite the fact that many of the antiques were valuable. This does not give the impression of someone experienced in burglary – more an opportunist theft. Mr Lewis died in vain, defending his home and property. Keys to the safes were found in a lady's handbag in a chest of drawers and there was no evidence that they had recently been used.

Detective Ernest Booth continued interviewing people who hadn't been at home on their initial 'sweep' of the nearby streets. He was again assisted by Detective Constables Atkins and Swift.

'On Saturday 27th, still accompanied by the above named officers we made a door-to-door enquiry at the following streets:- King Street, Queen Street, Prince Street, Edward Street, Brynderwen, South View, Conway Road, Bushy Park, Helpstone Terrace, Fairview Avenue, British School Lane, Upper George Street, Broadway, Amberley Place and Catholic Lane. I obtained no useful information. On 31st May, acting on instructions from Police Sergeant Davidson, I interviewed Mr Bella Powell of Llanarth Street, Pontymister and obtained a statement from him to the effect that he had given his son Stanley, alias Tansy Powell, a Mason's Hammer on Saturday evening 27th May. This hammer, he'd stated had been his property for a number of years. In 1st instant I checked all stations in this division for Convicts on License Reporting here, but found none'.

Constable Lionel Swift wrote a similar report:

'The only information I obtained was from Charles Millett, 40, King Street and Frederick Griffiths of 143, King Street – copies of whose statements I handed in to Sergeant Bowkett the same evening.'

THE LEWIS FAMILY

Miriam Lewis, the late mother of the deceased man had moved to Plasmont following the death of her husband, Thomas in 1884. Thomas born in 1834 was a butcher from Carmarthenshire. She needed a large house to accommodate her family of eight children; Elizabeth (1862-1925), Walter (1863-1931), Sarah Anne (1867-1936), Thomas Henry (1871-1918), Frederick John (1874-1926), Miriam, (1876-1950) William Alfred (1880-1939) and Emily Edith (1881-1953). Emily commented after the death of her brother William;

'My Mother and Father were rich people. All of us were periodically in receipt of monies and property; also a private income. When my Mother died she left property and money to each of us. All the family continued in business and as they died out they bequeathed their property to the surviving members of the family and this has continued to this day.'

The South Wales Argus reported that at the time of William's death, the Lewis family (Miriam, Emily and William) owned about 200 properties in the Eastern Valley.

Miriam Lewis senior (nee Lloyd) was born in the small village of Llanfrechfa, around 1840. The Lloyd family then moved to Gorse House, Upper Cwmbran. By the 1861 census she was living with her husband Thomas at 2, Crane Street, Pontypool. Their neighbours the Littlehales family being also in the same trade as the Lewis'- their profession recorded as butchers and pig dealers.

Miriam Lewis died in December 1913. The Free Press reported at the time

'We regret to record the death of one of Pontypool's oldest and most highly respected inhabitants, Mrs

Miriam Lewis of Plasmont, who passed away suddenly on Tuesday night, from heart failure at the ripe old age of 71 years. She was the widow of the late Mr Thomas Lewis, butcher, of Commercial Street, Pontypool and came to Pontypool in 1861. She had lived at Plasmont for the last 20 years. She was a woman of wide and sound business capacity, a loving mother and one who will be missed by the family and a wide circle of friends. She was a Baptist all her life and attended the Tabernacle Baptist Church. Plasmont was a 'home' for Baptist Ministers and the cause has lost a faithful follower and supporter. The funeral, private and for gentlemen only, will take place at Penygarn Burial Ground on Monday at 1 o'clock.'

In her Will made in September 1893, Miriam declared Thomas Henry (butcher's assistant) and Sarah Ann (spinster) the executors. Her four daughters each received a feather bed and her trap.

The best piano by Hopkinson went to Elizabeth and Emily Edith. Elizabeth also received a portrait in oils and the bedroom furniture used by herself. The oil portrait of Thomas Lewis senior was left to Sarah Ann and Emily Edith received her Mother's gold watch. Other bequests of money and shops. in Commercial Street and Crane Street were divided amongst the males of the family, with the proviso that if they did not want the premises the females could rent them out. Plasmont was held in trust until the last child was aged 21 with anyone who wished to live there, paying 'board and lodgings' and maintaining the house for the four sisters if they wished to live there. Walter paid 7/-, Frederick 10/-, Thomas (described in the Will as 'being delicate') 5/- providing that they were still single. Should Elizabeth wish to live away from home she should be granted 8/- to provide for herself.

The attendance register at Penygarn Church records Miriam Lewis as a member of the congregation there in 1878 'from Crane Street'.[5]

Miriam junior, her daughter married Alfred Pritchard, they had a son Lewis who was a solicitor. At one time Alfred had been the manager of the Great Western Hotel in Cardiff. In the April 2nd 1911 census, sister Sarah was visiting. Emily married Watkin Watkins, a Baptist Minister. They lived in Danygraig Road, St Thomas, Swansea and Watkins (known affectionately in the family as Watty) was the chaplain to the Mayor of Swansea and pastor of Danygraig Baptist Church, Swansea. They had a daughter.

Elizabeth and Sarah remaining as spinsters, continued to reside at Plasmont with their mother and four bachelor brothers Walter, Thomas, Frederick and William. William lived away from Plasmont house during the weekdays conducting his drapery business at Cwm, Ebbw Vale, until 1932 when he retired from business and went to live permanently at Plasmont House. His sister Emily said that he had made a considerable amount of money as a result of his drapery business and originally started to put his money into property almost as a hobby, but when he retired as a draper he took up property management full-time. His three brothers had all died by this time; Sarah lived at Plasmont with a maid. She died in 1936 and subsequently William Lewis lived there alone.

---

[5] The mourners at the funeral of Miriam Lewis can be found in the appendix

Pontypool Victim's Work for the Town

"GAVE NEW COURAGE TO THE BUSINESS PEOPLE"

On Sunday mornings for about three hours Maud Barnett of Plasmont Cottage popped in and cleaned the kitchen and pantry and prepared his midday meal for cooking. Following the murder the Rev. W.G. Watkins (husband of Emily) spoke to the South Wales Argus about his brother-in-law. He said he was perturbed that Mr Lewis had been described as

'A recluse, living in just one room.'

An important aspect missing from the newspaper reports caused further anguish to his family. Mr Lewis was a quiet and solitary man, he was even called a miser, so many people might not have known of his generosity. Rev. Watkins recalled the bad times, not so far distant when Pontypool was in the depth of The Depression when Lewis was considered one of the benefactors of the town.

'At a time when Pontypool was in very low water and many hundreds of people were out of work, he undertook the great task of reconstructing many of the shop premises in the main shopping centre of the town and in the Clarence Street direction. What he did gave new life, new heart and new courage to the business people of the town. He was one of the best known businessmen in Pontypool and was greatly admired by the business fraternity for his keenness. He was a businessman who did much good, and he had a remarkable memory.'

THE HOUSE OF DREAD

Plasmont was situated on high ground, opposite St Alban's Catholic Church. In the photograph below, all that is left is the grassy bank where it once stood. The South Wales Argus described it as being

'Only 200 yards from the centre of Pontypool, a large rambling building, standing in its own grounds.'

Speculation in the town was that Lewis was having the house decorated with a view to getting married.

St. Albans Catholic Church – Plasmont House was on the left

The Daily Mirror headlines of May 25th 1939 boldly stated 'Slain in house of Dread'

and described how Miss E. Parker of Pontypool said that she had turned down Lewis' proposal of marriage

'Because I couldn't possibly live in his old house. It is so eerie and so many deaths had taken place there. Several times I implored Mr Lewis to leave the house but he insisted on staying there.'

In her statement to the police on June 2nd 1939 Miss Parker of Glencoe, Pontypool Road stated

'I did not like the house and would not go to live there under any circumstances.'

Under the headline 'Murdered Man's Broken Romance' the reporter also wrote

'Rumours are growing in Pontypool that Mr Lewis was planning to marry a woman of his own age. In conversation with some of his neighbours he was 'chipped' about the suggestion that he was having the house decorated to have a bride there.'

Chief Inspector Rees said.

'It can be well realised the internal condition of these seventeen rooms, when no person had been employed to keep them clean for over three years.'

The South Wales Argus reported Chief Constable Major Lucas as saying that the house was very neglected. In the bedroom in which Lewis was found, whilst it looked as if it had been ransacked, Lucas said that because of the of the ill-kept circumstances state of the rest of the house, the police first had to satisfy themselves that the bedroom's appearance was not the usual condition of the room. Mrs Barnett did a clean of the pantry and kitchen and prepared Lewis meal on a Sunday but the rest of Plasmont had been gathering dust since the death of Sarah Lewis in 1936. Inspector Rees added

'The house was very heavily furnished and every drawer, box or other receptacle packed with such ornaments us would suggest the Lewis' had been a family of hoarders in as much as the greater part was unworthy of storage. When the police searched the house they found in each bedroom, as each brother and sister had died, their respective clothing packed into brown paper parcels and left on their beds.'

A safe in one of the bedrooms

There were two safes in Plasmont – in these Lewis kept the title deeds of all his properties and his personal papers. An illuminating insight by a South Wales Argus reporter describes Plasmont on the day of the auction sale.

'Stepping through the portals of Plasmont, the scene of the unsolved Pontypool murder mystery was like putting the clock back 100 years. The rambling old mansion was chock-a-block with those knick-knacks so beloved of our great grandmothers. Enormous cases of stuffed birds vied for pride of place on the walls with heads of foxes, spreading antlers and pictures of celebrities of a by-gone age. Here and there one chanced upon an exquisite piece of china, an antique piece of furniture or a grand-father clock which sedately chimed away the hours in some dark and secluded corner on the stairs. Here and there a discarded album of family photographs gave one a glimpse of the people who had filled Plasmont with all these expressions of their personality. It would have been no surprise to see one of the high-waisted, crinolined ladies of the album step into the drawing-room and take up the zither harp which lay neglected in the dust of the floor'.

It could easily be understood why the Daily Mirror called it 'The House of Dread' – so many of the Lewis family had died there. The family, Mrs Lewis and her eight children had moved into the house after her husband had died. The house had previously belonged to Mr Conway – a well-known Pontypool Councillor, whose name is remembered in Conway Road. In fact the only two that escaped the curse of Plasmont were Lewis' two sisters Miriam and Emily who were the only ones of the Lewis family to marry and leave Plasmont under their own volition rather than via the undertaker's coffin.

Mrs Miriam Lewis, the matriarch of the family had died in 1913 aged 72. Thomas Henry had died in 1918 at the age of 47; he was described as 'delicate' by his mother. Elizabeth died in 1925 at the age of 63, Frederick John in 1926 aged 53 and Walter in 1931. Notably Frederick John Lewis took his own life at Plasmont. Under the heading 'Butcher's Tragic Death' the Pontypool Free Press of Friday 9th July 1936 states

'Verdict at Pontypool Inquest' – At Pontypool Police Station on Wednesday, an inquest was held by the Coroner (Mr D.J.Treasure) touching on the death of Frederick John Lewis, a retired butcher's assistant, of Plasmont, Wainfelin, Pontypool, who was found by a servant girl on Sunday morning, hanging by a piece of rope from the ceiling of the kitchen. Mr W. Lewis, brother of the deceased, gave evidence of identification and spoke of his drinking habits. His brother had a private income and his affairs were in order. Mr Cecil Stephen, who occupied a part of the house, deposed to having heard sounds about midnight on Saturday coming from the direction of the kitchen as if someone was snoring. Dr James Fleming, Pontypool said he was called to the house at 8.30 in the morning. Deceased had then been dead for some hours. Death was due to asphyxia due to strangulation. The Coroner said the evidence was sufficiently conclusive to enable him to return a verdict of suicide whilst of unsound mind. The evidence was clear that the deceased was a heavy drinker and as a result his mind might have become weakened.'

The funeral of Frederick Lewis was held on Wednesday 7th July 1936, the internment was at Penygarn Baptist Chapel Burial Ground, the Rev. E.W. Pryce Evans M.A. Pastor of Crane Street Baptist Church officiated. In his Will administration was granted to his brother Walter Lewis, retired cattle dealer – the effects being £1,490 13s 5d.

When Walter died in 1931 he had a well-attended funeral reported by the Pontypool Free Press

'A Pontypool Tradesman' – A Familiar Figure in the Town and Country

The Late Mr Walter Lewis.'

After an illness which had lasted some months, Mr Walter Lewis passed away at his residence, Plasmont, Wainfelin, Pontypool, on Saturday (February 7th 1931). By his death Pontypool has lost a familiar figure. He was perhaps one of the best known business men in the town and neighbourhood, having been for at least two generations the head of a successful retail as well as an extensive wholesale meat business. He was the eldest son of the late Mr Thomas Lewis, whose business premises were on the top of Crane Street, near the station. Mr Thomas Lewis was the youngest of three brothers, who came to Pontypool from Carmarthen in the middle of the last century. They were well known in their day, two of them being engaged in the retail meat trade, while the other was a cattle dealer. They were typical Welshmen, who were greatly respected for their frank and open manner and upright dealing. Mr Thomas Lewis died while his son (Walter) was quite a youth, but such was the latter's grit and keenness that he shouldered the responsibility of such a large business and carried it on, greatly extended in new premises until he retired a few years ago, chiefly through ill-health. Mr Walter Lewis was extremely sociable and unpretentious. He had beyond doubt business instincts of a high character, as his speculations in property amply justify. On matter of that kind his advice was often sought and found generally to be safe and sound. Mr Lewis was a faithful member of the congregation at Crane Street Chapel. He cared little for outward show or ostentation but he did much good in a quiet way. Many will miss him on that account. His illness, extending over several months was patiently bourn, and great sympathy is felt for his brothers and sisters in their bereavement. '

A profusion of floral tributes not only from family but reflecting Walter's standing in the community covered the vault. [6] The undertaker was Mr C. C. Pritchard.

Sarah Anne Lewis never married and died aged 69, at Plasmont House where she had lived with her maid. She was buried at Penygarn on October 24th 1936, the last one of the family to be commemorated on the red granite memorial. The names of William and his sisters Miriam Pritchard and Emily Edith are recorded in the burial book as is that of William Lewis. However the names have never been added to the memorial stone, which now lies in a state of disrepair. A sad reflection on a wealthy family, whose links with Penygarn go back over 100 years.[7]

THE INTERVIEWS BEGIN

The first relatives alerted to the dreadful news of the murder were Lewis' close family, sister Miriam (who married her husband Alfred Pritchard in 1906) – along with their son Lewis. Lewis Pritchard in an interview at Pontypool Police Station on 27th May with Detective Sgt D. G. Davies stated that the last time he had seen his Uncle alive was on Saturday 13th May, when he had seen him to talk about business. Since he had qualified as a solicitor in 1933, Lewis Pritchard, who lived with his parents at Cyncoed Road, Cardiff, had helped his Uncle in legal affairs, mostly with the purchases of

---

[6] See appendix for names of those who sent wreaths
[7] See appendix for Penygarn

property and preparing leases. He carried on his practice at 17, High Street, Cardiff.

Mr Lewis had also used Bythway's a well-known firm of solicitors in Pontypool but by 1938 his nephew had taken over most of the legal dealings for his uncle. He told the police that his uncle was in good health (apart from a hernia) he was not insured and had never married. He confirmed that he had seen approximately £50 in gold sovereigns and half sovereigns in the safes in the house; this would have been about 6 months before the murder.

His uncle had discussed with him the rising price of sovereigns and may well have sold them at a good rate. He said that the safes were always kept locked and his Uncle always carried the keys. He described him as 'fairly wealthy'.

'He was very reserved which would account for his living alone at Plasmont.'

He had accounts with various banks and at the Post Office and had valuable securities. In common with his tenants and possibly most of the citizens of Pontypool, Pritchard confirmed that Lewis collected the rents on Mondays, Tuesdays and Friday evenings. Lewis Pritchard's mother Miriam said that she used to see her brother William about twice a week but of late visits had been less frequent. She generally called in on him when she was collecting rent for her own properties. She last saw her brother on 20th April when he went to see her in Cardiff, accompanied by a lady friend, Irene Harris of Goytre, Pontypool. She believed that her brother had last banked his rent takings on Wednesday 17th May and therefore had a considerable amount of money in the house. Miriam also told the South Wales Argus reporter that gold sovereigns and items of jewellery were missing from Plasmont.

Lewis' other sister Emily Edith had married a man of the cloth – a Baptist Minister called Watkin George Watkins of Danygraig Road, Swansea in 1917 and went to live in Aston Parsonage, Oxfordshire. They had a daughter. On 5th June he was asked to make a statement at Pontypool Police Station with regard to the last time he saw his brother-in-law. Both the Watkins' were regular visitors to Plasmont – usually about once a fortnight. They also owned property in Pontypool and called to collect the rent. On these occasions, they called in at Plasmont for lunch and tea. They last saw Lewis alive on the fateful day of 22nd May.

On this day, they arrived at Plasmont at about 2 pm and their lunch of cold shoulder of lamb, bread and butter and a cup of tea had already been prepared by Lewis, who had eaten his meal earlier. During lunch Lewis took a glass of wine out to the painter Tom Brimble and joined him on the lawn with a glass himself. After lunch Emily, Watkin and Lewis talked about religion and property. Then both Lewis and Watkin along with Brimble went to the back of 52, George Street, the rented home of John William Taylor to inspect work that had been done. From there they looked at a shop across the road which had damaged grating and Lewis gave instructions to Brimble to repair it. Watkins also gave Brimble a similar job at one of his properties at 72, George Street.

Leaving Brimble they went to Sandbrook and Dawes, Watkin had a bill of £19 to pay and Lewis wanted to dispute a bill for what he believed to be an excess charge on a water tank he had purchased for one of his properties. Business completed Lewis returned to Plasmont whilst Watkins went to the Assessment Department of Pontypool Town Hall to discuss his Rates. He there paid his Gas and Electric bills. He then went to the rented home of Mrs Meaden of 48a, George Street to discuss installing a bath there. Arriving back at Plasmont at 4.45 pm tea had already been put up – boiled eggs, bread and butter and small fancy cakes and of course a cup of tea. Watkins noticed that there were two jugs of milk on the kitchen table (no refrigerators in 1939) and as they had used little of it for their two meals he estimated that there would certainly be some left after tea-time. Immediately following his tea, Watkins called in at 79, Osbourne Road to collect the rent. Returning to Plasmont he put a few plants in the garden and discussed the bay fronted dining-room window with Lewis. Watkins estimated that it would cost £10 to reconstruct but Lewis disagreed saying that it would probably cost more in the region of £25 and that was far too much. Three bottles of Guinness were produced from the chiffonier in the drawing room and they enjoyed these as they chatted.

Emily and her husband finally left Plasmont at about 6.30 pm with her brother in the front seat of the car. They called in to see Miss Truman, a florist of George Street (later named as one of Lewis' lady friends) for Watkins to ask her about rubbish deposited at the side of her rented house. Leaving her they continued along George Street into Commercial Street and by the Clarence Hotel turned onto the Crumlin Road. Having arrived at Sycamore House and the junction of Albion Road and Crumlin Road, Lewis expressed the wish to walk back to Plasmont and would hear nothing of Emily's entreaties to go with them to Crumlin and catch the bus home. Before he left them however, he did mention a trip to Droitwich (presumably to see Miss Harris, who was staying there for her rheumatism) a journey which he had already mooted with Emily hoping that Watkins would give him a lift there to see Miss Harris. Watkins had the Automobile

Association map to hand and estimated that it would be about 65 miles. Lewis said that it would be too far to drive in one day from Swansea to Pontypool and then on to Droitwich and return to Swansea (he didn't offer to put them up in Plasmont). His reply, according to Emily in her statement was 'let's cut it out'.

The Watkins' said goodbye, reminding him that they wouldn't see him until after Whit Monday but if he changed his mind about Droitwich, he could write to them about the trip. Asked by Chief Inspector Rees for his movements the following day 23rd May, Watkins said he was busy in the Swansea district and did not return to Pontypool. He called at his Bank, went to see the Mayor of Swansea, who was unwell and called at the General Hospital, Swansea in the afternoon. He also paid his garage fees, went to his Chapel – Mount Calvary Baptist at Danygraig, Swansea to see the fixtures for the Children's Anniversary, visited various old people and saw his secretary.

Taking nothing for granted the police in Swansea Central Station, 'A' Division on behalf of the Pontypool police followed up the statement made by Rev. Watkins. They took a statement from his next-door neighbour Thomas Davies, described as a 33 year old salesman of 66, Danygraig Road, St Thomas, Swansea. He confirmed that he regularly saw the Watkins leave for Pontypool every other Monday morning for the purpose of collecting rent. He also mentioned that on Tuesday 23rd May, the Reverend could be seen cleaning out his car which was parked outside the house, removing the mats and dusting them off. Local gossip also records that the Rev Watkins said to Mrs Crossby his next-door but one neighbour

'You remember me coming back on the Monday?'

THE MYSTERY OF THE KEYS

When the murder was first discovered it was believed that the main bunch of keys, always carried by Lewis, were missing. However, as mentioned previously, these were eventually found in an old handbag on the top floor, in the house. The bunch of keys also contained the keys to the safe. It is highly unlikely that a thief would have returned the keys to the handbag, which led police to conclude that the safes had been left open by Lewis.

However, on the landing outside Lewis' bedroom door, three other keys were found, (Dr Webster the Pathologist had noticed two of them and mentioned them in his statement). The keys were described as, 'Two HTV pattern and one Yale'. The 'HTV keys' fitted the outside kitchen door. Some significance was given to these two keys, as a week or so previous. Lewis had asked Brimble to have two new keys cut as he had mislaid the two he had.

Brimble said it would be a lot cheaper to buy a new lock and indeed had bought one for that purpose on 22nd *May* though it had not been installed. In his summing up of the case Chief Inspector Rees said that perhaps the back door key, together with the Yale key (which Lewis thought were mislaid) were in fact found when the thief or thieves rifled through the drawers in the bedroom, scattering the contents and threw the keys to the ground where they were discovered.

If the murderer had obtained entry to the house through an open window on the ground floor, he or she may well have left by the kitchen door – which had the key on the inside, leaving it unlocked.

The Yale keys on the landing

There was also a box lock and bolt on the kitchen door but Inspector Rees observed that there was a considerable amount of dust and cobwebs on the box lock, indicating that it had not been used for some time. The Yale key was a mystery, so whilst one contingent of police officers were asking Lewis' list of tenants when they had last seen him, another contingent was playing a game of fitting the keys into properties owned by Lewis.

After much diligent searching they finally found a lock that matched the Yale key (No. 16/A/816). Dozens of people were interviewed who might have had access to this key which opened the front door of Jacquemore's Wine Merchants, 13, Crane Street, Pontypool. The shop was owned by Lewis but rented to a Mr Ernest Emanuel Gershenson, a man whose father had emigrated from Russia. He was a wine merchant and had shops at Bargoed, Blackwood, Mountain Ash and Ebbw Vale as well as the one in Pontypool. He also owned

The Tiger public house in Merthyr which had a wine shop attached to it. He had wine shops in Gateshead, Southshields and Ashington in Northumberland. He took over the lease of 13, Crane Street in March 1937 for £52 per annum (exclusive of rates). Gershenson had been to Plasmont (which he described as 'the big house on top of the hill') on a number of occasions to discuss the shop and to sign the rental agreement.

'I found Lewis affable and inclined to tell you of his property deals and personal affairs,' he stated.

He had employed various women as Managers at one time or another. The first to run the Pontypool shop was Miss Elizabeth Ward from 17, Watchhouse Parade, Newport; she had previously worked in both the Newport and Cardiff (Queens Street) branches of Jacquemore's. She took over the shop when it was being painted and prior to the carpenter fitting it out. In his statement Mr Gershenson said that he assumed that the painter had handed to key over to the carpenter and subsequently to Miss Ward. Mr Gershenson said he had never received a key to the shop from Lewis, in fact he thought that there was only the one key, held by Miss Ward and he asked her to have another cut. In his statement

'At present I am holding a key', which he identified the Yale key (No.16/A/816) as the key to open the shop at 13, Crane Street.

Although not relevant to the murder, Jacquemore's had already been the subject of a police investigation. In the antiquated language of law, Jacquemore's had been charged subject to the Licencing Act of 1921:

'For that they, on the 4th day of December 1937 at Crumlin in the County of Monmouth unlawfully induce a certain person named Doreen Baker to deliver certain intoxicating liquor, to wit, Ruby wine at 1 and 2 Lawn Terrace, Crumlin, aforesaid, from a certain vehicle, to wit a horse and cart, without having the name and address of the person to whom it was to be supplied.'

The case was filed at the Llanhilleth Petty Sessions 4th January 1938. Samuel Gershenson was fine £4 and Jacquemore's Ltd £6. 'A summons was not served on Mr Ernest Gershenson and the case was not proceeded with.'

The mystery of the Yale key remained, Nellie Davies, from The Osbourne Restaurant (another Lewis property) was interviewed by Detective Adams on 2nd June. Mrs Davies confirmed that the restaurant was next-door to Jacquemore's Wine Shop. She stated that she had seen Mr Gershenson in the Wine Shop a number of times, including on a Sunday – sometimes with his wife and sometimes with 'a girl supervisor', presumably one of the managers. She felt sure he had his own key to the shop.

Miss Ward, the first manageress was interviewed about the Yale key, which she confirmed opened the front door of the shop. She had worked in a number of branches of Jacquemore's, Newport (which closed just after Christmas 1937), Queen's Street, Cardiff, 2B, Oxford Street, Mountain Ash, Ebbw Vale and finally on to the Jubilee Buildings, in Crane Street. She said Mr Gershenson gave her a key and she passed on a copy of it to Dora Elsie Comley of 16, St Matthews Road, Pontypool, who was a shop assistant there. Miss Ward supervised a number of shops but would return periodically to the Pontypool branch, so she retained a key for the premises. On the 4th July 1939, Doris Comely was replaced by a Mrs Roberts, Pontypool Road. Miss Ward left the employ of Jacquemore Ltd on the August Bank holiday

Tuesday of 1939 and left behind her front door key. She knew Lewis well and often spoke to him, she said

'He did not have a key to the shop as far as I know.'

In a further statement made to Chief Inspector Rees (and read over to her by Police Sergeant D.G. Davies) she said that Mr Gershenson must have had his own key as he had been in there on a Sunday and hadn't borrowed her key.

Dora Comley said to her knowledge that Miss Ward (Betty) had a key and so did Mr Gershenson. She said she gave her key back when she left in July 1938. There was a small incident at the shop one Sunday, at the rear of the shop was a small room, kept padlocked when the shop was closed (Miss Ward had bought a padlock from Woolworth's for the purpose). On opening the shop one morning, Dora Comely discovered that someone had been in the back room and disturbed some of her personal papers kept in an attaché case. On complaining to Mr Gershenson, he just said

'I wanted some paper', which she accepted as an admission that he had been in her case.

'Well, I think he got the lock off here' she said to Miss Ward.

Mrs Sarah Ellen Roberts of 1, G.W.R Flats, Pontypool Road was interviewed by Police Sergeant. J. Haines on she stated she lived apart from her husband William Roberts of 11, David Street, Ebbw Vale. Her employment at Jacquemore's started on 4th July 1938 and finished on the 10th September of that year, handing her shop keys (including the one to the padlock in the back room) to her successor Mrs Hanford. Mrs Roberts stated

'I am almost certain that Mr Lewis did not have a key to the premises for on one occasion he asked my permission to pass through the shop to inspect the upstairs room.'

Kathleen Hanford of 27, Broadway, Pontypool gave her account to the police. She said she lived at the above address for thirteen years, with her husband. She named her married son, Garad 'and one in school away'. Living near to Plasmont she knew Lewis well and had seen him on 22nd May outside Jacquemore's, where she was the current manageress. She walked with him along Crane Street at about 11.20 am to Daniel's the grocers shop. She said that when she started work at Jacquemore's she was given a Yale key (16/A/816) and one for the back room by Mrs Roberts, the previous manageress, she confirmed that Mr Gershenson had a key as he had been in the shop when she wasn't there and left a note for her about stock. Kathleen Hanford's husband Philip was also interviewed; he said he was not working 'through ill health'. He said he would go to the shop with his wife every Monday morning to help her stock take.

Barnett Gershenson the father of Ernest Gershenson – aged fifty-nine of 66, Newport Road was questioned by Detective Sergeant D.G. Davies and J. Haines, of his knowledge of the keys to the Crane Street shop on 3rd June. Though He confirmed he was a Russian and came from Carabelbroka, where he was born in 'sometime in August' of 1879. His parents were Gerlro and Sora. He had come to this country in some thirty years ago with his wife and two children Fanny and Ernest. He originally lived in Tredegar, then Cardiff, finally settling in the Risca area in 1923. Curiously he held the same occupation as William Lewis, that of a draper, though he visited his customers at home and sold goods on credit. He stated that his son Ernest was educated at Tredegar High

School, later going to work in London for J. Lyons and Co. From there he became the Manager of the Piccadilly Hotel, Manchester, where he stayed for nine years. He said his son

'Travels a great deal and I only see him on occasions. He is registered as an alien.'

He saw his son on 29th May 1939 when he arrived at his home in Risca at about 8am. They travelled to the Blackwood shop and for lunch had tea, bread and butter and chipped potatoes' and then to Merthyr. His son dropped him off at Newport Bridge saying he was on the way to London. The carpenter and joiner James Hamar of 34, Wainfelin Avenue, Pontypool said he was currently in the employ of Mr W. Gardener, Builder and Contractor of The Sycamores, Pontypool. He said he wasn't sure who had given him the front door key in March 1938, when he was employed for two days to put up shelving in the shop. However, he was sure it wasn't Mr Lewis, whom he knew well and had last seen on 22nd May by the Catholic Church in George Street.

Aubrey William Thomas (painter) of 6, Woodfield Road also had access to the key to the front door, which he picked up from the Osbourne Cafe next door. This would have been when the shop was being painted, the interior for Jacquemore's, the exterior for Lewis. By the time he had finished the work 'a young lady took charge' and he didn't see the Yale key again. Nothing in these interviews gave any indication of where the Yale key found on the floor in Plasmont came from, only the fact that it opened the front door of the Crane Street shop.

Needless to say the police were quick on his trail. In it he reiterated that he had been at home all day on Monday 22nd but on the 23rd he had an appointment with Robert Cormack [8]. He had been a regular visitor at Plasmont since he was a child.

The search for the origin of the keys took up a lot of police time and resources when they could ill afford a diversion.

Aubrey William Thomas attended Pontypool Police Station on 5th June as yet another person to have worked inside 13, Crane Street and who'd had access to the key.

He stated that until August 1938 he had been employed on his own account but currently he worked for Messrs William Arthur of Abersychan. In March 1938 Lewis had employed him to do some painting in the shop for Jacquemore's and at the same time he painted the exterior for Lewis. He borrowed the key for No. 13 from the cafe next door on that occasion. James Hamar of 34, Wainfelin Avenue was also at the Police Station on the 5th June. He was a carpenter and joiner in the employ of Mr W. Gardner, Builder and Contractor of The Sycamores, Pontypool. He had also worked at the shop putting up shelves for Jacquemore's. He mentioned that he had seen Lewis, whom he knew well, at about 5.45 pm on Monday 22nd May near St Albans Church in George Street. Hamar confirmed that he had not retained a key to the shop.

---

[8] Cormack dealt with the auction sale of the property at Plasmont.

WHO HAD ACCESS TO PLASMONT HOUSE?

Certainly the painter Thomas Brimble for washing brushes and access to the sink whilst he was painting as did his workmen. Also Maud Barnett from Plasmont Cottage for her Sunday morning clean and preparation of dinner – though neither of them mention having access to a key.

There was a rumour afoot, Mrs Barnett had encouraged Mrs Drinkwater to 'identify' Brimble as one of the mystery men seen in Conway Road, on the night the murder was believed to have been committed. This was after a photograph had appeared in the South Wales Argus. Brimble's movements around the time of the murder were carefully scrutinised, Madge Beese of Bryn Derwen, Richmond Road, Pontnewydd, described as a single woman said that on Monday 22nd May, she had a card 'bearing the name of Tom Brimble left at my house and it must have been left after 6.30 pm'.

Wilfred John Flower of 1, High Houses, Victoria Road, Abersychan a builder's labourer employed by Coles Brothers, Builders of Garndiffaith often saw Tom Brimble on the 7.10 am bus from Abersychan. Whilst the two didn't sit together he confirmed that in the six or seven weeks that he had been using that route, Brimble also caught the bus.

Fred Tudgay of Earlsemore, Cwmavon Road, Cwmffrwdoer was employed by Tom Brimble and had worked for him 'on and off for four years'. He gave a statement which described the daily routine a Plasmont. He said that in the third week of April, he had worked with Brimble, William Brimble (Tom's brother) and father Henry Brimble (known as Ebenezer) at Plasmont House. Cyril – the boy apprentice was also there. They were erecting a corrugated iron fence and applying a colour-wash to the exterior of Plasmont. Tudgay (unlike his employer Brimble) must have had access to a vehicle as he and William Brimble called at Sandbrook and Dawes to collect a hundredweight cask of paint.

Tudgay said

'With this we washed the outside wall from Broadway, along George Street, Conway Road and into the area of Plasmont House.'

For some reason they did not paint the walls of Plasmont Cottage, even though it was attached to the main house. All tools belonging to the workmen were kept in a garden shed opposite the back gate of Plasmont House. They generally started work around 7.30 am, and 'took their lunch on the job'. Lewis was seen out and about by 8.30 am and the milkman usually arrived at 9.30 am. Tudgay was unable to say whether or not the back door to Plasmont was locked in the night, it was always open when he arrived and he had few occasions to enter the house, except occasionally to use the kitchen tap. He confirmed that Lewis would be 'in and out of the house all day', leaving fairly early to collect the rents. He occasionally joined the workman in a cup of afternoon tea, once they all enjoyed a glass of wine on the lawn.

PUB GOSSIP

On May 27th, John Atkins, landlord of The Pineapple Inn, Pontypool overheard a conversation between two men at the bar. They were discussing a man they named as Fred Bullimore and said that he had a good idea who had committed the Pontypool murder. Atkins didn't recognise the men but they talked about seeing Bullimore 'at The Works' so assumed that is where they were employed. Within hours of reporting this conversation Alfred Edward Bullimore, was at Pontypool police station. John Atkins brother was Detective

Constable Reginald Atkins who was on the Lewis case. Bullimore was asked to account for the rumour. He said he lived with his wife and child at 36, Fowler Street and was a sheet mill catcher employed by Messrs Baldwin at Panteg (known locally as The Works). He said he knew 'Jack' Atkins the landlord of The Pineapple, New Inn as footballer. He also said that he'd never set foot in The Pineapple and rarely frequented any public house. Although, like everyone in Pontypool, he had discussed the murder with others he had never stated to anyone that he knew who was responsible.

'If any person has suggested that I knew who was responsible it is defiantly untrue' he said indignantly.'

Islwyn Jones aged 29 of 22, Gray Street; Abertillery was in the Golden Lion Hotel in Usk when Bert Gardener the licensee told him that two men were looking for lodgings.

'They had come down from Sunderland and had been in a cheap lodging house in Newport, where they had seen a man with a roll of notes'.

Although this was third hand information it was still considered important enough for a statement to be recorded by Police Sergeant Alfred Butter (No.219).

John George of Penyrehol Farm Abersychan a miner at R.O.F. Glascoed and employed by Nuttall's was in the public bar of the Beaufort Arms during dinner hour one day. He said the bar was full of R.O.F. workers and lorry drivers associated with the works at around 1.40 pm when he heard a man claim that he could put his hand on the man who had committed the murder. Unfortunately George said he did not know the man who made this statement.

On 29th May, Ivor Arthur Jones a photographer of The Arcade, Abertillery went to his local police station. He made a statement to Sgt Alfred Butler. He said he was in the Steam Packet Hotel some 5 weeks prior to the murder when he overheard a woman discussing a man she referred to as

'A rich old bachelor from Pontypool.'

He also thought she mentioned the name 'Lewis'. He reported that the conversation thus 'The woman said she had 'kept house' for Lewis or that he had asked her to. At that point she turned to Jones and said

'He asked me several times to marry him. I would rather remain a prostitute all my life than marry an old man. I would not mind having his money.'

After this she apparently referred to the fact that she would like to find the money he kept in his house. His description of the woman reads :- age about 40 – 45, plump figure, well preserved, about 5ft 6ins tall, dark hair, fresh complexion, dressed in navy blue costume, clean appearance. Jones added that she appeared well-known by the customers of the Steam Packet Hotel. The statement was forwarded to Detective Inspector Rees by Superintendent Eugene Davies.

Victor Bowe, landlord of The Winning Horse Inn, Shaftesbury Street, Newport went to the Pontypool police with news of a conversation he had overheard.

'At approximately 12.30 pm today, 25th May 1939 I was serving in my public bar when two men walked in, ordered beer and commenced to talk about the Derby Race. We were all looking at the Derby Herald newspaper and saw the account of Mr Lewis of Pontypool. One of the men said to me

'They'll have 'em when he comes back from Epsom' – the men were strangers to me.'

He described the men – one was aged about 30, 5ft 5ins, dark face, clean shaven, light suit and a very light tie. The other he said was also aged about 30, 5ft 7ins, clean shaven with a blue suit. He thought he would recognise the men again.

A lady called Mrs Margaret Trinder of 93, Upper George Street was also the subject of virulent gossip. Rumour was rife that she had been arrested for the murder. There was tittle-tattle on the train from Sebastopol to the Wern Hir Halt at Glascoed amongst the men going to work and her name has even been whispered to the author during researches as 'the one that did it'. This demonstrates how for many years, vicious but unfounded gossip can survive in a small town. However, there is no mention of an arrest in the Scotland Yard files, though like many others she gave a voluntary statement. Mrs Trinder's 'crime' was that she had been reported as spending money freely on Saturday 27th May whilst in the Cross Keys Hotel, Tudor Street, Abergavenny. She was with members of her family and spent upwards of £2, however said the informant

'This wasn't unusual for her as her husband has a good job at Pontnewynydd Steelworks' said one informant.

Apparently Mrs Trinder stayed in the Cross Keys until stop-tap, except for visiting her mother-in-law opposite. By the following day, it was reported by the gossips, she was back at the Post Office as she had run out of money.

Margaret Trinder knew Mr Lewis well having been a tenant of his for nine years at the time of the murder. She called at Plasmont, every Friday with her rent and said in her statement that she would often share a glass of wine with Lewis. Indeed she still had a wine glass belonging to Lewis but had made sure that Mr Pritchard (nephew) and Mr Watkins (brother-in-law) were aware of this. The last time she visited Plasmont was on 14th May at about 9.30 am when she found Lewis brushing up leaves in the garden. They had a brief conversation about repairs to Mrs Trinder's house. As for the 22nd May, she had gone down to George Street at around 6.05 pm to watch the South Wales Borderers marching through town and arrived back home in time to hear a boxing fight on the wireless which was around 9 pm. She didn't go out again but stood on the doorstep of her house, her husband Albert had been with her all evening. They went to bed about 10.45 pm but did not see anyone hanging about Plasmont. However the streets were still busy and there were a number of people passing about.

On the 24th May she went with Mrs Fowler to pick up her gas mask at George Street School, Albert Trinder was on a day shift but had chosen to work 6 am to 10 pm. Denying that she knew Lewis' habits she did remark that she had seen a woman taking the curtains down at Plasmont .

'She was wearing a dust cloth around her head. I was given to understand (by whom she doesn't say) that it was the woman he was going to marry....'

She last saw the woman about 3 weeks before Easter. She said it certainly wasn't Mrs Barnett doing the cleaning.

With regard to the allegations of free spending, Margaret Trinder said in her statement of 30th June that she had been visiting Abergavenny every Saturday since Easter of that year and was there over the Whitsun Holidays.

'I spent a great deal of money. My husband earns good money as last week I had £7 from him and I expect £5 or

£6 this weekend. My husband has a pension of 8/- per week and it is left and we pick it up in one large sum, that's how we had a good deal over Whitsun.'

Detective Constable Adams followed this story up and looked out of a window facing Upper George Street. From there he could see that anyone in the houses opposite had an excellent view of Plasmont and the front part of the grounds. He made enquiries at a number of houses in Upper George Street and at 89, he went upstairs to the apartment were Laura Amos lived.

'She has a gas stove on the landing where she does her cooking and therefore spends a good deal of time there. She is a woman who does not go out of doors much and is very often looking out of this landing window, which gives an excellent view of the front grounds of Plasmont which face Upper George Street.'

Eliza Brown, wife of Alfred Brown also of 89, Upper George Street said there had been no curtains on the windows of Plasmont since Sarah Lewis had died, with the exception of the window on the bottom right hand side of the house where the curtains were up and drawn. However she added that Lewis had put curtains at all the windows when the decorators were there.

RELEASED FROM PRISON

By June the police were clutching at any information and had decided to have a look at men who had recently enjoyed some time at 'Her Majesty's Pleasure' for violent crimes but were now on release. A considerable amount of police time was undertaken tracking down men all over Britain and obtaining statements to eliminate them from enquiries.

One man had been re-arrested and was in Cardiff prison for 12 months hard labour. Another was on a ship at Botwood, Newfoundland. One had recently been released from the Casual Ward of City Lodge, Cardiff. He was proven to be in the Empire Cinema, Tonypandy on 22nd May – having paid fourpence for a ticket to see the film.

However, one such recently released prisoner was Alfred Greenhow. He was a cut above the others; he had not been in prison for petty violence but for manslaughter.

WOMAN FOUND DEAD IN A WOOD.

MURDER CHARGE ON MAN'S ALLEGED CONFESSION.

The Leeds police were alerted to 'bring him in' with regard to the dates 22nd to 24th May. Greenhow had been released on April 27th 1939 to Penarth, where he reported to the Police Station there at 7pm, stating that he would be getting the midnight train from Penarth bound for Newcastle-on-Tyne, where he hoped to take up employment with Messrs Armstrong Vickers Ltd. He was expected to register with the police on arrival, but didn't turn up in that city. Greenhow, previously a seaman had been in prison serving 12 years for the manslaughter of Janet Macdonald a single woman aged 32. She had been strangled in Pontefract Wood, Headingly in May 1928. He had freely admitted to the killing, first confessing to a startled tram conductor at 11 pm, on a tramcar from Lawnswood. The conductor then flagged down two policemen, who were equally astonished by Greenhow's admission.

Described in the Nottingham Evening Post as a 'well built, sunburnt and good looking man with brown curly hair' he ended up in Dartmoor Prison. In 1932 he was one of 32 convicts in the dock for riot and mutiny in the prison.

'On January 24th 1932, at Princetown, Devon, being riotously and tumultuously assembled together, to the disturbance of the peace, feloniously, unlawfully and with force did demolish, pull down or destroy a building devoted to public use or erected or maintained by public contributions, contrary to Section 11 of the Malicious Damage Act 1861'.

A massive dock had been installed in the Courtroom to accommodate the charged convicts and their warders. The Court heard that prisoners had burned documents in the hope of destroying their records. Greenhow had been seen to comfort a fellow prisoner who had been injured by a bullet.

Despite this, on his release in April 1939 he hadn't been out of prison long when he made up for his confinement. Chief Constable J. Jones, of Cardiff, said that Greenhow was wanted at Newport and Barry Dock for shop-breaking and larceny.

Alfred Greenhow was finally tracked down on 27th July 1939 via a Metropolitan Telegram to Hull City Police.

'On or about 8th May 1939 he obtained employment on s.s. Marie Tofte as an able seaman, and sailed from Riverside Docks, Hull on the same day bound for Cette, France. He says he was employed by Jutland Steamship Company.'

Greenhow, interviewed by Detective Sergeant Thomas Picken of Middlesbrough Police confirmed that he sailed on the s.s.Marie Tofte on 8th May. Arriving in Cette, he was paid off and then travelled to Marseilles, where he stayed at the Sailor's Club in Rue Forbin. On 31st May 1939 he was repatriated by the British Consul and returned to England aboard the s.s. Glantilly Castle, landing in London around 10th June. Another false lead which took up many police man-hours only to produce another suspect with a water tight alibi.

WHO KNEW PLASMONT HOUSE?

The police wanted to interview those who might know the layout of Plasmont House, who had worked there or even just visited and what did they know of the Lewis family.

James Roderick of 5, Cambria Street, Griffithstown gave a statement to Chief Inspector Rees on May 31st. He said he was born in Pontypool on 15th July 1883 and had lived most of his live in the town, latterly with his wife and two daughters. At the age of 12 he started work down the mines where he stayed until he was 31, joining the Army in 1914. Having been wounded in France he was discharged home in 1919 and had held various posts as labourer, bookmaker and odd-job man. He had been on the dole since Christmas Eve 1938. Whilst he was doing casual labouring during 1921 and 1928 he did some jobs for the Lewis family on and off. He worked at Plasmont, whitewashing and tarring the outbuildings. He knew the Lewis family well and said he used to enter the house to have his meals, though he had never been upstairs.

He had last seen Lewis walking through Pontypool town centre some two months previous and heard of his death when he met a friend by the Co-operative Stores in Commercial Road.

This friend, Ted Young of Rockhill Road told him that

'Mr Lewis had cut his throat.'

Roderick said that on Monday 22nd May and Tuesday 23rd he was at home all day and in the evening after his tea and affirmed that he was nowhere near Plasmont House between the dates of 22nd May and 24th.

Linda May Morgan was interviewed at Pontypool police station on 1st June. She said she was twenty nine years of age, a domestic and she lived at 17, Buller Street, Cwmffrwdoer, near Pontnewynydd. Miss Morgan stated that she went to work for Miss Sarah Lewis at Plasmont House in 1936. Mr William Lewis was then living there permanently. She was the only servant employed there and was accustomed to clean in all the rooms. She worked there for three months and saw Lewis' sisters come and go and once heard a quarrel about money matters between Sarah and Emily. Mr Williams Lewis however was quiet and reserved. She confirmed that Miss Parker was a frequent visitor but didn't consider her any more that a friend to Mr Lewis. For some reason unrecorded she said that Sarah Lewis had forbidden her to talk to Mrs Barnett of Plasmont Cottage.

Mr David Clifford Udell of The Cottage, Broadway, Pontypool had known the Lewis family for over twenty years as an architect and surveyor. He had an office at 23, Commercial Street, Pontypool and had worked for the family in a business capacity. He was less than complimentary when talking about them.

'I knew the whole family and acted for all of them with the exception of the parents. They are and were people who valued money very highly and I would say they were grasping people.'

However, he said that William Lewis was not as bad as the rest of them and 'would spend money'. Though he thought that if one member of the family spent more than was considered reasonable by the others, they would be taken to task. As a frequent visitor to Plasmont he had the opportunity of meeting the family on their own territory. He was present when Sarah Lewis' Will was settled and said

'There was considerable discontent as to the manner in which the property had been divided. In fact I know that at all times there were petty squabbles over finance'.

He also noted that a Miss Parker visited regularly and felt that a marriage might take place between herself and William Lewis but added that the other members of the Lewis family and their spouses

'Did not take kindly to the idea.'

He ended his statement by saying that he knew there was always a considerable sum of money at Plasmont House.

John Russell Evans of Grove Lodge, George Street said he had lived at Grove Lodge for the last five years. He knew Lewis, having met him on business matters. He had worked for the Gwent Relay Company which brought him into contact with Lewis in connection with 'Way Leaves'. He said he had been in Plasmont House but at the time Sarah Lewis was still alive. He hadn't been in the house for over 12 months. As regards the 22nd May he said he was visiting a friend, Mr G. Morgan, of Springfield, Wainfelin, he was there from about 7 pm until 10 pm. The following morning, Evans said he was out and about in his garden nearly all day.

Francis Bruce Bowditch aged 27 of 34, Carw Road, Croesyceiliog, Cwmbran said in his statement to Detective Sergeant D.G. Davies that he had visited the house twice, the first time on Monday 15th May 1939. He was looking for a house to rent and had been to see Mr Dowell a local estate agent. However, Dowell didn't have any vacant properties on his books so he referred Bowditch to Lewis. Having called on Lewis he discovered that he didn't have any house to offer either. However Lewis said that his brother-in-law from Swansea would be in Pontypool the following Monday and to call back then. Bowditch returned on Monday 22nd at about 5.15 pm.

> 'As I entered the drive a clergyman walked out and I opened the gate for him. I went to the house and saw Mr Lewis who said I had missed his brother-in-law who had just left.'

He described the clothing Lewis was wearing

> 'Fawn trousers and waistcoat and a collar and tie, he had green paint stains on his shirt.'

Miss Ethel Parker, a lady friend of Lewis knew Plasmont quite well. She said when she visited she would go in through the front gate and to the front door, at other times though she used the back door. In winter, the front door was generally locked from the inside, which had been a more frequent occurrence since Sarah had died.

Someone who was adamant that he hadn't been inside Plasmont was William Thomas Hinds, a store-man for the Monmouthshire Regiment, Corporal (No. 44997). He stated firmly that he had never done any wiring in the House. He was able to account for his movements on 22nd May, the date of the Display in Pontypool Park as it was the day he 'joined-up for the Territorial Army.

His morning was spent undergoing various medical tests for the Army and in the afternoon he went to the Drill Hall. At about 5.30 pm he went home but was quickly out again to see the soldiers drilling in the Park. At around 8.30 pm he went to the Palais-de-Dance, returning home at 11 pm.

'Father was in bed in the kitchen' he said 'and I did not go out again that night.' The following day Hinds said he went to look for work at R.O.F. Glascoed

THE AUCTION

Then a surprising announcement in the press – the contents of Plasmont were to be sold by Auction on 19th and 20th of July – antique pieces, oil paintings and grandfather clocks said the Free Press, there were 373 lots and 256 went on the first day, the following day everything was sold. [9]

Anticipating demand – the admission was by catalogue only - smartly charged by the Auctioneers Robert Cormack at 6d. The many lots which included 3 pianos, two, nine piece suites, a 4ft 6in Italian vase made in 1752, cases and cases of stuffed animals, two 'all brass' Italian bedsteads and a brand new summerhouse were put under the hammer. The contents of the house were sold and scattered, though there are still people in Pontypool to this day who own a souvenir of Plasmont.

---

[9] The contents of the Auction Catalogue can be found in the appendix

Many more people had come to gawp at the house in which a murder had taken place, than to buy – 6d was worth it to get a look around the murder house and especially the bedroom where the body was found

Described by the Free Press as a chamber no bigger than the average bathroom (for those that had a bathroom, let alone an average one in Pontypool in 1939) it was a bit of a disappointment to those looking for something exciting, the wall paper splashed with blood had been removed and the reporter said that the room

'....looked out on to a hideous pink-washed wall – the room itself was decorated with pink paper and was thoroughly unattractive. Why it was used as a bedroom at all is a mystery when there are so many spacious rooms in the house?'

However, the writer in the South Wales Argus painted a wonderful still life picture of the interior of Plasmont

'It was like putting the clock back 100 years, the crowds that flocked to the viewing were able to tour the house. The rambling old mansion was chock-a-block with nick-knacks, it would have been no surprise to see a crinolined lady from one of the discarded photograph albums step into the drawing room and pick up the zither harp which lay neglected on the dusty floor. As expected the house was filled with sightseers willing to pay for a sixpenny catalogue'.

According to the South Wales Argus the house was stripped bare, people even buying up Lewis' clothes.

Police Diagrams of Plasmont House

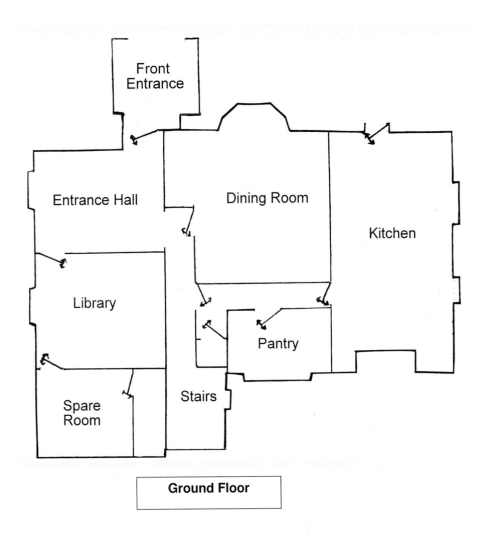

Front Entrance

Entrance Hall

Dining Room

Kitchen

Library

Pantry

Spare Room

Stairs

Ground Floor

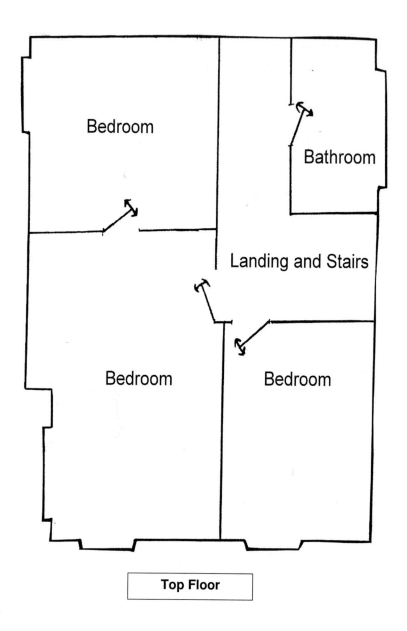

Bedroom

Bathroom

Landing and Stairs

Bedroom

Bedroom

Top Floor

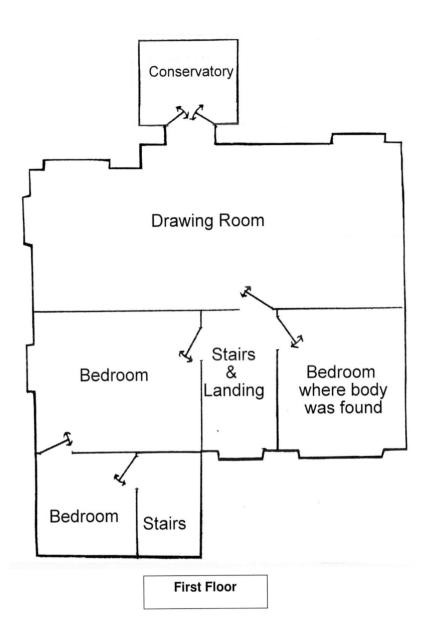

First Floor

Lewis' bedroom - the body was on the bed
on the right of the photo

FIND THE LADY

'Key to Mystery not Held by a Woman' said the headline in the South Wales Argus of 30th May. The front page article 'from our own correspondent' in Pontypool said that the detectives at Scotland Yard

'We're not attaching much credence to the suggestion that a woman might hold a key to the mystery.'

Rumour had been further fuelled when one of the wreaths at Lewis funeral had a card attached saying 'From Ethel with fond memories'.

William Alfred Lewis was known to have a number of lady friends, most of whom knew about each other, though there was considerable animosity between two of them – Miss Harris of Goytre and Miss Parker of New Inn.

Miss Harris's mother, of Maesycwmmer talking to a reporter of the South Wales Argus said

'My daughter had been friendly with Mr Lewis for a couple of months but did not give the proposal serious consideration. I don't think she knows of Mr Lewis's death yet.'

However the reporter from the Daily Mail was quick to locate her in Droitwich and pass on the bad news. (Annie) Irene Harris is described in the Daily Mirror as

'A tall attractive red-haired teacher, who lived with her sister and mother but at present was living in Droitwich.

She told the Daily Mail reporter

'I just laughed it off when he proposed to me the first time but I soon found out he was very serious. I told him that I could not marry him if he insisted on living in Plasmont as the house was too big and eerie. I could not have lived there. He wanted to marry very much. Perhaps we should have eventually married. I used to go to his house Plasmont fairly often. I knew he had other women friends, rumours that he was getting married started when he had alterations made to the house. I do not know whether the rumours concerned me. Perhaps they did.

When I came to Droitwich he saw me on the bus and I said I was staying until July. His murder has been a terrible shock to me... he told me he was forty three and he did not look much older[10]. I was fond of him and liked being with him and perhaps if he had promised to move from Plasmont I may have agreed to marry him. It is well known all around Pontypool that he was wealthy. He owned practically the whole of the town and streets of houses. He spent most of his time looking after his property and collecting rents. He seemed to live for his property transactions but it would not be fair to call him a recluse.'

Detective Sergeant D.G. Davies travelled to St Margaret's, Corbett Avenue, Droitwich to see Miss Harris, who had moved there 'for health reasons'. She suffered from rheumatism. She had met Lewis in April 1938 when he called at her house for business purposes. Miss Harris said that she and Lewis met occasionally and just prior to Christmas 1938, he proposed marriage. She wouldn't give him an answer however as he was just as determined to keep Plasmont as his lady friends were for him to be rid of it. They met every few weeks

'Every time I saw him he repeated his proposal of marriage.'

She also said that they wrote to each other. She said he didn't discuss his financial dealings with her but he did mention he had Gas and Water shares. On the subject of Miss Parker, Miss Harris said it was a one sided question. Whilst Miss Parker might wish to marry him, Lewis had no intentions of marrying her. She did say that Miss Parker had called at her home once, but she was out. Miss Harris had an alibi – confirmed by Mrs Bessie Hall, she was in Droitwich at the time of the murder.

---

[10] Though most people referred to Lewis as 'an old man'

Recalling the last time she saw Lewis on 29th April, she said she went to tea at Plasmont House, he proposed as usual and as usual she had refused. She was one of the few to venture upstairs at Plasmont.

'I was rather disgusted at the dirty condition of the place and was glad to get downstairs.'

Miss Harris recalled a visit to the Pritchard's in Cardiff when Lewis repeated his proposal of marriage in front of his sister Miriam. She told Miss Harris that Lewis had no intention of marrying Miss Parker, another lady friend.

Lewis' sister Miriam was confident that had he lived, Miss Harris would have been the chosen bride. This was based on Miriam's theory that he had decided to sever his friendship with Miss Parker in view of getting wed.

'She wished him to assign to her all his property, in case of death, prior to getting married.'

Miriam, reports this conversation to Inspector Rees on 3rd June. She recalled an incident in Cardiff. Miriam had put off a visit to Pontypool on account of illness and was sitting in the car, outside her house in Cardiff on Tuesday 23rd May when she was suddenly accosted by Miss Parker.

'Oh, here you are' said Miss Parker, 'I thought you were ill in bed, I'm glad I've caught you.'

I said 'What's the matter?'

Miss Parker replied 'I have come down to tell you what a rotter your brother is'.

I replied 'What's the matter, have you quarrelled with him?'

She said 'You know quite well, you are quite as bad as he is, fancy entertaining Irene Harris, you know that we have been keeping company for three years.' Miriam replied,

'I told her that I could entertain who I liked in my own house. At that point Mr Pritchard my husband came to the front gate and Miss Parker spoke to him, I asked if she would like to come in the house and have a cup of tea and wait until I returned from town, which would not be long. I drove off leaving her with my husband. I later learned from him that she did not go into the house, she also spoke to my son Lewis.'

In her statement on the 24th May, Miss Parker agreed that she had been angry with Emily Watkins (Lewis' other sister) when she discovered that Lewis had taken Miss Harris to visit the Pritchard's in Cardiff although she didn't recall calling him 'a rotter'. She did say that she had felt hurt and wished she had never called there in the first place.

Ethel Parker described as a spinster of Glencoe, Pontypool Road, New Inn said she last saw Lewis (whom she called her second cousin) in his dining room when she visited Plasmont at 5.30 pm on Saturday 20th May. She left at 8 pm

'He was in good spirits' she said.

In a Daily Mail article on Friday May 26th Miss Parker confirmed that marriage had been discussed between Mr Lewis and herself. Trouble arose however because Mr Lewis insisted that after the marriage they should live in his house Plasmont. In a further statement on 19th June, the visit to Plasmont on the 20th May took on a different complexion, there had been a quarrel between her and Lewis. She said

'During a conversation I had with Mr Lewis, he denied that he had ever proposed marriage to me. I knew this to be false, as he had repeatedly done so, and I lost my temper and slapped his face. He was not the least put out with me for doing it and we were quite good friends immediately after. Mr Lewis talked that evening of getting married and I asked him to whom. He had repeatedly spoken to me of Miss Harris, Miss James and Miss Humphreys and I asked him if it was Miss Harris.'

He replied 'No, but she's alright'.

In a further statement to Chief Inspector Rees on 2nd June, Ethel Parker expanded on her friendship with Lewis. She said she didn't really know him until he retired from his drapery business some 4 or 5 years previous, when he moved to live at Plasmont on a permanent basis, this was after the death of his brother Walter in 1936. Miss Parker's mother died in July 1934, at the time Sarah Lewis lived at Plasmont and she was a great comfort to Miss Parker, who became a frequent caller. William Lewis had also helped her in business affairs following her mother's death. Miss Parker continued to visit after Sarah died and she said that whenever she visited, Lewis would tell her about his property or tenants and helped her purchase a house in 1938. However, he never discussed banking or money affairs in her presence. Miss Parker was convinced that before Sarah Lewis died, it was her wish that Lewis and Miss Parker should marry.

Following the death of Sarah Lewis, Miss Parker continued to visit William Lewis once a week. They would often discuss his property dealings, had even spoken of having the interior of Plasmont decorated. She also said that he was a secretive man who seldom expressed his future intentions. The Lewis sisters Mrs Emily Watkins and Mrs Miriam Pritchard were on good terms with their brother and she said he wasn't one to harbour a grudge or grievance and if someone did something to upset him, whilst he might be outspoken at the time, he would quickly forget it. Inspector Rees was of the opinion that Miss Parker would have consented to marriage with Lewis, if only he would give up Plasmont House for a more modern property. He also noted that Lewis dallied with the other ladies (and told Miss Parker that he did) in an effort to make her jealous and agree to a wedding.

Miss Parker mentioned another lady friend of Lewis, Miss Edith James of Llancayo, near Usk. Lewis and Miss James' brother had been apprentices together in the drapery trade with Howells of Cardiff. There was also a Miss Humphreys of Griffithstown in the frame.

'He appeared delighted that so many ladies were taking notice of him.' she said

Vera Humphreys, secretary of 25 The Avenue Griffithstown said she met Lewis during a business deal, which was conducted mostly by letter or in the presence of her father and brother.

'Mr Lewis proposed to me but I treated the matter as a joke' she said.

Emma Harrison of 30, College Road, Pontypool saw Mr Lewis every day, as he used to call at her stall in Pontypool Market around about 11 am, to collect his daily paper. She said that the last time she had seen him was the morning of 22nd May.

Another lady who worked in Pontypool Market was Edith James from Llancayo, near Usk. She was seen by the police but apparently declined to go to the Police Station to make a statement. She said she knew Lewis merely as a customer who called at her dairy stall in the Market. However, letters discovered when the police made their search of Plasmont, disputed this declaration. Correspondence was found from Edith James to show that she had invited Lewis to spend a few days holiday with her. This was in 1938. She had also accompanied him on a visit to his sister Miriam, in Cardiff on one occasion. She recognised a pair of gloves found at Plasmont as ones that she had purchased from Fowler's of Pontypool some three Christmases ago as a Christmas present for Lewis.

Morgan Jones of 24, Fowler Street in a police interview with Police Constable Parfitt (No. 167) said he would not allow his daughter Haggie to work at Plasmont

'Owing to the fact that the girl previous left, owing to William Alfred Lewis conduct towards her.'

Mr Jones said that he had been in Plasmont Cottage visiting the Barnett's and had played the piano there.

He alleged 'I have known Mr and Mrs Barnett to say that they have had to go into Plasmont, to quieten Lewis and his sister and they have had to punch them about.'

FRIENDS OR ENEMIES?
The Scotland Yard detectives were, in lieu of any other evidence, working on the possibility that there was someone with a grudge against Lewis, perhaps someone who owed him money. The Argus reporter suggested that someone, somewhere suddenly had a lot more money to spend and that person may also have the gold sovereigns that were missing from one of the safes. In his article Questions for Detectives'' on Monday 5th June he states;

'Here are a few of the problems to which answers are being sought. Did Lewis leave the two safes open. Did he meet anybody after leaving George Street School at about 8.45 pm, and if so, did he take that person to the house, or was his assailant already in Plasmont? Why, if robbery was the main motive, was a tin box, containing about £100 and sovereigns, left under the bed on which Lewis was murdered? Did Lewis leave his keys in a handbag in a drawer in a top room, buried beneath other things, or were they put there by the murderer? Was it a murder of passion, or for fiscal gain? Was the murderer a man or woman? Discovering that some of the bank notes found in the tin box had been issued less than a week previously by the Bank of England, confirmed that the contents of the box were from Lewis's last rent collection round.'

Did William Alfred Lewis have any enemies? He seemed a nice enough chap, described as 'affable', well regarded by those who claimed to know him, (these were mostly business acquaintances.) He seemed to have no close friends.

His tenants only had to ask for a repair and it was arranged swiftly, He was well respected by them. Lewis it seems was a solitary man and kept himself to himself, apart from his penchant for the ladies. Many people have referred to him as 'the old man' – he was only 59 when he died but his demeanour harked back to earlier times. He was short – about 5ft 4ins, quite slight, weighing around 10 stone and always wore a bowler hat and a brown checked suit when out and about.

John Matthew Cope of Bryngwyn Place, Pontypool was the Deputy Chief of the Pontypool Fire Brigade. He had known Lewis for many years describing him as

'A man of peculiar habits, reticent and secretive.'

This description is in direct contrast to other witnesses who attested to the fact that Lewis told everyone and anybody about his property portfolio. Cope and Lewis would have a beer together occasionally, the last time was about 3 weeks prior to the murder.

'He was not a mean man' he said' 'but stood his ground. I have drunk with him in the George public house. He has never mentioned women to me. I have been to Plasmont House but not for the last twelve months.'

The first rumble of a quarrel involving Lewis came in a statement made by Charles Fenwick Jones, a tinplate worker of no. 6, Old Estate Yard, Pontymoile, Pontypool. He said that about 3 months previous he was returning from the Town Forge, when he passed Billy (William) Allen and Lewis talking, he said he heard Allen remark

'I wants another dollar and I will bloody have it.'

Jones also noticed that Terry Hurcombe was on the other side of the road at that time.

Police Constable Ellis Blease (No.26) made an interesting discovery – had Lewis decided to sell Plasmont? Perhaps the entreaties of his various lady friends finally had some influence in this matter. Police Constable Blease doesn't say where he obtained the information but in a statement made on 26th May he said that to his knowledge some 16 months previous, a number of men went to see Plasmont House with the object of buying it for a nightclub and they were given a guided tour of the house. He said in a statement that these men were George Tomboline – Butcher of Pontypool, Moss Mayers of Abersychan, Ted George of 17, Conway Road,

Tom Crook a baker of Old Furnace, Nat Hillman from the Argus or Echo newspaper and Acker Lewes from The News, Pontypool. Was this just idle gossip?

A lady from Abersychan contacted the police to say that some years previous a member of the Brimble family had murdered her three children and had then committed suicide. Certainly no information has come to light about that incident; it would have been the talk of Pontypool. An anonymous postcard addressed to 'The County Constabulary, Pontypool' said

> 'It is freely discussed at our Six Bells Colliery that Brimble the Painter and Decorator knows more about the Murder than any other living person. Many testify he has loitered quite a lot there lately. PLEASE keep him under observation.'

However Inspector Ivor Rees was adamant that Brimble had neither opportunity or reason to kill Lewis.[11]

WHEN DID YOU LAST SEE MR LEWIS?

The Pontypool police were meticulous in their search for witnesses who had seen William Lewis in the days before his death. There were many conflicting stories. He had been seen in Pontypool Park watching the Military display, he had been seen walking along George Street and he had definitely been seen having a gas-mask fitted. Through the newspapers and cinema screens the police appealed for people to come forward. One of the first was a young lady revelling in the wonderful name of Golden Lindsdale Hurcombe of 64, Albion Road who gave her statement to Detective Constable

---

[11] The police found no evidence of murder and suicide as alleged above

Victor Adams at Pontypool Police Station on 31st May. The South Wales Argus reporter described her as

'The Girl in White Overall who was taken to the police station in a patrol car.'

She stated that she was a butcher's assistant and was 17 years of age.

'On Monday 22nd May 1939 I was walking along Albion Road towards Clarence Corner. It was 6.45 pm I saw Mr William Lewis walk out of Lower Park Terrace. I spoke to him and asked if he was going down to the Park. He said he might later on but that he was going to Pontymoile first to make a few calls. I am positive about the time because it was before I went down the Park to see the Territorial's.'

In mentioning the Park, Golden Hurcombe refers to the 25th Anniversary of the South Wales Borderers. Many of those who gave statements recalled that they had attended the display.

A later sighting of Lewis was made by Cathleen Green of 14, Albion Place. She stated to Police Constable Pring (No.56) that she lived with her husband Albert Bernard Green at the address stated. About 8.20 pm. on Monday 22nd May she was just leaving St Alban's Roman Catholic Church (next to Plasmont) when she saw Lewis leave his home. He was carrying a letter in his hand which he posted in the pillar box a few yards down the road, on the opposite side. After posting the letter he retraced his steps and went back into Plasmont. She said that he was wearing a dark maroon suit and a bowler hat.

Pontypool was gearing up for the forthcoming war and gas masks were being issued throughout the town. The final public sighting of William Lewis was by Edmund Williams, 17, Brynderwen, Pontypool. He said to Detective Constable Adams

'I am an Air Raid Warden, I knew the late Mr W.A. Lewis personally. He came to George Street School at about 8.30 pm on Monday 22nd May for the fitting of his Gas Mask. I fitted it and he seemed in good spirits and passed the remark that he hoped that he would never have to use one. He was wearing a brown suit and a bowler hat.'

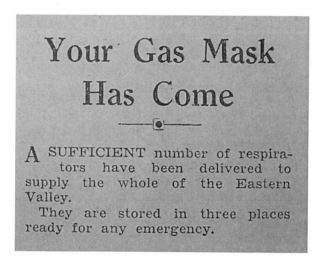

Your Gas Mask Has Come

A SUFFICIENT number of respirators have been delivered to supply the whole of the Eastern Valley.

They are stored in three places ready for any emergency.

In fact a number of people confirmed that they saw Lewis at the gas-mask fitting, Mr A. H. James, Divisional ARP Warden for Pontypool told the South Wales Argus correspondent that Lewis was there a little longer than other people,

'He thought he should have a different size mask than the one the Warden provided.'

The postal service was far different in 1939 – three deliveries a day, including Sundays and the majority of the post was delivered within twenty four hours. Thus James Henry Howells, the newly appointed postman on 'third delivery' (he had only been on that particular shift since Sunday 21st May) was called to the Police Station and gave a statement to Detective Constable Adams at 8.15pm on 25th May.

'I reside at 66, Broadway, Pontypool and I am a postman. Since Sunday 21st May 1939, I have been engaged on the third delivery and would reach Plasmont, Conway Road about 4 pm each day. Whenever I deliver any postal packages there, I put them through the old fashioned letter-box at the side of the house, without going down the steps or through the back gate. I have not delivered any correspondence to Plasmont this week. I walked down past this house about 4pm on Tuesday 23rd May but saw no-one outside or inside the premises.'

Another postman was interviewed, this time by Police Sergeant Haines. Stating his name and address as Hubert Charles Williams of 6, Victoria Road, Pontypool (where he lived with his wife) Williams said that he was attached to the Head Office of the G.P.O (General Post Office) in Pontypool. He was the 'morning and mid-morning' postman. He had delivered mail at Plasmont on Monday 22nd (two or three letters) and also on 23rd (three letters) and 24th (one letter). They had all been delivered in his morning round and he said his usual time of arrival at Plasmont was 6.55 am. He also used 'the old fashioned letter box'.

'It is in the top on one of the windows, in the kitchen, the letters dropping onto the windowsill on the other side.'

He confirmed that he had not had to use the back-door when he made deliveries and was therefore unable to say whether it was locked or not. The letters delivered by Williams the Postman on 22nd May remained unopened. The police considered this a vital clue, it suggested that Lewis had not opened his post since mid-morning of 22nd May.

There must have been a queue of witnesses as various police officers were called in to take statements, all laboriously written out in longhand and still using the old fashioned terminology of 'Who saith' when recording the words of an interviewee. The statements were written in a formal manner, using stilted language which wouldn't have tripped naturally off the tongues of the witnesses. The police were committed to using their own terminology, however this didn't influence the essence of what the witnesses said.

The next statement comes from the milkman who gave his account to Police Sergeant D.G. Davies. The milkman was Wilfred James Williams of Perthellick Farm, Pontnewydd aged 18. He said he was employed by Mr E. H. Humphreys of the same address.

'I deliver milk and do other jobs on the farm. Mr Lewis of Plasmont was, to my knowledge, a customer of Mr Humphreys for twelve months. I used to deliver a quart of milk daily between 9.30 and twenty minutes to ten every morning. I used to open the side door, go into the yard, into the kitchen, pick up the two jugs and put a pint of milk in each. On Monday 22nd May I delivered the quart of milk. I also delivered on 23rd May. On Wednesday 24th May I went into the kitchen and the two jugs were still on the dresser, untouched. This was the first time that such a thing had happened to me while I had been delivering milk. I did not know what to do.'

Williams called next door, at Plasmont Cottage and seeing Mrs Barnett said

'Do you want any milk this morning?' She replied that she didn't have milk. Williams said

'Mr Lewis, rather'.

'Doesn't he want any?' Mrs Barnett replied.

The young milkman now thoroughly confused said

'No, the milk is still in the jugs from Tuesday.'

On hearing from Mrs Barnett that possibly Mr Lewis had 'gone away' he said 'Good morning' and left.

Mr Albert Barnett, of Plasmont Cottage wasn't formally interviewed until 28th May by Police Sergeant D.G.Davies, despite the fact that he had been party to finding the body – if only as guardsman at the door of Plasmont House when Brimble made his search. Barnett states his age as 54, living at Plasmont Cottage with his wife and daughter Pricilla. He also explained the set-up of Plasmont Cottage.

'I am a haulier and work at Tirpentwys Colliery, Pontypool. I have lived at Plasmont Cottage for the past nine years. The cottage consists of five rooms which are really part of the big house. There is a separate entrance to the Cottage, to get admission to Plasmont House you have to go through another door through the back yard. In the bedroom in which I and my wife sleep there is a door leading to the big house but in fact this has not been opened since we have been there and the door has been papered over the whole of the time.'

Despite living next-door for nine years Barnett explained initially that he had only been in Plasmont House a couple of times, and on those occasions, on the ground floor - the kitchen and dining room. However he recalled, some six or seven years ago he did go upstairs to help move a bed. He knew the layout of Plasmont as his wife cleaned for Mr Lewis. He said that the bedroom used by Lewis was on a floor lower than the bedroom occupied by himself and his wife. In fact it adjoined their kitchen and they often heard Lewis turn in for the night. Barnett said that for the previous two months he had been on the afternoon shift at the colliery 2.30 pm – 10.30 pm. He normally arrived home at around 11.30 pm and he sometimes heard Mr Lewis about at this time.

The Barnett's said they were friendly with Lewis (though a statement made by Morgan Jones belies this fact) and would often pass the time of day either in his back-yard or the kitchen. The last time he saw Lewis, Barnett said, was about noon on 22nd May. He left for work as usual at 1.30 pm and returned at 11.30 pm, walking his usual route along Conway Road from Osbourne Road, passing Plasmont on the way. He saw no-one on Conway Road or in the locality of Plasmont. It was not unusual, he said, to find people urinating against the wall of the house as they made their way home. He had often had to remonstrate with them. When he arrived home, Mrs Barnett was already in bed. He confirmed that he had heard nothing unusual during the next two days, though he did note that Lewis wasn't around. He was used to him being away for a day, visiting one of his sisters, though he generally wasn't known to stay overnight. Barnett said his wife first alerted him to the fact that Lewis hadn't been seen, after her conversation with the milk-boy on the previous day.

She had also spoken to Brimble who was anxious to have the windows open at Plasmont House so he could continue painting. After his breakfast Barnett went into the garden of

Plasmont, where he found Brimble mixing paint. Mrs Barnett followed shortly after him and the three of them discussed the fact that Lewis had not been around for the last couple of days.

Mrs Barnett had also spoken to a Mr John Sullivan who was on his way to collect his dole money. He knew Lewis very well, both men having been at the same school. He also tended the garden at Plasmont House. Sullivan said that on his return, he would go and look inside Plasmont to ally Mrs Barnett's worries. Barnett said to his wife

'The best thing to do is to notify the Police.'

However Brimble said

'It's no use to hesitate. Let's go and look for him now.'

As they went toward the door of Plasmont Mrs Barnett cried out

'You are not going in there without me.'

Brimble had preceded them and had gone upstairs, the Barnett's followed and had decided to search the ground floor. They were in the kitchen, about to go down the steps to enter the dining-room. Brimble rushed downstairs and the Barnett's knew immediately that something had occurred.

'He's there right enough, with a pillow over his head.'

Barnett offered to go for the Police but Brimble said

'No – you stop here with your missus and I'll go for the Police. Keep everything quiet until they arrive'. Mr Barnett said

'I then went back to the cottage and kept the wife quiet'.

Which was probably not an easy task judging by her insistence at becoming involved in the search.

Mrs Barnett was keen to add to the story when the Police arrived. In a formal statement she stated that she had three grown up children – one daughter and one son being married and living away from home. The youngest daughter called Pricilla (but whose full name was Leah Pricilla) aged 24 remained at Plasmont Cottage and worked for Mr and Mrs Evans at Ardlui, Wainfelin. Mrs Barnett said she knew Miss Sarah Lewis quite well – she lived at Plasmont house with only a maid to keep her company in the large house, although her brother returned on a Sunday and went back to Cwm on the Monday morning. On Sarah's death in 1936, her brother William had retired from his drapery business in Cwm and had moved back to Plasmont. Mrs Barnett then became his cleaning lady on a Sunday morning, preparing Sunday dinner – tidying up the downstairs rooms that were used. These would be the kitchen and larder, the dining-room, hall and porch. She had the impression that there were only 12 rooms in Plasmont since the division that created Plasmont Cottage but in fact there were seventeen.

Mrs Barnett had not been upstairs at Plasmont since Sarah Lewis had died. She said that William Lewis was very particular that no-one should go upstairs. Mr Lewis, she said was very regular in his habits and described his daily routine to Chief Inspector Rees. On a Sunday morning Lewis would be about the house cleaning the upstairs rooms. This belies the description of the dusty rooms noted by the South Wales Argus reporter. Perhaps Lewis was just keeping out of the way of Mrs Barnett as she cleaned down stairs. He would sit down for his Sunday dinner at about 2 o'clock – often having a snooze in his chair after dinner. It was his habit to retire to bed between 10 and 10.30 pm but Mr Barnett had head him about the house at 11.30pm on some occasions.

Monday was a rent collecting day, he would rise about 8.30 am, have breakfast and then about 10 am, start on his rounds of his tenants, in Pontypool, Abersychan and Cwmbran. He generally returned home by 2.30 pm and made himself some dinner, after which he would be off on his rounds again until about 5 pm. Tuesday and Wednesday followed the same pattern. Thursday, Lewis spent at home, perhaps in the garden or doing odd jobs around the house. Friday was another rent day, though he did make some time for a bit of shopping. Saturday he was out and about most of the day, but returning home at meal-times. He always carried a large bunch of keys in the pocket of his jacket, and generally wore a brown checked suit but was known to have a blue suit as well.

The last time Mrs Barnett went into Plasmont (prior to the murder) was at 7.30 am on 21st May – to do her usual stint of cleaning, for which she received 3/6d a week. Lewis was up and about. Mrs Barnett prepared the Sunday dinner and had put it in the oven to cook. She left at 10 am as Lewis would generally finish off the cooking of the dinner himself. She next saw him at the door of Plasmont at 6 pm. From her front door she could see if Lewis was home, indicated by a light in the kitchen, the night of the 22nd neither she nor Pricilla heard anything unusual.

She confirmed that when Lewis went out collecting the rents, he would never lock the back door – just pull it closed. However, she believed that on retiring for the night he would bolt the doors – as she and her husband could hear the bolt being closed. It was rare, she said, for Lewis to have windows open. She described him to the South Wales Argus reporter

'As nice a sort of man as one would meet anywhere, and if he could do anyone a good turn he would do it.'

John Sullivan of 1, Queens Street, Pontypool had been working in the garden at Plasmont for some twelve years. He said that Lewis paid him no wages but tending the garden was a 'gentleman's agreement', Sullivan could use the garden to plant and grow vegetables for his own use, in return he would keep the lawns tidy. As he visited almost every day, he was in a good position to know of Lewis' routines and confirmed, as had the other witnesses, that he was a man of regular habits insofar as his rent collecting round was concerned. He commented that Lewis was a man who always seemed to be in a hurry. Sullivan's usual route to Plasmont was to nip over a low wall between his house in Queens Street and Plasmont. (Queens Street is directly behind where Plasmont once stood). He confirmed his conversation with Mrs Barnett. At about 9.15 am on 24th May he saw Mrs Barnett, she said that she had heard no sounds from Plasmont and that she was frightened. As he was on his way to the Labour Exchange, he promised her that he would go in and look for the old man when he returned. However by the time he did, Brimble had already made the discovery

'It's all over.' he said to Sullivan.

Sullivan later recalled that he had been in his garden on the Monday night and heard Lewis talking to someone.

'I think it was a woman' he said.

'I SAW HIM ON THE TUESDAY'

How many of us marvel, when watching Crimewatch UK how people can accurately pinpoint where they were weeks, months and even years before. Many people pin their memories to a family event or public occasion. Many people giving statements recalled that they remembered hearing of the murder in relation to the fact that it was the weekend of the South Wales Borderers display in Pontypool Park. Some men remembered that they were on a particular shift at work or others with a friend that they only met on a specific night. In the case of the Lewis murder statements caused confusion when some people claimed that they had seen Lewis after 22nd May, even when evidence from the Home Office Pathologist and others suggested that he hadn't been around to pick up the mail or the milk and neither the Barnett's nor Brimble had seen him.

William Allen, widower of 9, Rockfield Terrace, Pontypool who gave a statement on 24th May was convinced he'd seen Lewis on Tuesday 23rd. Allen was a builder and had been doing odd jobs for Lewis for about four years, so knew him well. In fact in his statement he swears to the fact that he had spoken to Lewis at about 11.15 am on 23rd – at Lion Cross. They discussed Larcombe's shop roof 33, George Street (a cobbler's shop).

'I asked him to leave that work stand for a week as I had other work to do. I know it was Tuesday morning because I know I was not in town on Monday'.

So convinced was he about the date that he went to Pontypool Police Station on 25th May and made a second statement, this time to Chief Inspector Rees. He started by explaining his present job.

'I am a jobbing builder and work at present for Mr R.M. Cormack, Estate Agent. I am demolishing some buildings in George Street. I started this job on Wednesday 24th May 1939, Derby day. Prior to this I was working for Mr Cormack at Cwymynyscoy, where I demolished three houses. I have actually been working as a jobber for about twelve years and for ten years of this, on and off I worked for the Lewis family of Plasmont. My work for the family was repairing and keeping property in good order. About three months ago I went to work at Glascoed Factory and left the service of Mr W.A. Lewis. The last job I did for him was a re-roofing job at Upper Bridge Street, which Brimble's men, I believe, finished'.

Allen mentioned jobs he had done at Plasmont, including slating the roof of the back kitchen, repairing the roof of Plasmont Cottage and taking up the bathroom floor to remove dead rats underneath. The last time he had worked at Plasmont was in 1938 – when he cemented in place ornamental flower stands that had blown over. He said

'I saw Mr Lewis practically every day. I would see him about town or when he passed my house to collect rent.'

He had seen him on 22nd walking down George Street with Rev and Mrs Watkins, she was having a shop converted into a house and the three of them were inspecting the work thus far.

In every circumstance William Allen makes a good case for his report of chatting to Lewis on Tuesday 23rd May. He accounted for Sunday 21st, he was at home cleaning and cooking for his two children Terence aged 15 and Edward aged 12, (on weekdays he had a woman calling in to do these tasks). He was widowed

'I buried my wife four years ago'.

In his third interview he recalled that he had indeed been in town on Monday 22nd when he met with Cale Jones, from the

Tranch who worked with Harry Vickery. He saw Cale at The Cross at about 10.30 and they discussed a tender, in which they were both interested, demolishing some houses in George Street. Cale decided he didn't fancy it and left Allen to go ahead. Allen then called in briefly to see James Whelan at his home 2, Castle Yard, one of Lewis' properties, to pay him 30 shillings for a job he'd done and then he went home. Later that evening he called on his housekeeper, Cecilia Williams (presumably the woman who came in to see to the children on weekdays) and took her to Pontypool Cinema. They saw the whole show and as they left the cinema they saw the soldiers returning from their show in Pontypool Park. He escorted Cecilia home to 3, Channel View, Penygarn, where she lodged with Mr and Mrs Gullett, leaving her at the top of Channel View to make the rest of the way home.

His route home then took him to the Cross, up George Street and down Malthouse Lane to his home at Rockfield Terrace.

This brings him back to his statement, he said he now realised that he had seen Lewis on Monday 22nd. Lewis was with his sister Emily and the Rev Watkins walking through George Street, on their way to inspect 'the new house of Mrs Watkins.

> 'By 'new house' I mean that Mrs Watkins has had a shop converted into a house and I think I saw all three going in. This would be about dinner time'.

Up until then Allen was the only person to have claimed that he saw Lewis on the 23rd, the Tuesday. All other statements indicated that Lewis hadn't been seen by anyone since the evening of the 22nd. The pathologist was satisfied that Lewis' body had been dead for over 48 hours. Nevertheless Allen had been unshakeable in his belief that on 23rd he saw Lewis. Allen describes how he went to see Mr Robert Cormack,

Cross Chambers, Crane Street about 11.30 am and collected the payment for a job at Cwmynyscoy. Having pocketed the £6 he saw Lewis at Pegler's Corner. They discussed the job and he asked for a week's grace before he started it. He returned home to have dinner then went to the Clarence Hotel, where, with Cecilia Williams he caught a bus to Newport. On the way they stopped off at the Hanbury Arms in Caerleon for a drink then continued their journey to Newport about 3 pm. After some shopping in Newport they caught a bus around 9 pm to Pontypool where he and Cecilia parted, returning to their respective homes.

Needless to say the Pontypool Police were hot on his trail, trying to confirm the date that he last saw Lewis. In fact at one time Allen became the subject of gossip in Pontypool as 'the murderer', probably because he had been working for Lewis and the fact that he was known to have been interviewed. There is nothing in the police report to substantiate this and his movements were accounted for. As a result, sightings of Allen were important. He was seen by William Henry Jenkins, 9, West Place, an unemployed lorry driver walking towards the Clarence Hotel with a woman on 23rd May.

James Whelan was asked to corroborate Allen's statement. He confirmed he lived at 2 Castle Yard, George Street, with his wife and five children. He was currently unemployed but had been at Elled Colliery, Pontypool until three weeks previous. His house was owned by Lewis, who always called on a Saturday for the rent, the last time he had collected this was on 20th May. He remembered Billy Allen coming to see him to ask if he would like some demolition work in George Street. Whelan asked Allen if he could sign off the dole and when Allen said 'No', he said he couldn't do it. Allen mentioned that Lewis had asked him to strip a roof at Larcombes. Whelan lent Allan a pick for his demolition job.

Bertram Jenkins of 'Leamside' Broadway, Pontypool gave an interesting insight to the workingman's hours in the pit when he gave a statement affirming when he last saw Lewis.

'I am a colliery repairer employed at Hafodrynys Colliery. I start work at 11 pm, leaving home at 10 pm for that purpose. I finish work at 6.30 am, arriving home at 5 minutes to eight every morning. After having breakfast and a bath I go to bed and remain there until 5 o'clock in the afternoon. This has been my practice for the last eight years.

On Sunday nights I do not work, therefore on Monday mornings I get up from bed about 1 pm. After a wash and dinner I go into town to talk to my friends. This has been my practice for many years because I do not have any other times to see my friends in the afternoons unless I get up from my bed for this purpose. I cannot remember when I got up from bed before 5 pm on a normal working day.

On Monday 22nd May, following my usual custom I came into Pontypool, George Street at about 3 pm. I was standing outside Woolworth's Shop talking to someone, (I cannot remember who), when William Alfred Lewis passed. He was walking towards the Cross, that is, in the direction away from his home. About 4 yards from me, William Allen was talking to a man not known to me. This stranger is a short man, about 5ft 1ins. About 28/30 years of age, respectably dressed.'

As William Alfred Lewis passed William Allen, the latter called him and they spoke together for two or three minutes. While they were talking the short man left them, walking up George Street in the direction of Wainfelin. Lewis left Allen and a few minutes after the stranger returned and when I left George Street, Allan and the stranger were still talking. I know this was on the Monday before the news of the murder became public knowledge. When I got up from bed on Wednesday morning I heard of the murder.'

Next to be interviewed was Robert Manson Cormack, Auctioneer and Estate Agent. He lived at 99, Sunnybank Road, Griffithstown and he gave his statement to Police Constable William Ackland (No. 259). He confirmed that he had known William Allen for many years and had often given him work. On or about 15th May 1939 he gave Allen a contract to demolish three houses at Cwmynyscoy. Allen called in at his office on 22nd May to say the work had been completed and to pay his rent as the property in which he lived was owned by Cormack. A contract for £30 was agreed for Allen to demolish three houses in George Street, as Cale Jones had decided not to tender. Allen also mentioned that he would shortly be receiving a contract from Mrs Pritchard of Cardiff (Miriam, Lewis' sister) to demolish another three houses adjoining the ones had had just agreed to demolish for Cormack. Allen left Cormack's office at around 11.15 am. Cormack went to the bank at about 2.30 pm. Near Lion's Cross he saw Thomas Brimble, whom he knew well and who was also carrying out repairs. Brimble said that he had completed the work at Conway Road and would be please to accept any more work from Cormack.

Police Constable Ackland had his own statement to make. He said that he was stationed at New Inn. On Tuesday 23rd May he was on the 2.50 pm bus from Pontypool to New Inn. At the

Clarence he saw William Allen board the bus, he sat in the rear seat. He also saw Mrs Williams

'With whom Allen resides. She also boarded the bus at the Clarence but sat in front of Allen.'

Yet another person claimed to have seen Lewis on 23rd this was Herbert Hicks of 2, Armory Terrace, Pontypool. He said he passed him walking up George Street and said 'good morning' Lewis just nodded his head.

'I am sure it was Tuesday and I'm sure it was Mr Lewis. He was dressed in a brown suit and a bowler'.

Albert Dyson Larcombe was next to be interviewed, he lived at 33, George Street where he ran a shoe shop, his landlord being William Lewis. His roof had been leaking for years, initially Dan Young repaired it, then Billy Allen patched it up. Finally some six months previous Lewis had instructed Brimble to strip and re-roof the place. He added to his statement

'About 14 days ago around 14th May, I saw Billy Allen talking to Mr Wheland.'

The significance of this statement will be understood later.

Another witness came forward to say that he had seen Lewis on Tuesday 23rd. Alfred Worthington, colliery haulier, Tirpentwys Colliery, lived at 18 King Street with his wife and family. He recalled his movements of the past few days, which lead to his belief that Lewis was alive on 23rd. His statement made to Chief Inspector Rees, is thus.

'During the week commencing the 22nd May I was working the afternoon shift 2.30 pm to 10.30 pm' (the same as Mr Barnett of Plasmont Cottage) when I am working the afternoon shift I usually go to The Fountain Public House, George Street, for a drink. On Monday 22nd May I went to The Fountain between 11pm and 11.30, I cannot recollect who I saw there that day.

I went again to the Fountain on Tuesday at about the same time, and on Wednesday. When I was coming down the street on Wednesday I met a couple of women who live opposite me, one of them is Mrs Daniels. They told me that Lewis had committed suicide, I said 'That's strange, I saw him yesterday'. One of the women said 'you couldn't have done, it happened on Monday night you couldn't have seen him yesterday.'

Worthington then waivered a bit and wondered if it had been just the Monday he'd seen Lewis but concluded

'I still think I saw him on both days, at about 1.30 pm. This would have been when he was catching the bus to work.

Another Tuesday sighting was by Frederick Weller, lorry driver, 9, Queens Street, Pontypool. He gave his statement to Police Constable William Holt. (No.39). He explained that as he was driving a car down George Street at 7 pm on Tuesday he caught a glimpse of a man he believed to be Lewis between Trueman's Shop and the White Hart Hotel. Lewis was wearing his bowler and a dark suit. Weller said he'd known Lewis for a number of years.

By now sightings of Lewis on the Tuesday night were coming in thick and fast. On 14th June, John Silas Morgan of Bushy Park, Pontypool was seen by Chief Inspector Rees. He said he was a supervisor for Briggs and Co. of Leicester, Boot Factors and Drapers. He stated he knew Lewis very well and saw him almost daily. On one occasion Lewis offered him £50 if he could persuade Briggs and Co. to rent one of his shops or the same amount if he could find a tenant. He went on to describe seeing Lewis.

'On Tuesday 23rd May I travelled by bus from Blaenavon to Pontypool where I arrived about 6.45 pm. I then met Miss Spencer, who is employed at the same firm as myself. Miss Spencer resides at Gamyverw, Blaenavon. I met her at a workshop and went to Turner's Restaurant where we had tea and afterwards returned to the workshop in Osbourne Road where we arrived at about 7.55 pm. After leaving Turner's tea shop and walking through Osbourne Road on the left hand side, going up, when near the chapel I passed Mr Lewis. I did not mention to Miss Spencer that we had passed him, although I had intended on many times to point him out to her as the man who offered me £50. I am sure it was Tuesday night, because Miss Spencer had been to Newbridge. I only meet her on Tuesday and Friday nights and on Friday 19th May I was not with Miss Spencer in Osbourne Road and I am certain that I was with her when I saw Mr Lewis. It could not have been the previous Tuesday because when I heard of Mr Lewis' death on 24th I mentioned it to a boot dealer near our premises in Blaenavon that I had seen him the previous night.'

The dealer, David William North of 14 Wainfelin Avenue, Pontypool disputed this. He claimed that

'I can definitely say that Mr Morgan did not say anything about seeing Mr Lewis on the night prior to speaking to me. He did not mention seeing Mr Lewis at all on the night prior to his death.'

BRIMBLE THE DECORATOR

As the person who found the body, Thomas Brimble could not avoid suspicious gossip. Had anyone given it thought it would have been obvious that he would be the last man to contemplate murdering Lewis. It would amount to killing 'the goose that laid the golden egg'. He and his various odd-job men, mostly his father Ebenezer Henry Brimble, brother William and 'the lad', Cyril were all in full time employ since he had become the main builder, painter and decorator for Lewis, looking after all his properties Nevertheless, the police were obliged to check his movements. If the 22nd May 1939 could be called a typical day in the life of Tom Brimble it can be seen from the various witness statements that he was seen working at almost every hour of the day. Leaving home around 7 am and still calling on customers (tenants of Lewis) right up until 9 pm at night. The first to give a statement was Esther Jones, wife of William Jones of Bronyglyn Bungalow, Cwmfrwdd, Abersychan, she said she saw Tom Brimble at 10 pm on 22nd May. She knew him well as he had previously supervised the decoration of her house. She said

'I made certain business arrangements with him.'

This puts Brimble well away from the murder scene. Mrs Jones doesn't remark on his demeanour but that is probably because he was exactly as he usually was – and she knew him as he had supervised the decoration of her house some time previous.

Inspector Rees from Scotland Yard describes Brimble in his summing up of the case;

'Thomas Brimble is a painter and decorator, who lives at The Firs, Waterworks Lane, Abersychan. He is married, has two children, and employs five men and two boys, including his father and brother. To commence, I will say that this man is financially embarrassed and can get no credit in the locality. About November 1938 he started doing repair work for the deceased man, and apparently they concluded their business amicably and with mutual satisfaction, for we know that the deceased introduced Brimble to his sister, Miriam Pritchard of Cardiff and to his brother-in-law Rev. W. G. Watkins, who both own properties around Pontypool. Brimble did work for both of them. '

Madge Beese said she was a single woman, living at Bryn Derwen, Richmond Road, Pontnewydd. In December Brimble had called at her home to discuss redecorating her house. On 22nd May she found Brimble's card on the mat and said it could only have been delivered after 6.30 pm on that day.

Brimble's father Ebenezer gave a statement and said that he worked for his son Tom. He described the work that they had been dong at Plasmont 'colouring walls, erecting a zinc fence and putting stones on a wall'. He didn't know about any lost keys and neither had his son mentioned them. He first heard about the murder when he required some materials whilst 'working at Chimp's place near The Clarence' and went up to Plasmont. 'When I got there Miss Barnett told me that Mr Lewis had been murdered. This was on a Wednesday, the day when the news of the murder was made public'.

John Henry Cooper of 9, Chapel Street, Pontnewydd said had seen Brimble on the afternoon of the 22nd, when he called on him to confirm that he would shortly be painting the exterior of Cooper's shop. However, when he talked to his son, John Lyndon Cooper, he realised that Brimble must have called between 7.30 pm and 8.30pm. The two Coopers' voluntarily went back to Pontypool Police Station to correct the original statement. Meanwhile the South Wales Argus reporter despite pursuing Brimble failed to get a scoop, 'he has been warned not to divulge anything that he has said to the police'.

Wilfred John Flower of 1, High Houses, Victoria Road, Abersychan, described himself as a builder's labourer, working mainly in Pontypool. His employers were Coles Brother's Builders, Garndiffaith. He knew Brimble as they caught the same bus from Abersychan each morning – the 7.10 am. Fred Tudgay was one of Brimble's workmen, having been with him for nearly four years. He lived at Earlesmere, Cwmavon Road, Cwmffrwdoer. He described the work that he had been doing at Plasmont. He had assisted 'Henry Brimble'– as Ebenezer Brimble (Tom's father) was known, along with William Brimble (Tom's brother) and 'the boy Cyril' to paint the exterior walls of Plasmont. He said he had 'fetched the paint from Sandbrook and Dawes in a hundred-weight cast' so it can only be presumed that Tudgay had transport as none of the other builders mention owning a car or van. The colour-wash was mixed with lime and they painted the outside wall of the house from Broadway, along George Street, Conway Road and into the area of Plasmont House. They didn't paint the walls of Plasmont Cottage. All the builders kept their kept their tools and materials in a shed in a garden opposite the back gate of Plasmont. He said he had been into the house but only as far as the kitchen tap directly inside the kitchen door. He started work at about 7.30pm each morning 'and took lunch on the job'. He saw Lewis about the house around 8.30am and the milkman usually called about 9.30am. He was unable to confirm whether the back gate or back door were ever locked, the gate was always open when he arrived for work in the morning. Lewis joined the builders in a cup of tea some afternoons and on one occasion offered them a glass of wine.

William Brimble aged 21 confirmed that he lived at The Firs and that he had five brothers. Tom, Ralph, Jack, Trevor and Ivor. He said that Ralph lived in Sidcup and hadn't returned home to Pontypool for about two years. Jack lived at Wadden, near Croydon and was last in the district at Christmas 1938. Trevor worked for the Blaenavon Company as a driver and lived at 17, Wan Street, Blaenavon and Ivor lived at 12, Clarewarn Street, New Inn, Pontypool. He stated that he had, under the direction of his brother Tom, started work at Plasmont in April. It is now we learn how much work was being undertaken at Plasmont. William had put up a fence, made two swing doors for the garden opposite the back gate of Plasmont and helped his father colour wash the exterior walls in Broadway, George Street, Conway Road, plus the back of the house and the space between the lean-to roofs.

He said that he had been into the kitchen of Plasmont and that was to wash his hands. He generally went to Mario Quadrilli's for lunch but occasionally ate his lunch on the job. He had fitted a swan-neck pipe and rain water head on the top left corner of the first floor conservatory, using a ladder to reach it and he and Cyril had completed the flooring in there. He took a piece of glass from the dome to Farrows, glass dealers of Newport, for bending and rolling comparisons and had made a template from a portion of the top of the conservatory. He said it was not uncommon for his brother Tom to go into the house as he and Lewis often discussed building work on the rented houses and shops.

William Brimble was working at Plasmont until the Monday before the murder. On the Monday he was working in Cwmbran for the Rev Watkins of Swansea on a house and shop. On the morning of 22nd May he had fixed a new lock on the door of Mrs Trinder's house at George Street. He had also been to 6, Nicholas Street with a new lock. The locks had been purchased at Sandbrook and Dawes by Tom Brimble, they were rimlocks. However, William discovered that the lock at Nicholas Street was a box lock, so rather than cut the door to fit the new lock he oiled and repaired the old one. On the evening of the 22nd Tom Brimble had called at his house at about 10.30 pm to tell him not to come to Plasmont the following day as he wanted him to finish off a job in Abersychan.

Cyril Hawkins who was a builder's apprentice aged 15 and lived a 1, Top Road, Garndiffaith. He had assisted William Brimble to put a new conservatory floor down and fix a water pipe. He climbed the ladder with the timber and put it through the open window. Joseph Leonard Parker of 6, New Street said that Tom Brimble the carpenter called at his home to inspect the front room floor at 8.30 pm and left at 9 pm on the 22nd May. Rosina Jones of 58, Commercial Street, Pontnewydd said that Brimble called on her between 7 pm and 9 pm, looking for her sister, Laura Poulton as she was not at home. At 10.30 pm on the night of 22nd May, Brimble was at home, in the company of his wife and brother until midnight. He was preparing estimates as a result of the calls he had made to prospective customers earlier that day and his wife confirmed that he didn't leave the house that night.

In the past William Lewis had also employed as builders Dan Young of Clarence Street, Mr Mears of Abersychan, Gardener of Crumlin, William Allen of Pontypool and a Mr Thomas of New Inn.

STRANGERS IN CONWAY ROAD

In a small town like Pontypool, strangers rarely went un-noticed but in 1939 there was a great influx of workers from

all over the country converging on the lucrative building works at Glascoed. However, the sighting of strange men around the area of Plasmont meant more statements to be taken by the Pontypool police. Some had seen strangers on the night of the murder, the 22nd some in the days afterwards.

One anonymous description of the strangers appeared in the Argus, 'One was about 5ft 5ins wearing a collar and tie, respectable appearance. Not a working type. The other was about 5ft 6ins, also of respectable appearance and not a workman type.' Detective Constable Swift interviewed 17 year old ('I will be 18 years of age next July') Frederick Griffiths of 43, King Street. He was employed at Glascoed by Nuttall's the contractors

. 'At about 10.30 pm on Monday 22nd May, I was coming home from the pictures with Ken Millett, (who lives opposite Mundy's Shop on Broadway). When passing the front gate that leads into Plasmont, which is opposite the Roman Catholic Church, I saw two men aged around 25 years. One was dressed in a blue pin stripped suit and the other wore a raincoat. One did not have a hat. One was standing between the door and the door post (the door was open) and the other man was in front of him on the step.' Griffiths was subsequently quizzed by Chief Inspector Rees, and recalled that it was the man in the blue suit who had no hat, he had light hair. Both the men were of medium build. Griffiths added that what he had described as a gate was really a wooden door. He said that he wouldn't recognise the men again. Kenneth Millett of 26, North Road, Pontypool who was with Griffiths (and was seen by other witnesses) could not remember seeing anyone in the gateway to Plasmont.

Leslie Williams, 3, The Avenue, Wainfelin said he was employed as a lorry driver. He remembered where he was because it was the day when the soldiers were in the Park. On that day he finished work about 9.45 pm. He walked home through George Street, along Wainfelin Road and when he reached Conway Road, at about 10 pm he saw two men standing up against the railings of Plasmont. He described one of about 30 years of age and 5ft 9ins, he was of thin build, wearing a brown mixture cap, light trousers and a brown sports jacket. The other man was older and bigger built and was wearing an overcoat with a belt on it. Williams himself, he said

> 'I was wearing my grey mixture smock. The two men were strangers to me. There are generally men stood at this corner.'

Detective Constable Victor Adams said that he had taken the statement down in his Official pocket book.

Francis Edward Taylor, whose relatives still live in Pontypool, also saw strangers and he was able to give a very detailed description of them. His account reflects on the fact that most people knew each other in that area of Pontypool. He came forward voluntarily after an article appeared in the Pontypool Free Press asking for sightings around the area of Plasmont. He stated to Chief Inspector Rees that he was a single man, a steel-fixer at Glascoed and lived with his parents at 32, Edward Street. On Monday 22nd May he was returning home at about 7.55 pm and when going along Conway Road near Plasmont he noticed one man standing at the green door, which leads to the back of the property. Another man was standing about 5 yards away in the opening leading to the back door of the house. He was adamant that the men were not from Pontypool.

'They were strangers to me and I feel satisfied that they were not local boys. Had they been, I feel sure that I would have known them. The man by the gate seemed to be looking for a way into the grounds of the house. I did not think it important at the time but after reading in the paper that two men were seen about there I thought it best to let the Police know. The man standing by the gate was about 25-26 years of age, aged 5ft 7ins, sallow complexion, clean shaven, high forehead, fair hair brushed back, slim build, he did not have a full round face but rather a long face, he was dressed in a fawny coloured sports jacket or check pattern – about 1in square and dark flannel trousers. No hat, I'm definite that I would know this man again. The second man was about the same age, slightly shorter than the other man, thicker set with strong shoulders. He was clean shaven and I think his hair was dark and wavy. This man was dressed in a dark suit with a pin stripe. I think he was carrying a mackintosh or raincoat on his arm. This man had no hat.'

The two strangers also attracted the notice of Mrs May Drinkwater who lived at 29, Edward Street with her husband and daughters Doreen and Betty. Mrs Drinkwater had previously 'identified' Brimble as a stranger she had seen in Conway Road, after a photograph of him appeared in the South Wales Argus.

At around half past ten she and Doreen were returning from a concert given by children at the Mount Pleasant Sunday School. The show was called 'The Magic Rose' and finished around 9 pm. They went directly home but popped out later for some fish and chips and called in to Turner's Fish Shop in George Street. On their way home, arriving at the junction of the Broadway and George Street at about quarter to eleven, they saw two men walking from Broadway into George Street. The men crossed the road and continued along to Conway Road. They stood near the pillar box outside St Albans Catholic Church. As the Drinkwater's passed the two men, one of the men started to walk up the road in the direction of Wainfelin but the other said 'This way' and they turned into Conway Road and walked up the middle of the road, as did the Drinkwater's who were taking their time, enjoying the fish and chips. When they arrived opposite Mrs Bessie West's house at 2, Conway Road, May Drinkwater noticed a couple sitting on the windowsill there. She made a joking remark about a courting couple to her daughter Doreen who remarked

'No, it's those two men.'

They continued on the way home and when she passed Mrs Shott's shop she glanced back and saw the men still there.

'The man who spoke was very tall, slim and muffled up, wearing a dirty raincoat. He kept his head down and his hands in his pockets. He walked with a slight stoop. The second man was between 27 to 30 years of age, fresh face, appearance of working out of doors, neck appeared to be clean (*an unusual observation in the street lamps of Conway Road*) as though his hair at the back had been cut very short. He was well built and about a head shorter than his companion. He wore what appeared to be a mixture coloured overcoat, with a belt all round'.

She estimated that it was about 10.50 when she and Doreen arrived home.

The following day Tuesday 23rd, May Drinkwater chatted to her next door neighbour Ena Turk and asked if she knew whether Mrs West had taken in lodgers, recalling the men sitting on the windowsill the previous night. Mrs Turk didn't know but obviously told someone else as the enquiry got back to Mrs West, who had also seen the strangers (but not on her windowsill). Bessie Louisa West was a widow with five children, the eldest of whom was Doreen Pricilla. On 22nd May Doreen had been to the Palais Dance Hall, leaving home at 8 pm. Her mother Bessie at home with the other four children had gone to the front door to await the return of Doreen from the dance. She also saw two strangers coming up from the steps leading from the backyard at Plasmont. From her house it was possible for her to see the backdoor of Plasmont. In the run up to war, the street lighting had not yet been turned off.

> 'One man's hand was on the door, as if he was closing it but I couldn't actually see whether the door was open or not owing to the shadow from the tree. The men walked out onto Conway Road, past Plasmont Cottage, turned right and then up Wainfelin Road'. They seemed unhurried.'

She estimated their ages as 35 – 38 years and noted that one wore an overcoat, she wasn't too sure about hats. At the end of her interview she said

> 'I didn't see much of their faces, and I should not know them again'.

This statement would be refuted later on.

Doreen Pricilla West aged 17 gave a statement, saying that she lived at 2, Conway Road with her widowed mother and siblings and as a job assisted an aunt 'selling green-grocery' in Pontypool Market. She concurred with her Mother's statement that she had been to 'The Palais-de-Dance' on Queens Street for the regular Monday Dance Night. When the dance finished at 11 pm a young man called Cliff, (she didn't know his surname but he lived in Pontnewynydd) was kind enough to accompany her home. He left her at the corner of Conway Road and George Street satisfied that other couples, also on their way home, were not far behind and that she wasn't walking alone.

Norman Albert Spencer, aged 25, an electrician of 46, College Road, Penygarn was walking from the Power Station in Osbourne Road and past Plasmont on the night of 22nd May at around 11.10 pm. He noticed that the electric light was on at the entrance to the front gate, though the house was in darkness. The light at Shott's shop was also on.

Following Doreen West and also returning home after their night out were other young women (whose mothers were no doubt also at the doorstep awaiting their arrival). Mavis Cornfield of 40 Edward Street and Maureen Lewis of 10 Edward Street were close behind her. In addition, a number of couples that Doreen had seen at the Palais-de-Dance (though she didn't know their names), were strolling home in the moonlight. Most of the courting couples passed Plasmont to continue up Conway Road. Doreen didn't see the two men but it was of sufficient interest for her mother to comment on two strangers near Plasmont that she had seen some half an hour ago when she arrived home.

Doreen Drinkwater's dancing companion Cliff was quickly located by the police, his full name was Clifford James

Collins of 6, Bryn Terrace, Pontynewynydd. He confirmed that he had walked Miss West home

'As far as the end of the Catholic Church, opposite the rear end of Plasmont.'

Having chatted for a few minutes they went their own separate ways. He ended his statement with

'I have never pushed my motorcycle up over George Street'

(This sentence is never explained in the evidence). Inspector Rees thought that Collins was 'somewhat mistaken' in the times he gave to the police as Tomboline suggests that it was after 11pm when he saw Collins.

Mrs Hilda Hubbert of 3, Conway Road gave her statement to Police Sergeant W. Davidson (No. 7) on 24th May at 6.45 pm. She saw Lewis leave his house about 6.30 pm on Monday 22nd. He was wearing a dark suit and went in through the door at the bottom of the steps at Plasmont. The following day Bessie West her next door neighbour mentioned that two men had been sitting on her (Mrs West's) windowsill at 11 pm. She had even asked her children to turn off the wireless, so she could hear what they were saying but she couldn't hear anything. When she went to the door they were walking up Conway Road. Later on she saw them coming from Plasmont – one was wearing an overcoat with a tie-up belt. She added ominously

'I heard banging toward Lewis' house'. However, Mrs West was seen on a number of occasions by the police and emphatically denied that she

'Had ever told Mrs Hubbert such a thing.'

Adeline May, wife of William Tudor Fenwick who lived at 2, Amberley Place gave her own version of 'the two strangers'. It was recorded in Police Sergeant W. Davidson's official notebook at her home at 5.45 pm on Friday 26th May. At about 10.40 pm on Monday 22nd May at 10.40 pm she was standing outside the Devon cafe, Upper George Street chatting to friends Mr and Mrs Alfred Brown.

'Two young men came along from the direction of town, walking in the road. As they were passing us, one of them came over to me, as if he was going to speak to me. I had my baby in my arms. He said nothing but lurched back into the road, and he was then called by the other man, who had gone ahead. Both men then went into Conway Road, and I lost sight of them. Both men appeared to be drinking and the one seemed the worse than the other. I should imagine they were in their twenties. The one who came over to me was wearing a dark suit and a light cap. The other was wearing a lightish suit and no headgear. Neither had an overcoat on, they were both strangers to me'.

She parted from the Brown's and went home and saw

'Nothing unusual in the vicinity of Plasmont House'.

She added to her statement on 8th June saying that she thought the two men had come from George Street. She thought that she might know the two men again. William Thomas Watkins who lived at 18, Conway Road said

'When looking from the bedroom of my house, I can see along the road to Plasmont for a distance of about 20 yards. On Tuesday 23rd May I went to bed about 11 pm and after switching off the light in my bedroom I looked through the window down Conway Road to see if there was anybody about. I then saw a man aged I should say, under thirty, about 5ft 7 ins in height and wearing a dark suit. No overcoat. I cannot say whether he was wearing a hat or not. From the time I first saw him he came towards our house, with his face towards me for about 4 yards. He then turned and walked back for about 16 yards. He was then looking towards Plasmont House.'

Police Sergeant Bowkett took a statement made at noon on 24th May by William Charles Cox of 29, Twmpath, Pontypool (but curiously signed by Thomas E. Cox) said

'I am a school caretaker at British School, George Street. At about 2.30 pm on Tuesday 23rd May I was walking down Conway Road to my employment, when I saw two men emerge from the garden gate of Mr Lewis' house. Both were well dressed. I heard them arguing as they were passing from the garden but I was unable to distinguish what they said, but it sounded as if they were arguing about business. Neither man was Mr Lewis, as I know him well. Both men were strangers.'

Wilfred George Evans, who gave his profession as 'Sea Captain' of Ardlui, Wainfelin went to Pontypool Police Station at midnight on 24th May where he saw Police Sergeant Bowkett. He said that he had seen a man earlier that day (at 12 noon)

'Open the front garden door and start to come down to the House'.

At that time Evans was in his kitchen with the maid Leah Barnett. He said the man saw them, turned around and went back out again but not before he was identified by Leah Barnett as 'The boss painter from Lewis's'.

Evans sent Leah to the Post Office. She later told Evans that she had been joined by the man on her walk into town, but tried to 'get rid of him' but he persisted in his attentions and talked of the murder. Evans finished his statement by saying that as a near neighbour of Plasmont he would scour his garden for a weapon.

Samuel Harris of 89, Upper George Street (a fishmonger) gave his statement on 28th May to Police Sergeant D.G. Davies at Pontypool Police Station. He said he lived at Upper George Street, with his wife and family on the northern side of Plasmont. He said he worked at Turner's Cafe on George Street. On Monday 22nd May he started work at 9 am until 11 am. Then went back to work at 3 pm until 11.30 pm. Although the cafe closed he stayed chatting to the manageress, Miss Williams until 12.15 am on the Tuesday morning. He then left, with his wife and Miss Williams and walked along into Upper George Street, escorting Miss Williams home along Wainfelin Avenue. Mr and Mrs Harris then went to their home, directly opposite Plasmont House, he estimated that it would be about 12.30 am when opposite St Albans Church, about 10 yards from the junction of Conway Road and Upper George Street, a man appeared on the opposite side of the road. He was walking towards Merchants Hill. As the couple walked down Wainfelin Road they hadn't heard footsteps, so when the man appeared without warning, Mr Harris looked at him, though he said it was too dark to see anything plainly. He was close enough however to note the stranger's belted raincoat and that he was about 5ft 6ins tall and of a sturdy build. Both he and the stranger locked eyes as they passed each other and he continued to look at them until they reached their front door. Harris remembered that as they walked Miss Williams's home a light could be seen in

Plasmont, when Harris glanced up again on arriving home, the light had been extinguished.

Another collier of Tirpentwys Colliery gave his account of two strangers. He was also on the afternoon shift. Charles Millett of 40, Kings Street recalled walking home from work and seeing two men, one in a Burberry raincoat the other in a lightish suit. He heard one say

'I couldn't have it so I shoved it across the table'.

He continued past them as they remained half way up King Street. The time was about 11.30 pm. He said he would not recognise the men again and that they were about 200 yards away from Plasmont. He also added

'I should think from their appearance that they were two men from The Dump'.

When Detective Constable Swift called at 40, King Street to follow this statement up, Mrs Swift confirmed that her husband had said that he'd seen two men 'drunk' by Plasmont – he thought they might be from The Dump – Glascoed, Usk.

Someone who walked past Plasmont at 11.10 pm was Norman Albert Spencer of 46, College Road. He gave his account of the 22nd of May to Detective Constable Adams at the Police Station.

'I am 25 years of age and an electrician'.

He said that he had walked from the Power Station in Osbourne Road, up George Street and then to Conway Road, passing Plasmont. He saw no one near the house but the electric light at the front gate to Plasmont was illuminated and the one near Shott's Shop. Plasmont House however was in darkness.

Arthur Henry Lewis Brown of 14, Bushy Park, Wainfelin was walking from town with his friend William Guest of 6, Queen Street. They walked through Upper George Street into Conway Road. They passed Plasmont at about 10 pm but saw nothing suspicious.

Finally someone gave a statement saying that he knew where the two mystery men worked, though he didn't know their names. Phillip McDonough, a haulier at Tirpentwys Colliery, aged 31, lived with his mother at 6, South View off Conway Road. He was returning from the Forge Hammer public house in town about 11.20 pm on 22nd May when he passed two men who he described as strangers though he said that he knew that they worked at the Glascoed Factory. He saw them standing talking at Malthouse Lane, just by the bridge. He thought that the one would be 40 – 44 years of age, 5ft 7ins and wearing a brown trilby hat and a dark, possibly blue suit. The other man was in his thirties, stocky build, wearing a grey lounge suit and grey cap. As McDonough crossed the bridge he saw three men at the bottom of Broadway, Jack Price, Jack Beese and George Tomboline.

As he passed them they parted company Price walking up Broadway whilst Beese and Tomboline went toward Wainfelin. As McDonough walked into Conway road he saw Doreen West at the Church boundary wall chatting to a young man. They were right opposite the rear entrance to Lewis' house. He also noticed Bessie West on the pavement in front of her house, watching the young couple. After he passed Mrs West he heard Doreen leave her young man and run to her house. Doreen had noticed two other young women who were strolling back from the dance, Maureen Lewis and Mavis Cornfield but they had seen nothing unusual when interviewed by the police.

In a second statement Mr McDonough said he was friendly with the landlord of the Forge Hammer pub, Tom Blewitt. He went there almost every night and often helped out by washing glasses when the place was busy. Such was his relationship with the Blewitt's that he generally stayed to supper. The pub closed at 10 pm and by the time the place was cleaned and supper eaten it wouldn't be until 11.15 – 11.30 pm before he made his way home. Since he made his initial statement, he had thought further about the strangers near Plasmont and gave a more detailed description of one.

'I know the short man uses The Castle public house. He is inclined to be a bit bandy and walks with a pronounced swagger, speaks with an accent which could be Irish as far as I can remember. He has prominent eyes'

McDonough said the other man was a complete stranger.

William Price named by McDonough as one of the three men he saw on his way home from the Forge Hammer was interviewed by Police Constable D.G. Davies. He had been to Pontypool Park with his friend Jack Beese to see the display given by the South Wales Borderers. They had stayed until about 8.30 pm when they made their way to the Comrades Club in Market Street. They stayed there until closing time at 10 pm and then stood outside chatting to George Tomboline. They had met him in the club earlier. By about 10.40 pm the three of them set off home. They saw Phil McDonough pass and then made their respective ways home. Jack Oliver Beese of Belmont, Wainfelin Road and Vincent David Tomboline (identified in statements as *George* Tomboline) of 55, The Avenue, Wainfelin agreed with the statement made by Price.

Herbert John Thorn of 50A, Brynderwen was a steel-worker for Partridge Jones and John Paton Ltd. Pontnewynydd

Works. He used Conway Road on his way to and from work and stated that for the previous fortnight he had noticed two men, always standing near the entrance to the Catholic Church (St Albans). He had also seen them in Pontypool town between the Town Hall and Barclays Bank. He described them as 'Roadster types, around 35 to 40 years. About 5' 10 ", medium build, both wearing knotted scarves, one might have had a red or green pullover. Dressed in rough clothes, one was wearing corduroy trousers and one wearing cloth trousers. One had a heavy brown belt almost 2 inches wide and had pockets high up in the waist of his trousers. Both were well built the shorter being of bigger build than the other'. He had not seen the men since the 22nd. Police Sergeant Davidson (No. 7) took the statement.

People also came forward to say that they had been in Conway Road and had seen no-one, strangers or otherwise, George Cornish of 'Glenview', Conway Road said that he was a Colour Sergeant in the 2nd Mons. Between 12.30 am and 12.45 am, he and fellow soldier James William Duncan a Sergeant in the South Wales Borderers, were returning from the Drill Hall in Osbourne Road via Malthouse Lane, Upper George Street, over the Fountain Bridge and into Conway Road. Both men were in uniform yet strangely no one claimed to see them and they were not mentioned in the list of 'two strangers' seen by everyone else on that night.

On 30th May Police Sergeant D.G.Davies was approached by Stanley Tew, a fruiter. He said that his house, 41, Rockhill Road backed on to the Afon Llwyd river and the door in the fence leading to it was usually kept fastened. On Tuesday 22nd May at about 12 noon he saw a man in a check cap (light in colour) brown fawn sports coat and flannel trousers. He was sitting on the bank of the river. He was there until nearly 5 pm and during that time, he and Tew discussed the murder and the stranger said he lived near Plasmont.

Tew was disquieted by the man's behaviour as not only had he trespassed on to the ground at the rear of his house he had also forced his way through some railings and entered the private grounds of Pontypool Foundry. He was also acting in a strange way said Tew

> 'He behaved suspiciously and was scratching some loose earth and walking up and down the river bank'

Two strangers with a motorbike then entered the confusing list of suspects. John Richard Palmer a window cleaner of Silverdale, Broadway gave his statement to Police Constable S. Parfitt (No.167). He said that on 22nd May he had left a house

> 'Where I was listening to the wireless and passing St Albans RC Church saw two men pushing a motorcycle towards Wainfelin. The head light of the machine was full on and this dazzled me. I could not describe the men who were pushing the machine.'

Kenneth Lewis of Forge Bungalow, Gilwern spotted the motorcycle before he saw the two men. He was the Manager of the Hafod Garage, Brynmawr. In his statement to Chief Inspector Rees, made at his place of work on 14th June he stated that on Monday 12th June he had arrived in work at 8.30 am and on the grass verge was a motorcycle. Attracted by this he noticed that there were two men sleeping nearby in the hedgerow. He went over to the men and one of them asked the time. On enquiring if the motorcycle had broken down one of the men replied,

> 'Yes, petrol trouble and clutch trouble'

and went about fixing the machine. He said they had travelled from London, leaving Marble Arch on the day before. He then got on the motorcycle and drove off, returning ten minutes later with some food, which he said he had bought in Brynmawr. At about 3 pm on that afternoon, one of the men went into the garage to ask if they could leave two haversacks, which they would collect later. He said his mate had caught a bus to Ebbw Vale. At about 6.30 pm the stranger then left saying that he was thinking of going to the pictures in Ebbw Vale, Brynmawr or Cardiff. No one ever returned for the haversacks but when the police later collected them they contained only working clothes.

Arthur Simpson, a bus driver of Alma Street, Brynmawr said that he had seen the motorcycle on the grass verge at five o'clock on the Monday morning.

Also on 14th June Acting Police Sgt G.A. Hibbert and Police Sergeant Frederick Salter, both stationed at the Police Station, Brynmawr, Breconshire had been called by a member of the public to say that two men had been seen hanging around Taylor's Filing Station near the ruined cottage called White House, situated alongside the main Abergavenny-Merthyr Road, Brynmawr.

'They were in possession of a motor cycle',

In the company of Police Constable Jones (No.15) Hibbert saw a Cotton 346 cc Motor Cycle, registration number CXM 465. On the machine was a Road Fund License No. J13000426, expiring at 30th June 1939. It was issued by Liverpool County Borough Licences, date stamped 19th April 1939. The machine was on its stand and had two Army valises strapped to the rear carrier. On investigating, he found clothing and tools in these. There was no sign of the two men, so leaving Constable Jones guarding the motor cycle, Hibbert searched around and found them near an archway in the hollow almost directly behind the filing station, about 100 yards from the main road.

Interrogating the men he found that one was Nicholas John Concannon, aged 26 – 30 years (it isn't clear why he didn't give a more accurate age). He described Concannon

> 'as about 5ft 8ins, flat features, deep dark set eyes, dark hair, square shoulders. He was wearing a grey cap, blue jacket and vest, Electrical Trades Union badge in the button hole of his left lapel of his jacket, with blue overalls over his trousers.'

The second man he identified as John Leslie Jones aged 30 years, 5ft 7ins, round features, fair hair, sun-burned complexion. This man was hatless, wearing a cycling pullover with a zipped front., grey trousers 'with dirty spots thereon'. Both men said they were Irish. Concannon had a Provisional Motor Driving Licence No. 19681, issued to Nicholas John Concannon, 88, Garmoyle Road, Liverpool 15. It was dated 19th April to 18th July 1939. He also produced an insurance certificate in respect of the motor cycle, issued to J.L. Jones on condition that the vehicle could be used by Concannon if he holds a Driving Licence.

This was issued by Merchants and Manufacturers Insurance Company. 15 – 18, Lime Street, London. Hibbert asked Jones to produce a driving licence and he said it was in his kit on the motor cycle. However, after searching through his bag, he said he must have left it at home and the same for his Registration Book. The men said that they had left Liverpool on Wednesday 7th June and visited Whitechapel, London to look for work. While they were in London they had a slight accident which had bent the front number plate, bending it back and removing some of the white paint. They intended to have it repainted. They said that they had worked at Ebbw Vale Works for Lightfoot and Co. and were travelling on to Cardiff, calling on their way at the home of Mrs Morris, Tybryn, Rassau, Beaufort, with whom they had lodged previously. Both men were taken to Pontypool Police Station for further questioning.

John Leslie Jones confirmed his address in Liverpool and said that he'd been born in Kennington on 11th November 1909. His parents were dead and he lodged with Mrs Concannon, the mother of his fellow motor cyclist. He said until August 1938 he had worked at his trade, that of an electrician, in Liverpool, the Midlands and London. He moved then to Ebbw Vale and worked for about three and a half months at John Lightfoot and Co. of Manchester, who were contractors. He returned to Liverpool and was employed by Grayson Rolla Company, shipbuilders for five weeks, then to Tate and Lyle at their Liverpool Works where he was employed fitting up air raid shelters and telephones, he stayed four months there. After a bout of 'flu he was now off work – until he and Nick Colcannon decided to look for work back at Ebbw Vale. Leaving Liverpool at 4 am they motor-cycled to Shrewsbury and then to Ebbw Vale., where they arrived at in the early evening, Concannon then went off to see a Mr Meek, who was the area secretary for the Electrical Trades Union. Having failed to meet him the two met up again and slept the night in a barn. With nothing to do they also slept most of the next morning until trying to see Mr Meek again.

The following night they returned to London bedded down in a Salvation Army Hostel, Westminster. Still looking for work they ended up at Abergavenny, not unnaturally looking for somewhere to buy petrol. They called in to see a friend of Jones', Douglas Armstrong at a house close to the Sirhowy Inn, Sirhowy but he wasn't in. Having travelled so much in the last week or so they discovered that tools they had lost on a previous visit to Ebbw Vale had been located by the Cardiff Constabulary and they could be collected from Mr Meek. Back to Brynmawr on Monday 12th June they found somewhere to sleep by the side of the road, which is where Police Sergeant Hibbert found them. They confirmed the story of the abandoned kit bags, also described as Army valises or haversacks. These had caused consternation, they were blood-stained.

Jones said that he could explain this – during their various travels they had picked up a dead rabbit and a dead hare, which they tied to one of the haversacks. The rabbit he said, had been attacked by a stoat, the hare had been run over. They gave the dead animals to the proprietress of a cafe in Gloucester – opposite Cory's Garage, no money exchanged hands.

Another pair of strangers had been sighted in Pontypool. Gloucestershire Constabulary were alerted by Scotland Yard via a phone call at 6.40 pm on Friday 26th May, to seek out brothers William and Albert Maggs

> 'With a view to obtaining statements as to their movements on 22nd, 23rd and 24th May.'

The brothers had been seen in Pontypool at the time of the murder. They were tracked down to 18, Grange Avenue, Hanham near Bristol, where they lived with their mother. Interviewed by Detective Constable P.Griffin (No.104) and accompanied by Police Superintendent W. Wakefield, William Maggs was described as about 5ft 11ins in height, 30 years of age, clean shaven and well built. His brother Albert Edward Maggs, about 5ft 9in, 38 years of age, clean shaven and very well built. They showed Detective Constable Griffin two halves of return railway tickets and the following day went to Staple Hill Police Station with a view to returning to Pontypool

'To clear up the matter of their presence there on the days in question.'

They gave the following statements to the Bristol police: William Maggs said

'On Monday 22nd May 1939, I was staying with my brother, Albert Edward Maggs c/o Mr Blair, 51, Abbotsford Place, Glasgow.'

He explained that he wasn't in work, as his job as a tunnel worker on a sewerage works for Messrs John Drysdale had ended because of a fire. The Maggs brothers caught the 10.45 pm train from Glasgow that evening arriving the following day in Pontypool at about 1 o'clock in the afternoon. After their epic journey from Scotland, they made for the nearest public house on the left hand side of the Railway Station having left their luggage, comprising of three suitcases, a brown paper parcel, a green trilby hat and two mackintoshes at the left luggage office for a fee of 1 shilling. At the public house they had bread and cheese and some beer. They then went to the next pub along the road where they stayed until closing time – in 1939 that meant 3 pm. They enquired of lodgings and were advised to see Mrs Carlos, whose address they couldn't recall for the statement, however she had no vacancies so they walked along until they saw a park and settled on a bench to sleep. They left the park around 5.30 pm and on the way, saw an old man and they asked him about lodgings. They explained that they were looking for work at the Ordinance Factory, Glascoed. They tried other lodging houses until they were finally taken in by Mrs Lily Horswill, of 115, Pontypool Road, who lived at that address with her husband and sons. William Maggs offered to pay a deposit for the room and proffered a £1 note from a large roll of notes. These notes Mrs Horswill said were discoloured.

'They were a brick colour, the same colour exactly as the working clothes worn by the brothers.'

Returning to the railway station for their belongings William Maggs was unable to find his left luggage ticket, so he showed his unemployment book as proof of identity. They stayed the night at Mrs Horswill's having come back the 'the worse for drink. The Maggs brothers were less than impressed by the wages offered in Pontypool and decided to look for a job elsewhere. Whilst they were at the house Lily Horswill noted that Albert had a large roll of money, which he made no effort to conceal. The following morning they left their lodgings for Pontypool railway station where they each purchased a 7d workman's return ticket to Glascoed. On arriving at the works they asked a crane driver if Taff Jones was working there, the reply was

'No, but Bristol Gunner is here and he is packing up today.'

The Maggs brothers knew Bristol Gunner, who apparently had one eye and was a tunneller like themselves. They considered that if Bristol Gunner was leaving, the work couldn't be much good, so decided to return home to their lodgings via the nearest public house. They were lucky at The Ship Inn, where the landlord accepted a 10/- bet on 'Romeo' in the Derby, the commentary of which they could listen to on the pub radio. Not lucky enough to win their bet however, they walked to the bus stop, only calling in to buy some bananas on the way to their lodgings. Deciding to seek work in Bristol they caught the 8 pm train, which stopped in Newport and they had another trip to a pub whilst waiting for a connection, finally arriving home at 10.20 pm on Wednesday 24th May.

William Maggs said that on leaving Scotland he had about £15 or £18, saved from his wages of £4 - £7 a week. Whilst in Pontypool he was wearing a grey cap, blue tweed jacket with leather cuffs and brown striped moleskin trousers. He explained that these were his working clothes and covered in reddish mud. Albert concurred with his brother's statement, except to add that he carried £57 in savings, in an old brown leather wallet. When he was living in digs in Glasgow, an altercation blew up between himself and his landlady's sister when he discovered 10/- missing from his pocket. She admitted to taking it, as a result he had been briefly arrested in Glasgow on 12th May 1939 on a charge of assault. At that time he had £63 in his possession, noted by Detective Sergeant McNabb, who suggested that he bank it. He was also wearing red stained clothing.

The two men were described by Lily Horswill – Albert Maggs was aged about 40/45, about 6ft, big build and clean shaven He wore a brown suit and fawn raincoat. William Maggs was about 38, around 6ft, big build, dark and heavy face, clean shaven. He was also wearing a dark brown suit and fawn raincoat.

Checking up on the alibis of the Maggs brothers, their movements in Pontypool were carefully followed by the local police. In Dixon's Fruit Shop in Market Street, Gwendoline Evelyn Daniel of 2, Moreton Street, Pontypool said that she had seen the two strangers at about 4.20 pm. Her attention was taken by a 'very thick wallet' that one of the brothers pulled out of his pocket. However, he paid for the bananas in silver coins. She thought he might be Irish and he said to his brother 'I bet she's a Welsh-un'.

Albert Perkins of 14, Park Street, Griffithstown a Parcel Porter, employed by the Great Western Railway Company at Pontypool confirmed William Maggs story of the lost luggage ticket. He questioned Maggs about the contents of his luggage and satisfied with the unemployment card Maggs produced, he allowed him to reclaim his possessions once he had signed an indemnity form. Mr Perkins handed over the form to the Pontypool police. Alfred Sydney Attwood, 15, The Avenue, Griffithstown employed as a 'Light Porter' agreed with Perkins account but added that when he last saw the men they had been drinking and one was complaining of the amount they had been charged for lodging in Pontypool

'I've got £100 in my wallet which I have worked hard for and I don't intend to give it away freely'.

Mr John Ridd of the Great Western Railway police went to Pontypool police station accompanied by the GWR Booking Clerk, Alfred Percy Coles of 26, Charles Street, Griffithstown. Coles also saw the Maggs brothers. He was on duty from 12.45 pm to 9.45 pm and at 7.40 pm sold the two men single tickets for Bristol, being paid with a £1 which was produced to the police and identified as No. A68A 207575. The tickets cost 5/8d each. Mr Coles also saw the wallet stuffed with notes, one of the men said

'This money was hard earned at Glasgow'.

Coles continues 'I noticed that there was a peculiar mark on what I could see of the £1 notes and this caused me to closely examine the note I received from the man. I noticed it was discoloured on the back and edge and discoloration being red and I thought it might be a stain. In view of what I read in the newspapers I thought it was best that Police should know about the discoloured note in case the red mark is blood'.

MORE STRANGERS

Following a tip-off, Pontypool police asked the Newport police to trace a 'Norman J. Griffiths of London' who was seen in the company of another man, could these be the strangers? Following information Detective Sergeant H. Parker went to The Modern Cafe, 2 Commercial Road, Newport where he examined the Visitors Book. John Tampini owned the cafe but 'Griffiths' had been see by his daughter Yolandi when he booked in on 25th May and she described him in great detail.

'He was about 39, 6ft, thin build, very thin face, pale complexion, fair wavy hair, small fair moustache, Full denture upper jaw, wearing a grey pin-striped suit, light blue shirt with white pin-strip and brown shoes with heavy soles.'

Miss Tampini also said the man was of effeminate appearance. Griffiths had told the Tampinis' that he was born in London, but that his parents were Welsh. He was married but separated from his wife and was in Newport on business as a traveller for a brewery firm.

Griffiths left The Modern Cafe at about 7.30 am on 26th May, leaving behind an overcoat and a parcel (believed to be containing shirts). He called back for these items at 8.30 pm that day in the company of a short, stout man dressed in grey sports clothes. When it came to paying for his lodgings he produced 4/6d but was very dissatisfied when he was asked to handover more. He said he had been looking for cheap lodgings of 3/- or less. Apparently he had called at a number of possible lodging places in Newport, 28 Ebenezer Terrace being one. Elsie Skinner of that address said that Griffiths was looking for cheap lodgings but decided not to stay there preferring instead The Modern Cafe. Yolandi Timpani had seen Griffiths in Newport sometime between the 22nd and 24th May, however a phone call from Detective Sergeant Davies of Pontypool suggested that Griffiths wasn't a suspect and Detective Sergeant Parker from Newport could stop searching for him.

On 29th May, William Jones, a labourer of Robert's Lodging House, Bridge Street, Blaenavon was walking down the Crumlin Road from The Race. Shortly after passing the Gypsies camp he looked over the railway line and saw a man who seemed to be looking for something.

> 'He was middle aged, stout build, sports coat and flannel trousers and wore a trilby. 'He was searching for something and looked suspicious, I think the police ought to know' said Jones.

It wasn't until June 17th that Mary May Griffiths, of Coed Cae Cottages, Llanhilleth Old Church, Aberbeeg made a statement about strangers. She went to see Detective Constable Lionel Swift to say that whilst in her garden, chatting to next-door neighbour Mrs Willets, they both saw two young men, in light coloured mackintoshes. Neither wore a hat and it was evident that they were in a hurry as the kept glancing back down the road in the direction of Pontypool. Mrs Griffiths made particular notice of the men as despite it being 'such a fine, hot morning', the men had their coats fully buttoned up. They went through a gate by Parfitt's, which would lead them to Six Bells.

Bertie John Butcher who described himself as a licensed victualler of the Green House pub at Llantarnam, Cwmbran who gave a statement on 14th June said that about three or four weeks previous a lorry pulled up and three people got out, two men and a woman. They sat outside the pub and had a drink and some food. He described the woman as of 'disreputable' appearance. One of the men was tall, with a Birmingham accent and dressed in working clothes. The other man he said, was short, with a Scottish accent and 'roughly dressed'. No one had luggage and they left after the food heading in the direction of Newport.

Joshua George, 5, Gwent Street went to the police station on 30th May. On the previous day he said, he and his wife had been walking in Pontypool Park when approached by a stranger, who had been sitting on the bank, near the Grotto.

> 'Can I see the place where the murder was committed, from here?' he asked George.

> 'I told him where the place was and pointed out where the house was but that he would not be able to see it owing to the trees in the park.'

The stranger asked if it was on the way to the Football Grounds and George said it was. As George and his wife entered the Grotto he walked with them.

'He mentioned the Llanfrechfa murder[12] and said that no doubt Sullivan did the two'

George also said that this very morning he had been in the Hospitality Inn, Pontypool and a Mr Johns of Crumlin Road had told him that he had been seen by the police (no statement on file) as he had seen a man in a dark suit of clothes. His description of the stranger matched that of the man seen by the George's.

'Name unknown, about 5ft 6ins, clean shaven, aged 45 – 46 years. He was wearing a dark suit, low shoes, blue socks, check shirt, collar and tie and a cap.' His shoes were rather worn said George – but he was otherwise respectable.

Another citizen who felt he ought to report a sighting to Police Constable S. Parfitt of Pontypool police was John Edgar Butcher of 24, Penywain Street, Wainfelin. He was a bus driver for Western Welsh, Pontynewynydd and said that on 29th May he was driving for a private hire from Pontypool to Evesham. On his return journey, at around 6 miles from Gloucester he spotted a man 'of the tramping class'. This man he said, was wearing a bowler hat and jacket 'very similar to that worn by Mr W.A. Lewis'. He explained that he knew Lewis well and should any clothes be missing from Plasmont, perhaps this information would be useful. The tramp was about 5ft 10ins, with a dirty face and 'a definite leer on his face.'

---

[12] William Sullivan killed Margaret Thomas at Llanover in 1921. He was the last man hanged at Usk Prison

Caleb Jones of 'Pleasant View', Club Row, Tranch was working for H. Vickery, Builder and Contractor of Wainfelin. He said that

> 'Two foremen from the Aluminium Works at Glascoed live with a painter at Wainfelin Avenue. The painter's name is Perce Parsell. He has told me that the foremen have discussed in front of him certain things connected with the murder of Mr Lewis. Mr Parsell has heard one of the foremen say that on Monday, 22nd May there were two men at the Ammunition Works with no money or no food – they were absolutely flat broke. On Wednesday these two men 'had money to burn'. He further stated that he had overheard a conversation between the two foremen to the effect that they suspected some persons at The Dump (ROF Glascoed) of committing the murder and it would be an easy thing to destroy any evidence by dropping the article – keys etc. into the concrete'.

A lead at last, albeit fuelled by gossip. The police invited Benjamin Percy Parsell (Perse) to give them a statement and he was interviewed on May 27th by Police Sergeant D.G. Davies. Parsell said he was a painter and decorator by trade, carrying on his business from his home address of 64, Wainfelin Road, Pontypool. His two lodgers Cecil Haynes and George Hill came from Malvern and had taken work at the Ammunition Factory at Glascoed. They paid full board and lodgings and whilst Haynes used to go out to the pub occasionally, Hill rarely went out, even though he had a motor car. They left the house at 7 am each day returning about 7 pm. They went home to Malvern on a Friday night and came back to Wales on the Monday morning, going directly to work.

Mrs Grace Margaret Parsell in her statement confirmed their habits, saying that as lodgers they had both been 'perfect gentlemen' who drank little and had never given her any trouble. Having been away for the weekend, the next time she saw the pair was about 7 pm on Monday 22nd May. Haynes went out about 9 pm Hill stayed at the lodgings. Haynes returned around 10.30 pm.

'He had not taken any drink' said Mrs Parsell.

On the evening of 23rd May, the pair arrived back from work at the usual time of 7 pm and sat with Mrs Parsell on the lawn, until they went for a drink for half an hour, returning home at 11pm. That night they were going to Usk (as confirmed by Hayne s in his statement) and had planned to get home to change.

'We are going to a bachelor party tonight, Mother', one of them said.

However, they sent a boy to Mrs Parsell to say that they wouldn't be home until later as they had gone directly to the party. It wasn't until she saw them at 11pm that evening that she mentioned the murder close by.

'Good Lord where, what was the motive?' One asked and Mrs Parsell replied 'Robbery I expect by what the Argus says.'

and with that she handed over a copy of the South Wales Argus for them to read.

'It was on Derby Day' that I mentioned the murder. I am not sure but one of them said in a joking manner 'I wonder if it was those two fellows we saw splashing their money about?'

It seemed that Parsell might have exaggerated the extent to which his lodgers knew of the murder, he stated

> 'All I can say is this. One night, after the murder of Mr Lewis of Plasmont, Haynes and Hill were talking and one of them said to the other 'It's funny if it is those two fellows who were spending all the money'. The men were described as 'flat broke' one day and on the next 'had money to burn.'

Nevertheless, it was a small lead and the police followed it up astutely. Cecil (Jack) Haynes of Elm Tree Cottage, Little Malvern was called to the Malvern Police on 27th May. He said he worked for John Morgan Ltd. Contractors at the Royal Ordinance Factory at Glascoed and agreed that on weekdays he lodged with the Parsells. He said that George Hill had a brand new Austin 8 h.p. car and that they used to return to and from Malvern in that. He said that when at the Parsells, he and Hill slept in the same bed. Some 12 days previously he had been in The Castle Inn, where he met one of the men who was working under him, on the finishing gang.

The man was Wilfred Heys, he thought he came from Burnley. There were a number of Glascoed men in the pub and they joined in a darts game. Leaving the Castle about 10.15 pm Haynes and Heys walked together towards Turner's Fish and Chip Shop. Heys had been telling of a run-in he had with the police in Burnley and admitted to spending time in Parkhurst Prison for robbery, he said he was still on license. Haynes continued

> 'When we stopped outside the fish and chip shop Heys said 'I know where some easy money is, I shall get it at the weekend' and at the same time beckoned over his right shoulder. At this time I was stood on the edge of the

curb facing the street with my back to the fish shop. Heys was stood on my left facing towards the town. I said to him, 'You leave it alone and go straight'. He then remarked that that it was so easy he intended to have it.'

The men then continued on to their separate lodgings. Haynes said some 3 days later that he'd mentioned the 'easy money' remark to Hill, 'He just laughed' he said. Returning to Malvern on 20th May for the weekend, Haynes went to the police station there (on an unconnected matter concerning a fishing rod) and whilst chatting to the policeman's wife a mentioned the 'easy money' remark. In a statement made by Gladys May Hemmings, to her husband Police Constable Reginald J. Hemmings (No.306) she recalled Haynes words

'You will hear of a big robbery soon. There is a chap working under me who knows where he can put his hand on a good bit of money. This chap knows I could shield him because I could say he was at his work when it happened, he would see that I was alright for a few quid. You will see it in the papers soon – and he'll get away with it all right, he is an old hand at the job.'

Mrs Hemmings warned him for talking so freely

'You want to be careful what you are doing or you will be drawn into trouble yourself'.

She noted that he had been drinking and was very talkative but didn't take his words seriously as he was 'known for boasting'.

On Tuesday 23rd at supper time Mrs Parsell told Haynes and Hill that there had been a murder in Pontypool. They went to The Clarence and then to the Castle Inn 'for the sing song'. They met 'the usual crowd' in the pubs, Charlie Noon, Joe

Clarke and Fred Griffin, all fellow workers at Glascoed. As they walked home that evening, the news of the murder was on everyone's mind and each man had his own theory. Charlie Noon said that on the Monday previous, when he was on his way home from a dance, he saw a man coming out of Conway Road. He was in a hurry and was not wearing a jacket or waistcoat.

Encountering Wilfred Heys in work some days later Haynes said to him

> 'How about it Tich, it's Whitsun now, did you do that bit of a job? He had said to me that if he got the money he would give me a good dab in the fist so I could have a good time at Whitsun'.

Haynes didn't receive an answer either way but Tich asked him for a lend of a shilling. Cecil Haynes gave a description of Wilfred Heys to the police

> 'he is about 40 years old, about 5' 4", short in the leg, slightly bandy, long face, bald on top, dark hair turning grey and bad teeth.' He added 'he may have a scar on his stomach.'

This was apparently caused when he fell through a glass roof. The murder was the only topic of conversation at work or in the homes and pubs. George Hill came up with a rumour of another man. Working on scaffolding, Hill had overheard a conversation between someone called 'Sailor' and another two men. They knew of a workman who had been sacked, yet turned up in the days following the murder with a wallet stuffed with notes. However Hill and Haynes were still worrying about what Tich had said and Hill attempted to engage him in conversation but whereas in the past he was always willing to stop for a chat, he suddenly became uncommunicative.

The Pontypool police lost no time in contacting the Burnley Police as Tich Heys had returned to his home in Rectory Road, Burnley. There he was interviewed by Inspector Pullen with regard to his movements from 22nd May.

He said he was aged 32 (Cecil Haynes had thought he was about 40) and was a foreman joiner at R.O.F. Glascoed. Whilst in Pontypool he lodged at 4 Malthouse Lane, home of the Wests. He left for work each morning at 6.30 am to start work at 7.30 am. On the morning of 22nd May he was accompanied by Bill Jackson, who lived in the same lodgings. They walked to the Clarence Hotel where they caught a Red and White bus to R.O.F and arrived at the Time Office there at 7.25 am. The two men then had a walk of a mile before they arrived at the works. Clocking off at 6.30 pm, George Hill gave him a lift home and dropped him about 100 yards away from his lodgings. After tea and a change of clothes he went out to The Castle pub about 8.30 pm. He said he played darts and then went home. He slept in the same bed as Jackson, who was already in bed and didn't get up until the following morning to go to work.

One interesting fact that came out of the statement was that he wasn't a 'convict out on license' as he had claimed to his fellow workmates in Pontypool. His only conviction was a fine of £1 for being drunk and disorderly. Inspector Pullen noted

> 'He is strongly addicted to drink and of a very boastful nature'.

Heys was able to account for his movements whilst in Pontypool, which, like the rest of the men at Glascoed was a regular round of, work, pub and back to the lodgings. In his statement he never mentioned a conversation with Haynes about 'easy money' and was never challenged about this by the Burnley police.

Heys said he did know of a murder, he remembered Mrs West saying one day at tea-time that the murder happened somewhere near where they lived and that the murdered man was a miserly sort.

Despite living so close to the murder he said that he didn't hear of it discussed by the men on the bus going to work. He also said that it wasn't mentioned in his hearing in work or in the pub. This is despite the fact that he and 29 of his workmates were having a presentation and dinner at The Castle, Usk for a mate, Arthur Jones, who was getting married.

A murder in a small town like Pontypool in 1939 was national news, how could he have avoided talk of it? However despite some glaring questions resulting from his statement, this statement is the only evidence that Heys was ever spoken to on the matter, there is no follow-up statement made by Pontypool police. Charles Noon received a visit from the police at his work at Glascoed, they wanted to hear more of his sighting of the 'man without jacket or waistcoat'. He had been to The Palais-de-Dance on the night of 22nd May and had walked a young lady to the Crane Street railway station for the 11.40 pm Usk train. Walking home he turned into Conway Road and saw a man just standing there.

> 'He was dressed only in shirt, trousers and shoes. He was about 5ft 10ins tall, medium build, had a good head of hair and an upright carriage. I don't think I would know him again.'

Charles Edward Merchant of 36, Prince Street went to the police to report 'strangers' in Conway Road, seen by both him and his wife. At around 8.15 pm on Monday 22nd May, he said he was standing near Woolworths when he saw a black saloon car coming down George Street.

> 'The car I mentioned contained two half-castes, that's what drew my attention to it.'

On arriving home his wife mentioned having seen a car 'with two black men in it', about 30 yards from Plasmont.' Merchant saw another car start off from outside Plasmont at 8.45 pm.

> 'There was a man and woman in the car. The man was driving and the woman was sitting in the front seat beside him. He was dressed in a clerical suit and wore a light trilby turned down in the front. He appeared to be between 50 and 60 years of age. I could identify him.'

Merchant was on his way to a gas-mask fitting in the schoolroom at St Alban's Catholic Church and he arrived just before the session closed at 9 pm. Statement 213

There was another sighting of two men in a car by an un-named young lad. Now deceased, in his later years he always maintained to his stepdaughter that he had seen 'a limousine' draw away from the house on the night of 22nd May.

THE PONTYPOOL UNDESIREABLES

The police had an extensive list of no-good-boyos, otherwise known as 'The Pontypool Undesirables'. It included those recently in trouble with the law, or recently released from prison or probation. One by one they were invited to Pontypool police station to account for their movements on 22nd May. The Scotland Yard file contains the interviews.

One such, who vowed he was on the straight and narrow was Godfrey Phillips of 30 Edward Street currently employed at R.O.F. Glascoed as a chain-man. He remembered well that on the night in question he was at Pontypool Park (with most of the population of Pontypool) to see the South Wales Borderers display. He left there at about 9.30 pm and went to Savini's bar, which was very full. He stayed there for about half an hour then walked home via George Street and Conway Road. He said he knew Mr Lewis slightly and that he lived in the big house on Conway Road. He said he saw no one near Plasmont as he was walking home. He was keen to say that he now had a good job and was keeping out of trouble and didn't see the chap who had led him astray on previous occasions.

At Abertillery, Police Sergeant Phipps (No.85) had been making inquiries regarding Aubrey Powell, unemployed collier and bookies runner formerly of Montrose Villa, Commercial Road, Llanhilleth. During the week following the murder, Powell was seen to be spending money freely, (which was considered far above his income) on drink. He was in the habit of roaming the country singing in public houses. On Saturday 3rd June, whilst under the influence of drink, he quarrelled with his wife. She then reported to neighbours that he had a large quantity of silver and a roll of notes upstairs in a tin box. Early the following week he left for London, with the money. He also left without paying out winning punters for previous racing wins.

He wrote asking his wife to join him in London, saying that he had found a job on the A.R.P. Shelters and had a friend called Paddy. His wife stated that her husband had a single Omnibus ticket for 8d, which was the price of a single fare from Pontypool to Llanhilleth. Mrs Powell didn't go to London and on the night of 16th June, Powell returned home, entering his house by means of the back bedroom window. He alarmed his wife who was not expecting him home. He was next seen by Charles Hopkins of Merton Villa, Commercial Road, Llanhilleth, in what Mr Hopkins described as 'a concealed position' on the footbridge of Llanhilleth Railway Station. Hopkins said

'Hello, I have to have a second look at you, you look so brown.'

'That's the fresh and sea air, here's my train coming, I'm off' replied Powell.

However he waited until the train had come to a complete standstill before dashing down the footbridge steps and onto the train. Hopkins said that during their brief conversation, Powell seemed very agitated. Since Powell had left his wife, she was on Public Assistance but when he returned home he gave her £1 and arranged for all the furniture to be removed to London, 27, Prospect Road, Childs Hill, London NW 2. Powells was described as follows: aged about 27 years, height 5ft 5ins, a medium build, dark hair, tanned complexion and when he was last seen wearing a blue suit, cap and black shoes. There is nothing in the Scotland Yard file to show that Powell was ever followed up in London.

Two black men, also an unusual sight in Pontypool, were under suspicion. Emma Rose Blake of 9, Jubilee Terrace, Pontnewynydd, a married woman aged 63 gave a statement, on 2nd June. She remembered the date of a sighting of the saloon car as 6.30 pm Monday 22nd May as she was on her way down George Street, with her son William, on the way to the Soldier's Display in the park.

'In it was a dark man driving and a dark man sat beside him. By dark I mean black men, like the Indians about here.'

William Jack Blake, a twenty five year old steelworker agreed with his mother's statement and said he thought the car was green and black and a Standard 9. The car drew up and one of the men asked where 'T' Lewis of 2 Wainfelin Road, was'. Blake advised him to go to George Street School and ask there. He mentioned that he since found out that the men did not go to Wainfelin Road that night. However, the mystery of the two black men was solved when Gertrude Lewis of 2 Merchant's Hill, Pontnewynydd spoke to Detective Constable Adams. It transpired that the men were from Bridgend and had a stall in Newport Market. They purported to cure rheumatism. They were visiting her husband Stanley for that purpose on Monday night and had left at about 8.30 pm which would concur with sightings of them in the Plasmont area. Inspector Rees described them as 'quack doctors'.

Another man came under suspicion when he was overheard in a pub in Newport, discussing the murder. Enoch Thomas, Coal Tipper of Tregenna, Queens Hill Crescent, Newport was in The White Hart in Mill Street around 8 pm on Thursday 25th May when he heard a fellow drinker who seemed to have a lot of knowledge about the murdered William Lewis. ,

> 'This man stated he lived closer to Mr Lewis than his housekeeper Mrs Barnett', *(though as she lived in Plasmont Cottage which was part of Plasmont House, this wasn't possible)*. Lewis was worth forty thousand pounds.' he said. He also stated that 'Mr Lewis got two lovely 'bloody' bumps on the head'.

Another man at the bar called out to the one talking about Lewis

'Where are you living now Tancy?' at this the man downed his beer, pocketed his darts and left the pub.

In the Welsh Oak, Rogerstone near Newport the landlord William Richard Jenkins served a customer at 11.25 am on Saturday 27th May. This was Sidney Powell and his left arm was in a sling. One of the customers said

'What's the matter with your arm?'

To everyone's surprise, Powell slung the arm out of the sling and said 'Get out.' He then challenged other customers to a game of darts for 10/- but there were no takers. Police Sergeant A.M. Sutton (No 72) of Risca Police took this statement and passed it to the Pontypool Police Station.

It transpired that Sidney Powell, lodging at Amberley House, George Street, was a labourer at The Royal Ordnance Factory. He was working on No.5 Section Filter beds and had gone to the first aid centre at the factory where he had been treated by John Hails, who was interviewed in the Boiler Room of the factory by Police Sergeant. D.G. Davies. Powell had injured his knee when he was walking over a bank and the knee twisted. The accident had happened at noon said Powell, but he didn't report it until 5 pm, thinking it 'not too bad' at the time. In his statement, John Benjamin Hails, giving his address as 19, College Road, Penygarn and confirming his job as 'a first aid man' went on to say that Powell also showed him an injury to his left hand.

'The first a left fingers were abrased' he said.

After binding them up, he took particulars of the injury for the accident book, which he described to Police Sergeant Davies. It showed that

> 'At 10.15 am on 24.5.39 Powell was trimming a piece of old timber and a nail went into his fingers.'

There were apparently no witnesses to this accident. Hails later saw Powell who said he had been to his doctor about the twisted knee and was told it was cartilage problems and he had to have an operation

> 'I'm going to be a few weeks on the 'comp' *(compensation)* before it happens' said Powell.

This he apparently did because he went to Morgan's builders, bearing a medical certificate from Pontypool Hospital. His details were taken by John Leslie Donovan of 50, Malpas Road, Newport a clerk in the Compensation Department.

Work at Glascoed must have been severely disrupted by the number of witness statements taken by the police, who were asking questions about a lot of men employed there. John Lowe Bland, a pipe layer also gave a statement about Powell's hand injury. He stated that Powell was a labourer chiefly mixing compo, cement and sand and carrying pipes.

> 'One day within the last fortnight Powell came to me and said he had cut his hand by knocking on a nail'.

Bland advised him to report the accident and get it treated. Edward William Elliot lodging at 1, Park View, Goytre and working as a General Foreman said that Powell had never mentioned an incident with his hand.

Another man reported with an injury was George Lindsey. He had been frequenting the Unicorn Inn, Albion Road where the licensee was David Morgan. Lindsey was described as

> 'About 42, black curly hair parted in the centre and was in the habit of going to the pub with a pal name 'Joe.'

They were both tunnellers and were working at the Royal Ordnance Factory. Morgan said George Lindsey lodged with Stanley Metcalf in Albion Road. Sometime around May 24th Lindsey had arrived at The Unicorn with long scratches down the side of his face.

> 'I would think he would be a man who would be violent in drink'.

He added that Lindsey hadn't been seen since. When the police interviewed Elizabeth Margaret Metcalf of 67 Albion Road, she confirmed that Lindsey had now gone back to his home town of Wallasey, leaving on the Saturday. The day prior to that, she had noticed scratches on his face which he attributed to cutting himself whilst shaving. She had not seen him since. 'Joe' his drinking companion was traced and turned out to be another native of Wallasey, John Joseph Bates – lodging at No. 1 Back of Clarence Street, Pontypool was employed by Nuttall's Ltd as a foreman tunneller.

He said that the last time he'd seen Lindsey was on Saturday 27th

> 'As far as I could see he seemed all right'.

Detective Inspector Keith of Wallasey Police interviewed Lindsey at his home. He had left the job he said because he could not keep two homes going and was paying £1 a week for his board and lodging and 3/- bus fare out of a wage of £.9.0d. He had been working on the 'bougee' machine, which he described as a compressed air machine for mixing 'compo' which had caused a rash on both of his arms. Having been to see the doctor about this he obtained a certificate which he handed in to Nuttall's his employers. He then returned to Wallasey and was currently on 'the dole'. He'd come home on a Red and White charabanc, which had been hired by a number of Wallasey men returning home for the Whitsun holidays. The only scratches on his face he said were caused when he was shaving. He had not been out and about on 22nd or 23rd as he was working the 2pm – 10 pm shift. He said the landlord of the Unicorn was on the same shift as himself and they came home together at 10 pm.

No statement exists to explain why the police interviewed John Burgess of 23 West Place. He was interviewed at ROF, Glascoed on 16th June. He said

> 'I am a transport worker employed by John Morgan Ltd.' Glascoed. I do not know a thing about two men who were supposed to have seen a man coming from Plasmont House. If any person says I told him. That person is lying'.

Many of the men who worked at Glascoed only stayed in Pontypool or the surrounding district during the week, at weekends some of them returned to their homes. Numerous people with a spare room took in lodgers, some men having to share a room or even a bed. One such house was Amberley House, Upper George Street, Pontypool. The house was rented by Thomas Raymond Williams from a Mr King of Llantarnam for 14/- per week plus rates. Williams and his wife Lilly Ann had recently decided to take in boarders.

As well as their daughter Marie and Frank Victor Williams, his brother, the household consisted of Mrs Dinah Smith (a friend), Mr And Mrs R. Auker, William Watkins, James Claughan, Jeremiah Hallissey, Jeremiah Cronin, Mr James, V. Heeney, P. Toal, J. McArle and Sidney Powell. Mr Williams was a French polisher, working for Bevan and Co. Pontypool and left for work each day at 8.40 am and generally didn't see much of the lodgers. The police decided to interview some of the lodgers at Amberley House. First was Mr Horatio Auker, whose home was Wetlington, Norfolk. He shared a bedsitting room at the back of the house with his wife Mary and their child. He said he was employed by B.B. Sunley as an Excavator Driver at Glascoed and knew nothing of the murder. Mrs Auker said she mostly stayed upstairs and didn't mix with the other lodgers.

John McArdle, said he came from County Lough, Ireland and was a labourer employed by Dan Young, builder of King Street, Pontypool. He paid 8/- a week and shared two rooms with his friends Vincent Heeney aged 26 and Patrick Toal aged 24 were also from County Lough and worked for the same builder. None of them they said knew anything about the murder. Toal said that he had been at work from 7.30 am on 22nd May and returned home at 6.30 – 7 pm. He didn't go out that night. Jeremiah Hallissey, 29 from County Kerry said likewise and added that his friend Jerome Cronan had been in bed almost every night, suffering from stomach ache. Cronan had been working in a field behind the Beaufort Arms pub for Dan Young but was returning home on 4th June to Kenmaire, County Kerry and proposed to get a job with the local County Council.

One of the most unlikely suspects was seen on Caerleon Road, Newport. The police had asked for people to report anyone who seemed to have a large amount of paper money and one such was seen at Mrs Sadler's shop, 420 Caerleon

Road by John Wilson Western of 63, Aston Crescent, who was a commercial traveller.

On Tuesday 30th May, at around 11 am he was chatting to Mrs Sadler when a man came into the shop and asked to buy a sandwich. When he asked the price Mrs Sadler said

> 'Tuppence'. The man then said 'Tuppence, that's not enough, you will not get a living like that; take fourpence.'

and handed over that sum. He then told Mr Western that on the previous day he had won £50 at the Caerleon Races and given every man staying in the same lodgings a pound each. This evidence was enough for public spirited Mr Western to report him immediately to Pontypool police, though his subsequent description seems to rule the man out as no one in Pontypool had described such remarkable person.

> 'He was about 5'4" in height, thin face. His right leg had been amputated and replaced with a wooden leg. His left arm had also been amputated. He was poorly dressed, and was without collar or tie. He spoke with a strong Scottish accent. During my conversation with him he told me he came from Aberdeen and was on his way to Caerleon Races, where I presumed he hoped to make some money by playing a concertina he had in his possession.' This statement was witnessed by Police Constable Plummer (No.115)

> Anyone who had left the district recently was traced and all leads were followed up. Edmund Daniel James of 15, Pentwyn Terrace, Abersychan was traced to London. A father of 3 girls, two were at Pentwyn Terrace with his mother, the third at Greenford. He had been a collier but because of continued unemployment in Pontypool had

been sent to London by the Ministry of Labour, to train as a metal turner. It was established that he was on his training course on the days before and after the murder from 8 am to 4.30 on weekdays, for which he received a wage of 22/- a week, 17/- of which he paid in rent. He said he didn't have the means to return to Pontypool and in fact had borrowed a 'sub' from his mother as he was so hard up.

George Parkes, butcher of Conway Road Pontypool saw Lewis and a clergyman (presumably Lewis' brother-in-law Watkins) about 3.30pm on May 22nd .They were looking at some property in George Street and then walked down Trueman's Gulley. As he watched the two men disappearing someone he knew as 'Ginger' Roberts, who was clearly under the influence of drink came up to Parkes and said 'Wouldn't I like to go and smash his bloody face', indicating Lewis as he spoke. Councillor Greasley was passing and Ginger Roberts latched on to him and Parkes continued on his way to have a shave. Councillor George Greasley who lived at 50, Fowler Street was accosted by Arthur (Ginger) Roberts who seemed to have some grievance with Lewis saying 'Now Councillor, there's Lewis going down there with a Preacher, just talk to him.' Recognising that Roberts was 'slightly intoxicated' Greasley went on his way.

Arthur Roberts of 39 Fowler Street, a galvanised sheet drawer employed by Paton's of Pontnewydd didn't remember the incident at all but he had been in the Castle Inn and had consumed 'about 5 pints of beer'. He said he knew Mr Lewis very well though didn't give any reason why he should 'smash his face in'. Roberts claimed that he had heard on 24th May that Lewis 'had been knocked about'. His statement is signed with an 'X' as he stated that he could not write.

Cecil Howard Jeens (a retired ticket collector for GWR at Newport) of The Mount, Penrhiw, Risca, having seen a 'Stop Press' article in the Daily Express felt compelled to go to Risca Police Station to make a statement. He spoke to Police Sergeant A.M. Sutton (No. 72) 'There is a man, Donald Stephenson, who lives at Albert Avenue Newport'. He said that for a number of years Stephenson was a travelling draper. He may well have come across Lewis in his drapery business in Cwm as he travelled the valleys and knew Pontypool well. However, Stephenson developed an interest in Dog Racing and his previously successful business fell into decline, Jones described him as a 'down and out'. Jones described how he had seen Stephenson hanging about Newport station, asking people for 'a loan' of money and was taken aback one evening as he left his house to find Stephenson loitering nearby. This surprised Jones as he described his home as 'on the side of the mountain, well away from the main roads'. Refusing to lend Stephenson £3 he finally bought some cigarettes, from him 12 packets of 3d 'Players', which he assumed Stephenson had won in The Arcade, in Newport. 'I advised him not to do anything desperate' said Stephenson. 'In view of my knowledge of the above, I think it my duty to make this statement' Jeens added. He gave a description of Stephenson' he is about 5ft 10 ins, slim build, dark complexion, clean shaven, dark hair well brushed back. He wears a dark suit, soft collar and tie, dark socks with black shoes. He always wears a greasy bowler hat. Sometimes he wears a black coat and vest and pin-striped trousers.

Police Sergeant Sutton added a note to the statement that he had (via Newport Borough Police) found that the correct address for Stephenson was Tudor Road.

Another man who came under suspicion was Stanley Powell who said he was from Amberley House, Pontypool. Though his lady friend, Mrs Bennett a widow who lived in Mill Street, Newport, thought he was from Risca. She noticed that he suddenly took great interest in the newspapers, particularly reports of the murder. He knew of Lewis 'they must have been after his money' and he had his arm in a sling – and anyone and everyone in the environs of Pontypool sporting an injury was under suspicion in the days following the murder.

On 27th May, Powell turned up at Mrs Bennett's house, his arm still in a sling and suddenly said

'Look what I've got'

and produced a hammer from the sling. Mrs Bennett was taken aback and asked 'what have you got that for, are you going to 'out' me?' He replied 'You might laugh if you knew' and said that he wanted her to look after it, she described it as a slating hammer, her deceased husband had used a similar one, blunt on one end, sharp on the other. She refused to accept it and he left. Some days later they were having a drink in the White Hart, in Caerleon when a police constable approached Powell and took him aside.

'When he returned to me' said Mrs Bennett 'he was very pale. I said 'What's the matter. What was the constable talking about?

'Only about a murder up by me.'

He said no more. A couple of weeks later Mrs Bennett looked out of her front door and found two men talking to Powell. Later he said

'Did you see those men having a go at me?' '

She asked him what he had been up to.

'They were two detectives, somebody's shopped me. Somebody wrote a letter accusing me of having something to do with the Pontypool job and saying that I have the money that is missing.'[13]

'I said that if he had anything to do with the murder he should be a man, and admit the truth.'

She didn't see him after that date and he was never arrested.

Stanley Powell gave a statement:

'I am a labourer at Glascoed. Presently I am on compensation having signed ill on Wednesday 24th May 1939. I will received 30/- on Friday 2nd June as a first payment. I am married but live apart from my wife. I have two sons one is married and is a professional footballer, the other is in the Army in India. I started work in Glascoed in September 1938. Prior to working there I was engaged as a furnace man at Town Forge, Pontypool. I drink in The Little Crown, in Pontnewynydd and the Fountain in George Street, Pontypool. On 22nd May – 24th I was working a day shift at Glascoed. I start work at 7.30 am. I catch the train at Clarence Street Station at 7 am. and return home on the train from

---

[13] No letter to this effect in the Scotland Yard folder

Glascoed Halt at 6.40 pm. On 22nd May my train stopped at Crane Street Station at five minutes past seven. I went to my lodgings, Amberley House, had my tea and a wash and change and went to the Little Crown pub. I left the pub at ten minutes past ten, went home, had my supper and went to bed. I did the same on Tuesday and played darts with the landlord. On Wednesday 24th I worked as normal until about 3 pm when I walked over a bank and twisted my left knee. I had a previous injury to this knee on 15th November 1938, when I was buried in a trench at R.O.F Glascoed. I was laid up on the occasion for twelve weeks, receiving 30/- a week compensation.

When I twisted my knee on 24th I went to the temporary company office of my employers, John Morgan Ltd. to report the injury. It was dressed by an ambulance man, who also painted it with iodine. I filled in an accident sheet. Prior to that on Thursday 18th May, I was chipping back a concrete wall and a piece of concrete struck my left hand, causing a small injury on the second and third forefinger, and the first knuckle joint of the middle finger. To do the chipping I used a chisel in my left hand and the hammer in my right. I ought to mention that the injury to my middle finger was caused on Saturday by a nail in a piece of timber I picked up. When I reported my knee injury I also reported my hand, and at that time I said the injury had been caused on the 23rd, the previous day. He went to Dr McAllen's Surgery (who assisted at the Lewis post-mortem) on the way home from work and was seen by his assistant, who gave me a form to go to the hospital for an X-ray'.

On 25th May, Powell saw Dr McAllen's assistant again, (he also worked at the hospital) who told him that his knee 'would never be right again' until he had something done to his cartilage. Before his knee injuries, Powell had been notified by a ganger, Trevor Lewis that his employment would terminate on 24th May. He hadn't reported his injuries to the ganger Lewis or to the Accident Department however after leaving the hospital he took his Doctor's note to Glascoed, saw the clerk in the general office and signed his termination forms. Then he hitched a lift into Newport and went to the White Lion for about half an hour, he played darts with the landlord's son and this is where he met Mrs Bennett. He also met a man he knew came from Pontypool who mentioned the murder. Powell said 'I live opposite the house' meaning Plasmont. He mentioned that Mr Lewis was shorter than he was and also that he collected rents, but added that everyone in Pontypool knew that. Powell also said that the photograph in the South Wales Argus had been taken from his house. 'I might have said that he had two bumps on his head, because I'd heard this' said Powell.

'I might also have said that Mr Lewis was worth £40,000, for I know he was a very rich man'.

Mrs Bennett and Powell then went to the White Hart in Caerleon, where he chatted to the landlord. At the end of the evening they returned to Newport by bus and Powell saw Mrs Barnett home before catching the Pontypool train arriving about 11.30 pm. On the Friday after visiting the Little Crown, the Castle in George Street and the Clarence, he went to Glascoed to pick up his wages of £3.19.6d. He said his average wages throughout the year were around £3.10 shillings a week. On returning to Pontypool he met Billy Allen who was pulling houses down in George Street. Allen said he had given a statement to the police the previous night about his movements in connection with the Lewis enquiry. Powell said 'Billy Power, John Hancock of Abersychan, Jack Lodge and Jim Whelan were there. I talked with Allen about the murder. I had a feeling that there might be a woman mixed up in the case and said so'. The following day Powell went to Pontymister and The Welsh Oak and on to the Forge hammer at Risca. At 7.30 pm he returned to the Welsh Oak and had a game of darts for 5/- a side. At this point he took his arm out of the sling, where he was keeping his mason's hammer. He handed the hammer over the bar for safe-keeping whilst he played darts. In the days following the brutal murder of a man who had been attacked with a weapon, a man with an injury and with a hammer concealed in a sling hardly escaped attention. After the game of darts he collected his hammer and went on to The London Inn, in Newport and the White Hart in Caerleon. Returning to Newport he discovered he had missed the last bus home to Pontypool, so started walking. He said he saw P.C. Halt at about 5.30 am as he was making his way home. Powell said he had never been in Plasmont.

William Henry Power (referred to as Billy Power in Stanley Powell's statement) said that he met with the other men but they didn't talk about murder. He was an unemployed wheelwright of 24, Upper Bridge Street. He said he did a bit of lorry driving to assist his son, aged 15. The lorry was owned by his wife. Power said it was his custom to go to Tirpentwys tip every day to buy coke, from a character called Billy the Pant, which he used to sell around Newport and Cardiff. He said Fred Quillan of Granville Square, Newport used to take orders for him. He could account for his movements on 22nd May as he was moving to a new garage for the lorry, this was in Cwmynyscoy, the old garage was in Rockhill Road, Pontypool

The investigation brought forth people from all sorts of backgrounds and in this case a young wife fleeing from her violent husband got caught up in the investigation. Ernest Stewartson, Cadoxton, Barry had persuaded Ida Curtis to leave her husband and run away with him on Tuesday 23rd May. They arrived in Usk late into the evening and having no digs, slept in a field close to ROF Glascoed that night. Following many enquires the police tracked them down to Cadoxton, where they had returned. The police at Swindon were able to ascertain that Stewartson was in Swindon on 22nd and 23rd May and could not have been involved with the murder.

Edmund James, a man with a local reputation as a 'bit of a bad boy' was also seen near Plasmont but his brother Joseph Caradoc James a Turf Commission Agent of 3, King Street (the street behind Plasmont) was able to tell the police that prior to a month ago Edmund had lived with his mother at 15, Pentwyn Terrace, Abersychan. However he had lived in Baker Road, London since 22nd April. This was followed up by Detective Inspector Richardson of 'X Division' and found to be true. The police also followed leads on local 'bad boys' identified as William Henry Power, James Roderick, James Wilde, Frederick Horton, David Henry Williams, James Ralph and James Whelan. All were eliminated from the

166

enquiry, though David Williams implicated himself in the crime.

THE HIDDEN TROUSERS

Local no-good-boyo David Henry Williams had his arm in a sling and blood on his suit and knew that it was only a matter of time before he received a visit from the police. He had been arrested and previously jailed for house breaking. He had even mentioned to his wife Gwyneth Irene Williams that the police would shortly be knocking at their door.

> 'If they (the police) knew I was in Pontypool on the Tuesday they would be after me'.

As he had been in and out of prison, Williams was often visited by the police when there were robberies in the area. Williams lived in a two roomed house, Aber Cwm Hir Farm, Glascoed set right in the heart of the mountains. It could only be approached by a long cart track. It was described by Chief Inspector Rees as having

> 'No sanitary conveniences, the lavatory and well supplying water being some distance away in an adjoining field'.

Williams lived in this house with his wife and two of his three children. He had been employed as a 'casual', a borer, with Nuttall's at ROF Glascoed. He was wearing a sling because of an injury to his thumb. This was corroborated by nurse Gladys May Davies, at Pontypool Hospital as Williams had attended on two occasions on 3rd May and again on 3rd June, to have bits of steel removed from his finger-tips. She was present when the doctor lanced his hand on a table, protected by a mackintosh cover. Following the procedure she placed his arm in a cuff. She told Detective Constable Adams that as far as she could remember, there was very little blood and she didn't see any drop onto Williams' trousers. William's wife Gwyneth said that on 22nd May her husband had come home from work at 3pm. After tea she went to the pictures in Pontypool, while he looked after the children. She got home at about 10 pm and they went to bed at 10.30 pm. The following night, 23rd, she said that she had stayed home whilst he went to the pictures.

On 20th July 1939 (by now Williams was in custody) Flora Beatrice Giles his mother-in-law of Overdale, Wainfelin Road, Pontypool gave a statement to Detective Constable William Adams.

> 'Sometime in May of this year David Williams came to my house. His left arm was in a small sling, there was blood on his arm and also some blood on his trousers. They were grey coloured. I know David has another pair of trousers identical with the ones he was wearing that day. The ones he had on were his best ones and the blood on them was very noticeable, I think the blood was on the left trouser leg. The other pair of grey trousers was soiled as David used to work about the house in them. I have never heard David say that he had hidden any trousers or that he wished to hide them.'

It was Williams' behaviour in custody which aroused suspicion. He was in custody for robbing a house in Mamhilad at Pontypool having been picked up and was in court on 24th June. At that time there was nothing to connect him to the Lewis murder. Regarding the housebreaking, he had entered the house though a scullery window in the night and had taken 11 shillings. He was discovered by the householder and was pursued. He finally escaped by throwing himself over a hedge, though by then others hearing the hue-and-cry had taken up the chase. He ran into a wood and found a hiding place. However, he was captured by his pursuers and handed over to the police. As a result, he was taken to court and sentenced to six months hard labour. However, on his way to H.M.S. Prison Cardiff he escaped again.

After a couple of hours he was seen on the Usk - Pontypool Road and was re-arrested. At the time no particular significance was attached to his escape but on July 6th a message was received at Pontypool Police Station from the Governor of Cardiff Prison to the effect that two prisoners, Stanley Harold Griffey and George Harold Jones wished to make statements concerning a conversation they had in prison, with David Henry Williams. The particular interest being that Williams escaped in order to destroy some evidence which might be connected with the Lewis murder. Superintendent A. Gover and Detective Adams went to the prison to interview Griffey and Jones.

Griffey was in custody at Pontypool prison for 2 months for motoring offences when Williams was brought in on the housebreaking charge on 21st July 1939. He and Williams got into conversation and on the way to Abergavenny Police Station to be photographed Williams told Griffey that he had been near Plasmont House when the murder was committed.

'How do you know, because no one seems to know the time of the murder.' said Griffey.

Williams also explained that he had

'Diddled the police when the Scotland Yard had me under examination and took my clothes away.'

Williams revealed that he hadn't told the Police that he had two pairs of trousers to his grey suit, one blood-stained which he had hidden in a hedge near Glascoed, along with other items. He was worried that these trousers would implicate him in the murder at Plasmont House. When he was arrested he was wearing the clean pair. In Court when he realised that things were going badly for him and that his sentence would be more than three months, he thought that the trousers would be revealed by the falling of leaves in autumn. At that moment he decided to 'make a run for it' if the sentence was over three months. Jones corroborated this tale though neither of them paid particular notice of it until Williams' escape. The police spent days in the woods near Williams' home looking for the trousers, however the woods were thick and boggy and nothing was found.

Inspector Rees decided to interview Williams, Jones and Griffey again. This was on July 21st. Griffey stated he had been asked by Williams to find and dispose of the trousers as soon as he (Griffey) was released. He was serving a shorter sentence than Williams. The two men met again, making mailbags whilst in Cardiff prison, and at that time Williams said he was hoping for bail as he had one child very ill. When Williams was interviewed he said that the trousers had been left in a tree, and gave a description of the hiding place, which also contained the 11/- for which he was serving his current sentence. Williams was sure that if the police found the bloodied trousers they would associate them with the Lewis murder. However, he said he had an alibi for May 22nd and could account for his movements. He said he was at home from 2 pm until 6 am the following day, when he got up for work. He was certain of the date as, having heard of the Lewis murder he anticipated a knock at the door

'I expected Police would visit every man in the district convicted of housebreaking.' he said.

The trousers were finally located using directions supplied by Williams.

'Go to Waunfawr Farm, then through the hunting gate and across two or three fields to a blackberry hedge.'

There the police found a tin containing the money and some cigarettes. The trousers were less easy to find.

'Through New Inn Way, and at Berry's Corner go up the road and the trousers are in a tree up there.'

They were sent to Dr Webster, Home Office Pathologist at Birmingham for examination. Inspector Rees was confident that Williams had nothing to do with the murder, having satisfied himself that the explanation for the blood on the trousers came from the Mamhilad robbery. It was known that Lewis' blood group 'was in a very rare 'O' group' and the blood on the trousers was that of Williams.

Lucy Holbrook, shopkeeper of 35, George Street confirmed she knew the Williams family as they ordered goods from her shop and James Henry Mason of 21a, High Street, Garndiffaith – a steel-worker at Paton's Works, Pontnewydd said that he knew Williams but had not seen him for a number of months.

A different pair of trousers had been seen hidden in another hedge shortly after the murder. William Henry Jenkins, a timberman worked at R.O.F. Glascoed He lived at Small Cottage, Llanyrafon Farm, Llantarnam, Cwmbran. He said he was on his way to work at about 5.40 am on 23rd or 24th May, to arrive at the Newport to Pontypool Road to catch the bus, he had to pass through two fields. When he got to the stile in the second field which was alongside the main road he saw a pair of grey trousers, under the hedge about 10 yards from the stile on the field side. He went over to see the trousers and finding a piece torn out of one of the legs, he left them where they were. He saw Police Constable Isaac Moore (No.252) at Llantarnam Rail Station on Monday 29th May and reported his find.

Constable Moore said that he had seen Jenkins and his wife as they got off the train and that Jenkins had approached him immediately about his find. They went together to the spot where Moore took possession of the trousers. They were torn and inside the waist he saw a stamp 'City Lodge', which he knew was a Poor Law Institution in Cardiff. He interviewed Reece Beynon, the owner of Llanyrafon Farm and he said he hadn't seen the trousers in the hedge. He also saw Thomas Evans of Large Cottage, Llanyrafon Farm who had passed through the field on Sunday 28th May and he hadn't noticed them Thomas Waite of nearby Llanyrafon Mill hadn't been through the field for some time. P.C. Moore noted that there was a footpath running through the field, from the stile to Pontnewydd.

Another man who inadvertently implicated himself in the crime was Arthur Bernard John Martin of Pencisely Road, Cardiff. He worked for The Peerless Electrical manufacturing Company, London. He was interviewed on 3rd of June in Cardiff by D.S. Gordon Prosser. It is notable that Martin is the only person who says he was cautioned prior to giving a statement. This may prove significant. He had travelled to Weymouth and whilst there met a number of sailors from H.M.S. Royal Sovereign and they spent the day (21st May) drinking at various bars. They then decided to go to Bournemouth, Martin couldn't drive his car as he was in sling (he had fallen through a hatch on H.M.S Sovereign the previous night). Approaching Puddletown an R.A.F. Scout pulled them up as he believed the car was being driven in a dangerous manner. The passengers and Martin got out of the car and in Martin's word 'an altercation took place'. Martin said he would report the R.A.F. Scout to the police and demanded his details. In reply, the Scout asked Martin his name and where he lived. By his own admission Martin had had a few drinks and whilst he gave his correct name he said he made up an address, which just happened to be Conway Road, Pontypool. He further compounded the issue by being not too far from Branksome, where, on 23rd May Walter Dinnivan was murdered in similar circumstances to Lewis, i.e. a lonely man, battered around the head by an unknown person with a blunt object. However, after investigations by the Dorset police Martin was fully alibi'd by his drinking partners and was allowed to go.

It may have been assumed by Pontypool residents that with the coming War, the murder of William Alfred Lewis was no longer a priority. However, even in 1941 the Police were still pursuing people with a criminal record. One such, who had evaded interview in 1939 was Edward O'Hearne, who when he was in Pontypool stayed with William Allen, one of the builders used by William Lewis. In the words of the Pontypool Police

> 'He had made a hurried departure from Pontypool around the time of the murder.'

He finally emerged on 22nd May 1941 (curiously the anniversary of the murder). He had been arrested at Bicester, Oxford, for factory breaking. Detective Sergeant D. G. Davies was sent to interview him but was satisfied from enquiries made at Lindsay Parkinsons Ltd. Poole in Dorset, that

O'Hearne was working as a ganger for that firm in early May 1939 and as there was nothing to connect him to the murder it seemed futile, 2 years on to make further investigations. Nevertheless, it was another name to tick off the list. It transpired that O'Hearne had been back to Pontypool on a number of occasions since and was unaware that the Police retained an interest in him.

THE WEAPON

Police had searched in vain for the weapon used to kill Lewis. The South Wales Argus reported that Inspector Rees was seen to leave the house on Thursday 25th around 7 o'clock in the evening 'with a long object, wrapped up in newspaper' but this was later eliminated from the enquiries. The grass in the garden was mown and the area carefully searched. Probationer Recruit Ivor Jones, 6 Brecon Road, Abergavenny had found a piece of lead piping in an ornamental pool in the garden at the side of Plasmont. There was also speculation (amongst the public in Pontypool, rather than the police) that the assailant had used a shoe to batter Lewis. This rumour still persists. One elderly lady recently whispered to the author

> 'Shortly after the murder, we went on a Church day-out to Barry. I was only a little girl at the time. On the train, in each compartment everyone was talking about the murder, and they said it was done with a woman's stiletto shoe!'

This rumour may have been fuelled by a report in the South Wales Argus that a Newport woman, scorned by her lover had removed her shoe and holding it by the toe, inflicted dreadful injuries to his face. The South Wales Argus reporter speculated about the shoe as a weapon.

'It would probably have a rubber heel – a bare heel would cause much more severe wound and a rubber tipped heel, used with some force would probably be just the type of thing to inflict the injuries.'

However whilst high heels were popular and the stiletto had already been seen in the USA, it was unlikely that any woman wearing stiletto shoes in Pontypool in 1939 would have gone unnoticed. This rumour certainly muddied the waters for the police, who were looking for the eponymous 'blunt object'.

The overgrown garden at Plasmont House

Poster and newspapers carried appeals. In the cinemas the screens flashed with a plea for anyone with information to contact the police immediately. Percy Danter, a travelling showman, giving his address as 'The Fairfield, Pontypool', where his funfair was moving-in prior to the Pontypool Carnival said

'About 6pm on Tuesday 6th June we pulled our engines and a number of wagons into the Fairfield, Pontypool, when Mrs Winsper, who is residing with me, handed me an iron bar about 2ft 6 ins in length which she found near the entrance to the field.'

Mr Michael Joseph Flood of 96, The Highway, Pontypool also saw the appeal at The Park Cinema. He had lost an iron bar – from his stall in Pontypool Market. It was noticed missing on 19th May. Detective Adams went to Pontypool Market and his report to his senior officer says

'I have today made enquiries in the Market and was shewn a replica of the tool lost by Flood. It is a draw-bar. At one end is a fish tail shape for withdrawing nails. It is eighteen and a half inches long and weighs 3 lbs 6 ozs and the handle part of it is a round shape. I respectfully submit, Sir, that in my opinion it is too heavy a character to have inflicted the wounds on the murdered man's head.'

Detective Inspector Adams also checked the surrounding stalls and interviewed the errand boy J. Roberts of Bushy Park.

Flood, in his statement to Police Constable S. Parfitt (No. 167) also remembered his customers, those that generally called 'late' on a Friday, Mrs Hogan of Park Road, Mrs Hayward of Twmpath and possibly Miss Hogan of Upper Bridge Street (who rented a house from Lewis) but they all appeared unlikely suspects in the disappearance of his iron bar. The South Wales Argus was proud to point out that one of its newspaper boys had handed an artefact to the police.

'Typical of the desire of the public to help is the action of sixteen year old Rees Griffiths, a newsboy who lives in King Street, not far from Plasmont.'

Griffiths and a thirteen year old friend were walking along a lane between King Street and Queen Street when they saw a shining object. It was a motor-car club badge, about eight inches long, with a two inch grip, thin and with the words on it "Red X Tune-Up Club". This would have been a magic find for a young lad in 1939, a real trophy but he gamely handed in to the police.

On 14th June in a letter to Police Inspector Rees, Webster the Home Office Pathologist had been asked to look at various items found in and around the garden of Plasmont.

'The poker you sent some time ago bore no bloodstains. I also examined the piece of rusty spout found in the garden. In size this did not correspond to the wounds on the deceased man's head, the weapon being too small'. Further examination of the spout revealed a feather and 46 hairs, 45 of them dog hairs the remaining one bearing no resemblance to the hairs on the scalp of the deceased. The hairs and feather were deeply embedded in the rust and had been there for a long time. The feather did not correspond to the feathers in Lewis' bedding. A cloth and hammer also submitted bore no bloodstains.

'CHERRILL OF THE YARD'

Amongst the Scotland Yard personnel travelling to Pontypool from London on May 24th was Frederick Cherrill, such was his fame that he was known in the popular press as *The Fingerprint Man.* His evidence sent a number of men to the gallows and many others to long terms of imprisonment. It was said that he was responsible for solving more murders than any other policeman of his time. He pioneered the use of palm prints in the identification of offenders. In a case heard in the Old Bailey in September 1931, a burglar was convicted after a palm print was positively identified as his, by Inspector Cherrill.

He had started his career as a policeman in his early twenties and by 1937 had become a Chief Inspector, having spent most of his career in the Fingerprint Division. In 1950 he had a cameo part in the Ealing film 'The Blue Lamp.' [14]He was 47 when he was called to the Plasmont murder. The South Wales Argus reporter said that 'he had worked unceasingly to find an answer to the murder riddle'. In fact Cherrill went directly from the Lewis case Pontypool to Branksome Poole in Dorset, to investigate, what appeared to be a 'copy-cat' murder. On the night before the Lewis murder, May 21st 1939, Walter Dinnivan, a retired businessman was found in his large house, savagely battered around the head. Evidence showed that he had entertained a visitor, a glass, a beer bottle and a tipped cigarette were found. The Pontypool police and the Poole police began collaborating and interviewed likely suspects. The case of Dinnivan, unlike that of Lewis was cleared-up fairly swiftly. The glasses bore fingerprints and Cherrill of the Yard identified them as belonging to an acquaintance of Dinnivan. Joseph Williams was arrested and tried and was acquitted. The twist to this story is that Dinnivan's murderer, like that of Lewis, escaped the noose. Joseph Williams, found 'not guilty' in October 1939 stepped jauntily from the dock a free man. He was whisked away to a nearby hotel, by the famous News of the World reporter Norman Rae. After toasting his good fortune on the evening of his freedom, he woke Rae in the middle of the night shouting 'The jury were wrong, I did it'. He told Rae that he had indeed killed Dinnivan, 'but no one could touch him now'. A legal principle prevented people being tried for the same crime twice. The ban on "double jeopardy", which had existed for around 800 years, took effect in 2005 in England and Wales and in Scotland December 2011. However, Rae did not tell anyone until after Williams died, some twelve years later.

---

[14] Oxford Dictionary of National Biography

In the future Cherrill's evidence would go on to implicate John Reginald Halliday Christie of the murder of at least eight women. He was hanged in 1953 but not before what may have been another miscarriage of justice. Timothy Evans lived in lodgings in Christie's home and was hanged for killing his wife Beryl and baby Geraldine in 1950. Implications were that Evans had died for these murders, which were committed by Christie.

Chief inspector Cherrill '*The Fingerprint Man*' with Major Lucas, Chief Constable of Monmouthshire

Cherrill, who was awarded the MBE for his services to police work, has written of both the Dinnivan and Christie murders in his autobiography *'Cherrill of the Yard'*. However, he doesn't mention the Lewis case – despite its notoriety. Perhaps the reason for this can be found in the identification of the fingerprints.

He and Godsell completed their examination of Plasmont House on the 25th of May, 1939, resulting in three indefinable finger marks being found on the wooden bed head. One of these three fingerprints subsequently proved to be that of Police Constable James Thomas (who was the first policeman at the scene of the crime) while the others were made by Dr Webster the Home Office Pathologist and Inspector Burgess. For once Cherrill's speedy and accurate analysis of the fingerprints was not brought to public knowledge.

ROF GLASCOED

The building of ROF (Royal Ordinance Factory) Glascoed, some 5 miles outside Pontypool centre, had an immense impact on Pontypool and the surrounding district, which had suffered from the brunt of the Great Depression of the 1930's. Pontypool went from an area of heavy unemployment to suddenly finding employment for thousands of local men and women and requiring a great influx of workers (some of whom brought their families with them) from all over Britain. Men with expertise in tunnelling and building were required to create the 1,000 acre site factory which began construction in 1938. The land mostly agricultural, between Pontypool and Usk was acquired through compulsory purchase by the Government in response to Britain's preparations for the forthcoming and inevitable war. Surprisingly, the climatic conditions of Pontypool were considered ideal to handle the production of munitions and its isolation, surrounded by hills, an excellent location. The main aim of ROF was to produce ammunitions for the forces. It was a 'Filling Factory' – where shells, bombs and bullets were packed with explosives. Locals called it 'The Dump' and it is also referred to in the statements as 'ROF' and 'Glascoed'.

Suddenly in 1938/9 Pontypool was awash with people, mostly construction workers, requiring accommodation. Everyone in the town with a spare room took in lodgers, sometimes two to a room or even two to a bed. It wasn't an ideal situation, with nothing but a room to go back to, men spent their time after work in the public houses.

Shop-keepers, cafes and local businesses were glad of the extra trade. Local bus services also benefitted by the increased population of the town. Workers were bussed to the site and some hired coaches to take them back to their hometown during Bank Holidays. The majority of the construction was undertaken by John Morgan Ltd., of Cardiff. The factory, once complete generated its own power (steam) for heating, its own sewerage system and also an on-site railway, which linked to the Great Western Railway. Up to 13,000 people were employed at its height. In 1939, Inspector Rees described the town

> 'In normal times Pontypool has a population of just over 7,000 people.'

With ROF employing 4,500 in 1939, many of the workers were strangers to the district 'mostly Irishmen and Welshmen'. Some only stayed for a few days before moving on to another, more lucrative job. It was an ever changing population. Those who readily accepted the influx of visitors, the landlords, in general didn't keep good records and it proved almost impossible to trace some of the workers.

One element of the community who didn't welcome the ROF was the farmers. Fearing that men needed for work on the land were being lured by the better wages in construction. At the Abergavenny branch of the National Farmers' Union a report in the South Wales Argus stated

> 'Mr F.O. Price said he understood that some men were earning more than £4 a week at Glascoed.'

The matter had been taken up by the Ministry of Agriculture and the Ministry of Labour. Mr W. Beer, Chairman said

> 'We have no right to interfere with men obtaining work where they can earn more money. '

Mr J. P. Williams said that he understood that the idea of establishing the works at Glascoed was to relieve the unemployment problem in the adjoining industrial areas, but that would not be done if the works took men from the land. Contentiously Mr Beer said that

> 'The farmers should be in a position to pay the men the same wages as they were receiving at Glascoed'

Mr J.P. Williams replied 'We could never do that.'

The Chairman then said that the only solution was for the farm wages to be subsidised. Mr D. Rice Jones pointed out that land workers should not be taken on at the works. He blamed the authorities, not the men. The County Secretary, Mr Homfray Davies, had written to the NFU for names of employers, whose employees had deserted them to work at ROF but no names were forthcoming.

Mr Arthur Jenkins (Labour M.P. Pontypool) however took the opportunity of asking The Minister of Labour, Mr Ernest Brown, in M.P.'s Question Time about 'The over fifties'. He was concerned that local men over the age of fifty were not even being considered by the government in recruiting men for ROF Glascoed. Some men had been unemployed for many years, yet jobs were being given to younger 'incomers' to the town. Mr Brown said

'It is the normal practice of Employment Exchanges, which is being followed in this case, to submit local, suitable applicants to vacancies in preference to applicants from other districts. No discrimination against men over fifty years who have been long unemployed is made either by the contractors in notifying vacancies or by the Employment Exchange in submitting men to fill these vacancies. The only criterion observed is that the men are capable of performing the work offered. Detailed information with regard to the number of men placed on this contract and are aged fifty or more and have been unemployed for over a year is not available, but during the 14 months ended May 31st 1939, there was a decrease of 276 in the number of such men registered at Exchanges in the local recruiting area for this contract. This decrease was almost entirely attributable to the operation of the Glascoed Factory.'

Mr Jenkins however, wasn't convinced.

'Is the Minister aware that there are upwards of a thousand men in this area who have been unemployed for more than a year and are over fifty?'

In replying the Minister of Labour said that he was informed that the figure of 276 now in work was 'entirely due' to recruitment at Glascoed.

Magistrates were equally unhappy – the influx of men, who spent much of their leisure time in the local public houses saw an increase in 'drunk and disorderly' cases. The police had enough on their hands with the murder hunt without the extra work involved in keeping the town's latest citizens in order. Police Sergeant Davidson, who during his day shift was taking statements regarding the murder found his night shifts full of such cases. In one instance he was assaulted when four men from ROF were brought before Pontypool Petty Sessions. Thomas Durkin (22), Patrick Hynes (23) James Durkin (22) and Leonard Stroud (27) were scrapping in Osbourne Road. He attempted to separate them and remonstrated with James Durkin about, what was described in Court as his 'very filthy language'. Stroud then shouted

'Get back copper, or you will be killed.'

As he clutched at Police Sergeant Davidson's arm, Thomas Durkin was spoiling for a fight, shouting

'Let me get at the copper. One of his kind will not take me.,

He then rolled into the road and the other three tried to hold him upright. Stroud then tried to trip the policeman up

'I drew my staff and struck Stroud and then they all went away' said Davidson.

He managed to catch them up just outside the Griffin Press offices and Police Constables Mann, Pring and Holt, along with Superintendent Casey managed to get them to the police station but on the way Durkin was very violent and lay in the road. He was attracting a large crowd including a number of women and the policemen handcuffed him. John Scourfield of 74 George Street, was a 'have-a-go' hero. He said he was standing near the White Hart steps when he saw the men fighting

'Seeing an officer's helmet in the middle of it',

He waded in to give assistance. By now the fighters had their coats off and Scourfield witnessed the attack on P.C. Davidson and as he tried to help him, was also attacked, he described to the Court how he was hit on the chest with a flagon 'I still have the bruises now' he said. Police Sergeant A. Bowkett – another footslogger in the Lewis case, saw what was happening and rescued both Scourfield and Police Sergeant Davidson from further harm. Superintendent E. Casey said that three of the men were from Ireland and all worked at Glascoed and added

'I ask you to take a serious view of this case, we are getting a lot of trouble with these people now'.

Mr F.H. Davies, Chairman said

'The bench will certainly not take a light view of goings-on like this occurring in town. You and others will have to behave if you come to visit these parts'.

Thomas Durkin and Patrick Hynes were fined 40/- and Leonard Stroud 20/- and both he and James Durkin were sentenced to prison for a month. John Scourfield was commended by the Chairman of the Bench 'he acted very credibly in going to the assistance of the police' and Inspector Casey also voiced his thanks.

THE COACH CRASH

The resources of Pontypool police were already stretched to the limit, when on 29th May a coach, owned by Peake's of Pontypool, swerved across a road at a bridge, tore through a hedge and steel railings and dropped 15ft into the river. The driver and one passenger were killed and twenty one other passengers were injured. Elwyn George Thomas Palmer, the driver was aged 30, a young married man with two children of 6 Wern Terrace, he died on admission to Hereford Hospital. The passenger who died was Henry Whitcome, a widower aged 62, of 7 Twmpath, a mortar-man employed on the surface at Tirpentwys Colliery. His body was pulled from the river by rescuers. He had a family of seven children. Palmer was no longer employed by Peakes, but helping out for the day because of a shortage of drivers. The outing had been arranged from the Horseshoe Inn, Pontypool.

It was midnight and the passengers, who had enjoyed a day out in Worcester were merry and singing when the coached plunged into the Monnow. The drivers of passing cars scrambled down to the coach and smashed the windows with the starting handles of their cars. They also tore at the fabric of the roof to remove it and pull passengers to safety. The Free Press reported:

The injured were taken to three different hospitals – at Abergavenny: Ernest Horsman, 28 Chapel Lane, Pontypool aged 26, shock and a cut forehead. James Whelan, 2 Castle Yard, Pontypool, aged 43, concussion and abrasions. (Whelan had given a statement in the Lewis case). Alfred Williams, 7 Bunkers, Blaenavon aged 64, cut head and bruised ribs, James Evans, 2 Long Row, Upper Race, Pontypool aged 78, cut head, shock and concussion. James Morgan, 11 Chapel Lane, Pontypool aged 55, cut head and bruised face.

At Hereford : William Trinder, 9 Nicholas Street, Pontypool, Gwilym Morgan, 4 Forge Road, Pontypool, Edgar Pinney, 8 Chapel Lane, Pontypool, Alfred Groves, Coedcae, Pontypool, Charles Pinney, 2 Clifton Place, Pontypool, Ivor Newman, 15 Coedcae Place, James Rosser, 18, Park Crescent, Penygarn. Ivor Newman, Alfred Groves and Gwilym Morgan are the most seriously injured.

At Pontypool: John Purchase aged 76 of Chapel Yard, High Street, Pontypool, shock, lacerated eyes, ear and face. Thomas Waite, aged 29 of Edward Street, Pontypool, leg injuries and head lacerations. Ivor Morgan, aged 45, Mountain View, Pontnewynydd, concussion and cut lips. Ernest Evans, aged 45 of Crumlin Street, Pontypool, cut on forearm and head.

In addition five men were taken to Pontypool Hospital but were discharged after treatment – Harold Loveday, aged 30 of Edward Street, Pontypool, James Matthews aged 41, New Houses, Coedcae, Pontypool, John Rutter Welsh aged 36 of

Forge Row, Pontnewynydd, William Thomas aged 29, Ivy Cottage, Chapel Lane, Pontypool.

Ambulances were called to the scene but by the time they arrived many men had been taken by passing cars to the various hospitals.

Henry Whitcombe lived with his son and daughter-in-law, Mr and Mrs William Whitcombe and their four children. His wife had died a year, last September. He died from a fractured skull. He was buried at Panteg Cemetery. The Free Press reported

'Elwyn Palmer is reported to have bled to death after glass had pieced his armpit. He died twenty minutes after admission to Hereford Hospital. Palmer had played rugby for a number of teams since the age of twelve, when he was a member of the first Panteg Wern team to win the Schoolboys' Cup. Later he played for St James Rugby Team, for Newport Harlequins, and latterly for Cwmbran. Mr Palmer was the second of three sons of the late Mr James Palmer and Mrs Palmer of 2, Wren's Nest and has three young sisters. He leaves two young children a little girl aged seven and a boy aged two. He had been driving goods vehicles for around thirteen years and had recently been awarded a Road Safety Diploma.'

The inquest, held at South Herefordshire heard from the first witness on the scene, Mr Thomas James Watkins, of Hereford who said there were patches of fog around at the time. As he approached the bridge he saw a man in the middle of the road, running towards him waving his hands. Mr Watkins continued:

> 'I pulled up, and the man, who was covered in blood, told me that a bus had gone into the river. I got out of the car and saw what had happened. It is impossible to describe the scene, it was ghastly, injured men lying all over the place. The top of the bus and side had been ripped off and the only way to get to the vehicle and help the men, who could not help themselves was by climbing along a tree, which had been knocked down and was lying on top of the bus.'

At one time there were as many as twelve buses and cars on the scene, playing their lights onto the wrecked vehicle, while the rescue work went on. One of the first to know of the crash was Mr L. Crump, a farm worker of Grosmont Hill. He was reading in bed when he heard a tremendous crash. He could hear men's voices in the distance, so he dressed and ran to the direction of the bridge.

> 'The bridge was a danger spot' he said 'and has been the scene of a number of accidents. I could hear men's voices in the distance. I could hear a lot of noise but I couldn't understand what it was.'

The Coroner, Mr O.B. Wallis said that it was very difficult for the people at the scene to treat so many cases, particularly as they had to work in the dark. All of the passengers had been immersed in the river, their clothes were saturated and it was difficult under the circumstances to ascertain the injuries to each man. At the opening of the inquest Dr F.J. Hallinan, house physician at Hereford General Hospital said that he removed a large, triangular piece of glass, measuring 5 inches 2 inches wide at the base, which was deeply imbedded in the muscle of Elwyn Palmer's arm. The glass had severed the chief blood vessels of the arm, he died 20 minutes after admission.

Mr Garfield Lewis, High Street, Pontypool a boiler fireman at Pontnewynydd Works, escaped with bruises and shock. The coach he said had been on an outing to Worcester. The left Worcester around 6 pm and made a stop of a few hours at Hereford. They left there about 11pm. Originally he was sitting in the back of the bus but had moved to a seat in the centre shortly before the accident.

> 'The first thing I knew was that I went up in the air and my head hit the top of the bus. Then I was aware of water swirling around my legs.'

He managed to crawl out of the coach unaided. Although dazed and shaken, he kept his head, stood by the coach and did what he could to help others.

> 'One man' he said 'was partially submerged. He was an elderly man. I got hold of him by his coat and held his head out of the water. The trouble was we didn't know where the road was or where we were. The interior lights of the bus were still on.'

Some of the men managed to climb up the bank. A car that passed the scene contained Charles Prosser of Pontypool and Frank Broderick of London. Amazingly, they both knew Garfield Lewis and gave him a lift back home. Another passenger on the bus Mr William Thomas of Ivy Cottage, Chapel Lane, Pontypool a labourer at Glascoed said

> 'The coach was travelling at a very moderate speed. Before we realised what had happened we found ourselves up to our waists in water. I don't know if the coach was on its side or on its wheels when we landed in the river. We all did our best to see everyone was alright. I think everyone of us was submerged at one point.'

Mr James Matthews aged 41, a Blaendare miner had X-rays for a rib injury. He said that after the accident that they had to climb up a high bank to get out of the water.

'I had a hard smack on the forehead but I don't know what I struck, he said.

Mr Charles Vernon Jenkins, who lived in the same house as John Purchase, revealed that he almost went on the outing instead of Purchase. It appears that having bought the ticket Mr Purchase began to have 'cold feet' about going on his first ever coach trip and had tried to sell the ticket.

A verdict of 'Accidental death with no blame attaching anyway to the driver' was returned by the jury at the inquest at Pontdrilas.

According to the reporter at the Free Press, at one point a crowd of almost 200 holiday makers (the accident happened on Whit Bank Holiday), in buses and cars were crowding on to the scene as traffic was halted in both directions as roads leading to and from the Monmouth Cap bridge became congested and people left their vehicles to see what was happening. A police officer at the scene said

'The rendering of first-aid to the injured was very much impeded by the crowd, 75 per cent of whom were under the influence of drink. 'He added

'When a doctor went to attend the injured he was pulled back by drunken people and the police found it impossible to check up on the passengers of the bus, so they did not know whether any were still trapped under the wrecked vehicle.'

The Coroner, addressing the jury said that

'The evidence as to the state of the holiday-makers did not reflect in any way upon the driver, who was responsible for the safety of the bus. He was in his cab, partitioned off from the passengers. Any reflections on the way the passengers had spent their day or the state of sobriety in which they came back had not been connected, by evidence, with the driver. '

Richard John Pugh, a Hereford County Council surveyor, who put in plans of the scene of the accident, said the bridge – known as Llangua Bridge, was on the boundary between Monmouthshire and Herefordshire. Its narrowest width was 13ft 9ins. He produced plans for a new bridge over the Monnow to replace the present one, and for the straightening and widening of the road on each side.

James Whelan, a colliery surface worker who had suffered concussion told the court that he had been transported to Abergavenny Hospital after the crash.

He said that the outing had been organised from the Horse Shoe Inn, Crumlin Road by Gwilym Morgan. Weekly payments were made into the Outing Club. Leaving Pontypool just after 9am, they reached Worcester about 12.30

and left again at 6 pm. Some of the party spent their afternoon walking about, and some went on the river in boats. He was asked by the Coroner

'Did they have any drinks at Worcester?' He replied

'Some did, but no one was the worse for drink'. When questioned about Elwyn Palmer, Whelan said

'All I saw him have was a cup of tea'.

The coach had also stopped in Hereford from about 7.30 pm – 10.45 pm, where 'one or two' passengers had taken a drink. Whelan described the crash

'I was sitting on the right hand side of the bus, in the fourth seat from the front, next to the gangway. The first thing I knew was that there was a crash and the next moment we were down in the water. I don't know how I got out of the bus. I scrambled up the bank to the road in a dazed condition. I helped two men out. I saw one in the water and caught hold of him. I don't know who he was. I went up the road to get help. I stopped a car and told the people in it what had happened. Some of my 'butties' stopped other cars and they turned their headlights down into the water. I was taken by car to Abergavenny Hospital. The driver had to steady up several times to wipe the mist off his windscreen.'

Thomas James Watkins, a Hereford lorry driver, said that he had been to Barry and Cardiff by car and had been driving home when he was stopped on the Hereford side of the bridge by a blood-stained man, staggering into the road and waving his arms. Having heard that men were trapped in the vehicle below the road Watkins drove to the nearest garage and asked them to phone the ambulance and police. He returned to the scene to discover that by then the bridge was full of the passengers of cars and coaches, watching or impeding the rescue efforts. Watkins also commented on the patches of fog, so bad that on one occasion he had had to 'pull up dead. Otherwise, it was a moonlit night' he said. He had managed to get down the steep bank to the bus by grasping at a tree. He helped to pull the driver Palmer out

'He was unconscious. I asked the men to leave him by the side of the bus and cover him up, in fact I begged them to do that.'

However, Palmer was carried to the road, bleeding badly.

Watkins also described the bad road surface leading up to the bridge, saying that

'In some places it was bad enough to break stub axles and even springs'.

He also commented that the road was dangerously narrow, full of twists and bends.

Jack Phillips, 16 Victoria Terrace, Newbridge was a driver for the Western Welsh bus company. He was on the Worcester – Hereford – Newbridge route. He had been chatting with Palmer at Hereford.

'Did he seem quite competent to drive a bus?' asked the Coroner and Phillips replied

'Yes'.

Phillips' bus was following behind the Peake's coach and with Watkins, helped to extricate Palmer from the cab of his coach, through the side window. Some of the rescuers managed to get into the cab through the roof as it had been torn off. He agreed that there was a fog between Pontrilas and Monmouth, lying low across the road and blinding drivers.

Christopher Hale from the Newbridge Hotel, Newbridge who was a passenger in the Western Welsh bus also joined in the rescue effort to save Palmer. Despite the confusion someone had the initiative to do a roll-call to find out if anyone was missing. Police Constable Chance of Pontrilas said it was a fine, fairly light night but there were patches of fog near the river. He agreed with previous testimony that there were so many people milling about that it was difficult for doctors to adequately tend to the wounded.

> 'After breaking through the parapet, the bus collided with a tree on the side of the river, breaking the tree off. No doubt this broke the fall of the bus considerably.'

He noted that a quantity of bottles were found in the river 'about 30 or 40' he said to the Coroner.

> 'What sort of bottles - milk bottles?'

> 'No sir, flagons I think they are called' he replied. 'I don't know if any were full, the ones I saw were floating.'

The Deputy Chief Constable of Hereford, G. T. Brierly asked about the sobriety of the passengers and the sightseers. They had all been on a Whit Holiday outing, they were merry, one man was seen in a private car, sleeping on the back seat, totally oblivious to the situation. He also concurred that he had seen some sightseers try and pull doctors away, who were scrambling down to help the wounded.

Police Constable Franzen, Hereford was a trained motor mechanic and was at the time, in charge of police motor patrols. He said that examination of the bus revealed that it was in top gear with the hand-brake off. The steering was in the hard left-lock position. Apart from the damage occasioned by the accident, the vehicle was in good mechanical order

LETTERS AND POSTCARDS

The South Wales Argus reported on 20th September 1939 that

'Many anonymous cards and letters were received by the murder squad claiming to know who the murderer or murderers were.'

Frustratingly only a few of these still exist in the Scotland Yard file. What happened to the originals? One addressed to

The Detectives Department for Murder Crime

Scotland Yard

London

The letter came from a correspondent in Norfolk.

'Sirs, seeing in today's Daily Mail reward for help finding the murderer of Mr W.A.Lewis, I wonder if this is of any use in tracing him by investigation. Years ago a sensational murder, I think the name was Lee, a friend of one of the servants said it was the old lady's nephew but because he was a friend of Gladstone the police refused to countenance it.'

Another letter from Boars Hill near Oxford started

'No doubt you will receive many of these stupid letters which will no doubt waste your valuable time'.

The correspondent then went on to urge the police to look at the Lewis family

'I wonder if you have gone through the man Lewis's past and also his two sisters, it seems to me that the person who committed the crime knew the house extremely well. The man Lewis was a bachelor – why so suddenly eager to marry? Had he an illegitimate son anywhere? Perhaps he is lazy and Lewis had been supporting him. Perhaps he had got tired of doing so and realised this supposed son was just waiting for his money. Perhaps one of his sisters had a child – this is no reflection on his sisters, just theory. Why had he never married, or had he?

Please do not divulge my name and address as this is a very lonely place and after all, the murderer is still alive.'

An anonymous postcard suggested that Brimble should be investigated. Another tip off said that a woman in the Brimble family, some years ago, murdered her 3 children and committed suicide. There is no knowledge of this in the Brimble family, nor is it traceable in newspapers without further information.

Two clairvoyants offered their services, one from Cardiff described the 'murderers'. A letter was received – sent on 31st May and addressed to the Chief Constable. The original letters no longer exist – the following 2 letters are in typewritten form marked 'copy' and use the original spelling and wording of the writers.

'I am a clairvoyant and I am wondering if you would accept my services in connection with the Pontypool murder. Perhaps you are very sceptical about a gift such as mine 'but the proof of the pudding is in the eating' – I have never advertised, never solicited any clients and yet I work 16 hours a day. Everyday sees people turned away and they come from miles around, even from London just to see me. This strange clientele of mine includes scientists, government officials and engineers, Drs. of Science, bank managers, clergymen, solicitors, magistrates, H.M. Inspectors etc etc. The very positions they hold prove them to be men of intelligence – and yet they come back again and again.

I am very interested in crime and the criminal and so often have told people exactly how a certain crime has been committed and about the guilty person and so often when after a while the case has been concluded, I have been absolutely right. No doubt if I could stand in the room where the murder was committed I could help you very much. Despite the fact of how busy I am if you care to accept my help I will gladly give it. I have regretted on several occasions not offering my help – especially in the Torso case and Mrs Butley's (Bulley[15]) case in Porthcawl. I simply loathe publicity will you kindly treat this with confidence.

I remain yours truly I.R.

P.S. an enquiry at Bridgend Police Station will satisfy you to my being sincere and genuine.'

Another letter written on June 7th 1939 stated

'Re Pontypool Murder

Dear Sir

I wish to try and help you by giving you what I'm getting several days from my spirit friends. If you can follow it

---

[15] Alice Bulley was found drowned in her bath in 1936

all is well, if not, no harm is done only they refuse to give the address of the murderers.

Two brothers one aged 20. One aged 16 and a half of age did the murder. They were there at 1 pm and did the deed about 8.40 on the Monday night. They used a bed key and put it in their pockets. They wished to borrow £30 this being refused they murdered him and took <u>two</u> £100 notes from under the pillow, one of the notes has been offered to sum one in business for £80 one or two refused but one note has been passed for £40 down & £40 to come.

They live about 2 miles from the seen of the deed and the number of the house is 5, the St. or place not given.

If the above will give you a Clue all's well but keep my name out of it please.

Yours etc (aged 75)

There is no evidence to show that the police followed up any of these letters, it was (and remains) not unusual for people claiming to be clairvoyants or spiritualists to offer to help in the case of murder, missing persons etc

Another letter found at Plasmont shows that Lewis was interested in renting his properties to R.O.F. workers. He had evidently written to H. M. Ministry of Works, 43, Park Place, Cardiff as a letter sent on 22nd May was found, unopened. It was from a Mr Geaby, Estate Surveyor acknowledging that Lewis had properties for rent in Pontypool and seeking a date to view them.

TENANTS

Police Constable Parfitt (No. 167) drew the short straw and was sent out to interview all the tenants of William Lewis. Detective Noel Jenkins was drafted in to check three houses, he took his duties seriously only to find that his enquiries were in vain. Writing to Superintendent Gover, his senior officer, in somewhat archaic language he says

Sir

With reference to the telephonic communication received this day from Police Constable Parfitt, Pontypool, I have the honour to report to you that on Sunday the 28th May, 1939, I was detailed for duty at Pontypool and instructed to interview the occupiers of several houses, which I did with the following results:-

93, Upper George Street – no reply on each of the three visits, a message to this effect was left with Police Sergeant Bowkett (subsequently known to be Mrs Trinder's house, she was away in Abergavenny enjoying the holidays).

2, Conway Road, informed that Police Constable Parfitt had already made the necessary enquiries.

11, Railway Terrace – this house is demolished.

I have the honour to be

Sir,

Your Obedient Servant

Noel J. Jenkins

Meanwhile P.C. Parfitt started his enquiries and had much more success:

Christopher Clements of 'Avalon', Osbourne Road always took his rent to Plasmont. The weekly rental was 12/6d and he often let it go for two months. The last time he saw Lewis was on March 3rd. 'I went into the drawing room. I think I remained with him about 15 minutes. He was then his usual self and I have always got on with him alright and found him very decent'. Clements had repairs to his boiler in February

Lemuel Price was a greengrocer at The Shop, Hanbury Road, Pontnewynydd, he lived on the premises. He paid a monthly rent of £2.5s. Price said that Lewis was very irregular in his habits of collecting the rent, last picking it up on 15th March. He said he had been a tenant for 22 years but for the first 10 of those he only saw Sarah Lewis. Lewis took over the rent collection when she died. Repairs to the house had been done by William Allen, who had put a grate in the kitchen 'January last'. He had two months' rent in hand – waiting for Lewis to collect it.

A number of houses on the 'rent round' were owned by Lewis brother-in-law, the Rev

Watkins. 34, Clydach Terrace was one such, where Winifred Stephens lived with her husband. The rent of 13/- was paid 'every Monday fortnight' and the last occasion she had seen Lewis was on 27th March.

Robert Frederick Tuck, a poster sign writer of 53, George Street hadn't seen Lewis since March 27th, even though he generally paid a weekly rent of 12/- plus water rates. He did however see Lewis walking up Trueman's Gully on 22ndMay at around mid-day and Mrs Tuck had seen him at the British Schools, George Street where he was having his gas mask fitted.

Lillian Webber who lived at 25, Balmond Terrace paid 13/- a week to Rev Watkins. Occasionally Lewis would call in his stead 'Mr Lewis always appeared very decent to me but appeared a little nervous when he called. He was always like this and I never used to take any notice of him' she said. He called on 27th March and collected 26/-, 'consisting of a £1 note and small silver.'

Mary O'Donaghue of 22 Balmond Terrace had paid her 11/6d to Lewis for Rev .Watkins his brother-in-law on 27th March 'I have known Mr Lewis for a number of years and he has always been very good to me' she said.

On 27th March Lewis called in on 32, Osbourne Road on behalf of the Rev Watkins and was paid a rent of 12/3d by Elizabeth E. Hawkins.

Reginald Hawkins of 79, Osbourne Road rented a house from Rev Watkins and paid 12/- a week, on a fortnightly basis. When Watkins didn't call for the rent, Lewis would collect it and the last time he came was on 27th March. 'Mr Lewis was always of a shy disposition when he visited my home' he said.

The tenant James Gough gave a longer statement than the other tenants beginning 'I am a police constable in the Monmouthshire Constabulary and reside at 6, Grove Side Villas, St. Lukes Road, Pontnewynydd. I have been a tenant of the Lewis family for the past six years, first at 4, Fowler Street, Pontnewynydd and for the past three years at the above address. As far as I am aware, William Alfred Lewis was the owner and the weekly rental is 16/-. Unlike his regular routine, for some reason Lewis collected the rent intermittently and P.C. Gough had sometimes taken it to Plasmont. On the last occasion he saw Lewis 12th April, Gough having said he would like a bathroom put in, Lewis had apparently said 'I shall see Mrs Watkins', which seemed to suggest that the house belonged to them. In fact from that date onward Rev Watkins called for the rent 'Nothing was then mentioned about the bath'. P.C. Gough said of Lewis 'He was always sociable. He was an excellent landlord and said several times, I wish I could have all policemen as tenants, I would have no trouble'.

Vinton Harold Tanner carried on a business of 'General Dealer' at 84, Osbourne Road. He had last paid his rent of £2.6.8d (per calendar month) to Lewis on April 12th.

Mario Quadrilli was the proprietor of a restaurant at 23a & 23b George Street. The rent was £27.10s a quarter. He had last seen Lewis on 19th April. The last repairs to the premises were 5 years previous, when Mr Gardner of Pontypool carried them out. 'Lewis used to call about every three months for his rent. He was a very fussy sort of person'.

Florence Mabel Ricketts and her husband Walter Henry Ricketts lived at 19 Rockhill Gardens, he was a Clerk in the Labour Exchange. She said that on the death of Sarah Lewis some two years previously the house came into the ownership of William Lewis, however, he had always collected the rent prior to that. The rent was 12/4d weekly, which she used to pay on a monthly basis. She expected to see him again on 22nd or 23rd May, at his usual time in the afternoon having last paid on 24th April. 'I don't know much about him but he was always cheerful, and so far as I can remember when I saw him last he was his usual self.

Sarah Ann Burgham (widow) of 6 New Street, Pontnewydd paid a rent of 11/-, Lewis used to call every 4 weeks. He had last collected rent on 1st May and was due again on 28th May, by then of course he had been murdered. She did mention however that Tom Brimble had called on 22nd May at 8.30 pm to examine the floor boards in the front room. She said she knew little of Lewis, he just used to mark her rent book and leave without saying much.

Robert Ashleigh Poulson, aged 60 was the licensee of The Waterloo Inn, Trosnant Street, Pontypool. Lewis had bought the pub from Mr Knight of Abergavenny about 6 years previous. He stated that rent was £28 annually. Poulson said that Lewis was very regular in his habits and would always call in the morning, on a quarterly basis for the rent, and the last time he had called was 4th May.

> 'He put the money in his trousers pocket. He appeared as usual, very cheerful. He was generous in his way, he always offered me a drink when he called for the rent. I have known Mr Lewis personally for 40 years.'

Bessie Trueman was a green-grocer and general dealer and she carried on her business at 50, George Street and rented at £10 per four months. A 'Mr Pritchard' collected the rent on behalf of Mr Lewis' on 9th May (this presumably would be Miriam's husband). The premises had been painted quite recently by Brimble and an assistant.

Lucy Margaret Holbrook, a married woman, had last seen Lewis on Tuesday 15th May as she paid her rent of £2.2.0d fortnightly for the shop she occupied at 35, George Street. 'I knew nothing of his habits' she said.

Reginald George, steelworker lived at 51, Nicholas Street, the rent was 7/6d which Ellen George last paid to Mr Lewis on 15th May. Knowing she would be out when he next called she left the rent at Mrs Jones house, who lived nearby but it wasn't collected on 22nd May.

Mary Mabel Evans of 6, Woodland View paid her 13/- a week rent. She said that Lewis had bought the house from a 'George Morgan' in May 1938. 'Since I have lived under Mr Lewis I have found him very decent and all right to get on with. The only repairs that have been done were to the kitchen grate on 27th May, by a man I didn't know'. He had called on Wednesday 24th May and asked her to let the coal fire go out, so that he could do the repairs. He returned to fix it the following day. She described him to Police Constable Holt. 'He was about 47 years of age, short and stout. He had with him another man, aged about 56 who worked as a labourer.' This statement is interesting if only to show that someone was completing the jobs even though Lewis' body had been found.

She last saw him on 15th May when she paid £2/12s – a £1 note and twelve shillings in silver. She asked Lewis if he would call weekly but he said that he would return every two weeks

Ada Harris an 80 year old widow had lived at 15, Freeholdland, Pontnewynydd for 45 years. Lewis had owned the house and collected the 11/1d rent for the last three years. 'He called every Tuesday, never later than 11.30 am. The last being 16th May when I gave him 11/- in silver. He was always sociable but never sat down. He came with Tom Brimble and repaired the back roof three weeks ago. I have known him since he was a child and his parents, but he never talked about his affairs'.

Albert Larcombe, boot repairer of 33, George Street said, 'Lewis usually calls on a Tuesday for the rent. He last came on 16th May. There were repairs done to the premises a short time ago. They were carried out by William Allen and a man called Brimble.

Thomas Griffiths, a tailor, lived at 9, Upper George Street. He had seen Lewis in town on the previous Friday on 19th and had handed him a 10/- note. He commented that he thought Lewis was 'careless with money'.

At 8, Merchants Hill lived May and Joseph Donoghue, a steelworker. They had lived at the house for 17 years at a weekly rental of 11/1d. May Donoghue said the house has recently been painted by Tom Brimble and that he would arrange for repairs to the back of the house when the workman had completed their present job. She had last seen Lewis on 19th May at his usual time of around 5.30 pm.' Lewis said that he would have the back of the house repaired when the workmen had finished the job they were presently doing.

Emma Hussey aged 65, lived at 2, Mill Road with her husband Herbert John Hussey, a labourer. Lewis he recalled 'was regular in his habits, as far as collecting the rent was concerned. On 19th May I handed him a 10/- note and he gave me change of 1/6d. He put the 10/- note, loose in his trouser pocket, at that time he appeared as usual.' She said that Lewis had, only last week, put a new door knob on the front door and that they had a lot of repairs to the house, last Christmas by Dan Young, of Pontymoile. 'I always found Mr Lewis very cheerful.'

George Edmunds a retired collier had lived in his rented house, 5 Merchants Hill for 36 years, the rent being 7/6d. Lewis always called on a Friday at 6 pm and he had last seen him on 19th May when he gave him 7/3d in silver together with 8/6d in silver from Mrs Poulsom next-door at number 6.'

Margaret Trinder who lived at 36, Upper George Street used to call in to Plasmont and pay her rent of 11/-. She last saw him on Friday 19th May when she paid him with two half crowns and three two shilling pieces. Brimble was about. She had recently had repairs to the house – a door painted, new window chords put in and a lock replaced, which she gave to the rag man.

Arthur Bullock, aged 43 a fitter employed at Pontypool Gas Works lived at 1, Mill Road and paid 8/6d in rent to Lewis. He called regularly for the rent and the last time he saw him was 19th May at his usual time of 5.30 pm. At Christmas, Dan Young, builder, had carried out extensive repairs to the house, on behalf of Lewis.

The proprietor of The Osbourne Cafe, William Davies, said he paid a weekly rent of £1.2.6d a week and the last occasion was on Saturday the 20th May. He told Police Constable Blease (No.26) that he had recently started to do improvements to the inside of the premises and Lewis had offered to meet the cost 'halfway'. 'I always found him very decent and if I ever did anything for him he always gave me 6d for a drink'.

Annie Edwards, wife of Rowley Edwards last saw Lewis on 1st May. The rent was 10/-. 'He would just mark my book and leave without saying much'.

Susan Thomas aged 82 had been living at 1, Castle Yard for eighteen months. 'Lewis used to call weekly for the rent, generally on a Saturday and the last time he came was on 20th May. I do not know anything about Lewis as he said very little to me'.

Catherine Whelan of 2, Castle Yard said that Lewis called for her 7/- rent on a Saturday, the last time she had seen was on 20th May. She told Police Constable Charles (No. 190) that she was waiting for a replacement rent book

Richard Humphreys of 25, The Avenue described himself as 'a Loco Cleaner of Panteg Works' and said 'Mr Lewis purchased this house from me at the end of April this year. Mr Bythway, the solicitor, carried out the transaction. It might be noted that Vera Humphreys of the same address had met William Lewis during what she called 'a business transaction' and in fact been proposed to by Mr Lewis but laughed it off. Lewis fixed the rent at 12/6d per week, exclusive of water rate, and arranged to call the Monday morning of every fourth week to collect the rent. On Monday 22nd May, Mr Lewis called about 10.30 am and I paid him £2.10s in notes, comprising of two £1 notes and one 10/- note for the month's rent. Since acquiring this property Mr Lewis has had the outside redecorated and had arranged for several alterations to be carried out inside. Mr Brimble had the contract for the work and he was here on Monday and he was talking to Mr Lewis outside for about quarter of an hour'.

At 11 am on May 22nd Bert Hackett, steelworker opened the door to Lewis. 'He was in his usual spirits' said Hackett and Mrs Winifred Hackett handed over a £1 note, receiving 9/6 in change.

Mary Hogan lived in 10, Upper Bridge Street. Her daughter Mrs Kathleen Parfitt dealt with the questions from P.S. Bowkett. Mrs Hogan paid 8/9d a week and Lewis Eliza Brown (widow) of 17, Lower Bridge Street said that Lewis was regular in his habits and tended to arrive at 11 am on a Monday morning, 22nd May for the 9/- rent. She had been a tenant for the past 11 years. He had called at 11 am on Monday 22nd and Kathleen Parfitt paid the rent. She noted that Lewis had a large bundle of notes, loose in his inside coat pocket, they were not held together by a rubber band.

Mrs Einos Jones of 6, Nicholas Street usually paid her 11/4d rent weekly. Lewis usually called around 11 – 11.30 am. On 22nd May she was short of 4d. She said Mrs George, who generally left her rent for 51, Nicholas Street had forgotten on this occasion. Lewis said 'I'll call back' but that she hadn't seen him since 'This is remarkable that he did not call back as he seemed to me to be a man who would have called back for the money'

Pilate Kenhard of 34, Nicholas Street worked at the Royal Ordnance Factory and says he saw Lewis at 11.30 am on 22nd for the 9/2d rent. Lewis didn't have the full change and left owing Kenhard a penny.

Edith Highnam, wife of Charles Highnam of Pwllmeurig, Wainfelin Road had seen Lewis around noon on 22nd May when he called for the rent of 15/- . She gave him a 10 shilling note and two half crowns. and he had arranged for some window cords to be put in. 'A young man called about 2 pm on that day' but Mrs Highnam was on her way out and the cords were never fixed.

Cecil Morgan an unemployed shop assistant lived at 1, Bailey's Houses, Pontnewynydd. He had been a tenant for 10 years and paid 24/- a fortnight on a Monday about 1 pm. Lewis had been looking out for a house for a friend of Morgan's and when he saw him on 18th May he said there might be some news. However on Monday 22nd Lewis said he had bought the property in Albion Place for £230 but the current tenants did not want to move adding 'I do not like to turn them out'. Tom Brimble and Lewis had recently done some repairs at his house.

Mary Ann Winston of Gwynfa, Osbourne Road paid 16/- a week and she last saw Lewis at 12.30 on 22nd May. 'Mr Lewis was always in my opinion a little bit excited every time he called but I got on with him alright.

Rachael Johns said that Lewis owned her house at 83, Osbourne Road, it had been left to him by his sister Sarah. 'I have always found him a splendid landlord and liked him very much'. She said that she had two grates and the roof repaired by Mr Allen of Rockfield Terrace, who had worked for the Lewis family. She saw him at 12 noon on Monday 22nd when she handed over 12/10d for her rent.

Joyce Williams of 30, Clydach Terrace said Lewis called for the rent on 222nd May but she didn't have it and asked if he could return the next day 'He did not come' she said. 'I have always found him very lenient and if I did not pay him one week he would say, alright pay the two next week. The house is in my father's name, Benjamin Tovey, who is an unemployed steel-worker, I transact all his business for him'.

Mrs Eva Millett said 'I have known Mr Lewis for a number of years by sight and always considered him a jolly man'. She and her husband William Henry Millett, employed at Glascoed lived in 'an apartment at 61, Rockill Road, Pontymoile, the house was tenanted by Mr and Mrs Gibbs. He had called on Monday 22nd May at about 11 am for the 10/6d rent. 'He was his usual self and I asked him about letting me have a house and he said he had not got one just then'.

Doris Findlayson lived at 6, Upper Bridge Street, Pontypool with her husband. She paid 11/- per week in rent and had been a tenant for over two years. She had last seen Lewis on Monday 22nd May around his usual time of 11 – 11.30 am. The scullery taps had been repaired the previous week by Pontypool Gas & Water Co.

And some 6 months ago, Thomas Brimble had cemented the back wall of the house

Ethel May Watts had moved into 5, Upper Bridge Street 10 months previously. The weekly rent of 11/- was collected on Monday 22nd at around 11 am by Lewis, who had all the flooring in the house repaired before she moved in.

Mrs R. Davies of 37, Nicholas Street, a widow said that the house had been previously owned by Sarah Lewis and passed to William Lewis on her death. He regularly turned up on a Monday morning at 11 am but on 22nd May he was a bit late. She jokingly remarked to him 'I thought that you were married. He said I had to go to Pontymoile on business this morning'. The rent was 10/6d and there had been repairs carried out by Brimble the previous summer.

Florence Hobbs was paying 13/- for 5, John Street. She last saw Lewis at 11.45 am on 22nd May. She confirmed that Brimble had recently carried out repairs to her boiler and one of his workmen had repaired the window. She said that she didn't know anything of Lewis's habits.

Nellie Lewis lived with her husband Robert at 36, Clydach Place. The rental was 12/6d and she last saw Lewis at 12 noon on 22nd May. She commented 'Lewis was always nice with me'.

Bessie Turk the wife of Herbert Turk, a Private in the 2nd Bn. Dorset Regiment currently stationed in Aldershot lived at 4, Merchants Hill. Her rent was 8/6d and she last saw Lewis at about noon on 22nd May. She had left the rent with Mrs Regan who also lived at the house but who was away in London when Police Sergeant Maggs (No. 60) called around to take the statement.

George Trim working as a G.W.R. shunter lived at Grove House, Wainfelin – it was also known as 28 Wainfelin Road. He paid a weekly rent of 13/6d, every Monday and last saw Lewis on 22nd May at 12.15 pm. The house had recently been painted outside by Tom Brimble. 'Mr Lewis was always polite and I considered him to be a good landlord' said Trim.

Mabel Jones, wife of Edmund Jones, brickworker had only been a tenant of Lewis since 16th May. They lived at 76, Hanbury Terrace, Pontnewynydd. She saw him on 22nd May at 12.45. He said 'Thank you, it's a nice day' and marked her rent book 'W.A.L.'

Henry Brotherton of 51, George Street, Pontypool said he was a miner. He paid Lewis 12 shillings a week. On Monday 22nd May he called at about 2.30 pm for the rent. 'He seemed in his usual mood' said Brotherton

Mrs Adeline Manship a widow of 16, Lower Bridge Street had paid her rent of 8/6d on 22nd May, as it was a forthcoming bank holiday he said he would come the next Saturday instead.

Mrs E. A. Harris was unable to pay the 8/6d rent when Lewis called on 22nd May – her husband John was the tenant of 18, Lower Bridge Street. Lewis just said that he would return on the following Saturday.

Jane Batten and her husband William had lived in 72, Hanbury Terrace, Pontnewynydd for 30 years. Lewis collected the rent of 10/11d every second Monday, the last time being 22nd May. 'I gave him a £1 note and a half-crown and he gave me three-penny change. He was laughing and said 'You have plenty of money today'. I said 'You have the money, not me'. He never gave receipts but marked the book W.A.L. Mr Brimble repainted the troughing about six weeks ago. I asked him about a month or so if he was getting married, but he only laughed'.

Henry James Howes of the Singer Sewing Machine Shop, 12, Osbourne Road was aware that Lewis was his landlord but all financial dealings were done through the headquarters of the company at City Road, London.

Gladys Morgan lived with her collier husband Reginald at 12, Fowler Street, Pontnewynydd. The house belonged to Rev Watkins and either he or Mrs Watkins would collect the rent. Lewis would call on their behalf now and again, the last time being 10th April when Mrs Morgan called at Plasmont with her rent. 'He was always sociable and willing to do a good turn'.

Elizabeth Jones of 31a, George Street was a 51 year old widow. Lewis called monthly for the rent of £2.8.0d. 'I paid him £2 Bank of England notes and 4 two shilling pieces. William Allen had carried out repairs to the house in December 1938. When William Lewis called for the rent on 22nd May, she said 'he seemed rather worried'.

Arthur Bullock last saw Lewis around 6.30 pm on 22nd May, in Commercial Street, near the Town Hall. He was alone. 'I took particular notice of him because I thought he was wearing a new suit' he said. 'He never spoke to people on the street, so when I passed him I did not speak'.

John William Taylor lived at 52, George Street, he was a 62 year old chimney sweep. He was one of the last tenants seen on 22nd May when Lewis called in at 7.30pm 'I gave him a £1 note and he gave me 2/- change. That is the last time I saw him. There were repairs done to the house a few months ago by a man named Brimble. Lewis did not sign the rent book when I paid him the money, but said he was in a hurry, and would sign it next week. He appeared to be worried.

Ronald Rowles, a collier from 12 Albion Street had taken over the tenancy when his father Henry Rowles had died. Lewis was in the throes of buying the house and had put down a deposit of £10 towards the purchase to W. Jeavons, House Agent Pontypool. Rowles had met Lewis on one occasion when he took over the house. 'We are still remaining here, but are paying no rent pending completion of purchase.'

Anthony Bragazzi aged 40, was proprietor of The Express Cafe, Clarence Street and he gave his home address as 126, Osbourne Road. The Express Cafe was rented from Lewis at £20 a quarter. 'He was always a cheerful and nice man and he always treated us to something in the shop when he called and he did this on the last occasion'. Mr Bragazzi had last seen Lewis 'about a month ago' when he had called for the rent when Bragazzi was in his Osbourne Road Shop. Allen's the builders had done repairs in the shop and to the chimney.

Superintendent Alick Briggs was approached to assist the Pontypool police and he sent Police Sergeant Bowkett to check the ownership of three addresses in Pontypool. Charles Williams of 82, George Street said that his house was owned by Miss Trueman, not Mr Lewis and 84, George Street was owned by the occupier, Mr James Dowle. Mr W. J. Evans of 72 George Street lived in a house owned by the Rev Watkins to whom he paid £1.4s.

The butcher's shop at 25, George Street belonged to William Lewis and Trevor Rees Williams and his brother Norman were in partnership there. 'Lewis was due to collect the rent on Tuesday 23rd May but did not do so'.

Violet Harris, married woman, of 7, Upper Bridge Street was out when Lewis called on 22nd May for the 9/- rent and it remained uncollected by Mr Lewis.

Mrs Adeline Manship a widow of 16, Lower Bridge Street had paid her rent of 8/6d on 22nd May, as it was a forthcoming bank holiday he said he would come the next Saturday instead.

Mrs E. A. Harris was unable to pay the 8/6d rent when Lewis called on 22nd May – her husband John was the tenant of 18, Lower Bridge Street. Lewis just said that he would return on the following Saturday.

Vinton Harold Tanner carried on a business of 'General Dealer' at 84, Osbourne Road. He had last paid his rent of £2.6.8d (per calendar month) to Lewis on April 12th

Sarah Ann Burgham (widow) of 6 New Street, Pontnewydd paid a rent of 11/-, Lewis used to call every 4 weeks. He had last collected rent on 1st May and was due again on 28th May, by then of course he had been murdered. She did mention however that Tom Brimble had called on 22nd May at 8.30 pm to examine the floor boards in the front room. She said she knew little of Lewis, he just used to mark her rent book and leave without saying much.

Violet Harris, married woman, of 7, Upper Bridge Street was out when Lewis called for the 9/- rent and it remained uncollected by Mr Lewis.

Nellie Lewis lived with her husband Robert at 36, Clydach Place. The rental was 12/6d and she last saw Lewis at 12 noon on 22nd May. She commented 'Lewis was always nice with me'.

Florence Hobbs was paying 13/- for 5, John Street. She last saw Lewis at 11.45 am on 22nd May. She confirmed that Brimble had recently carried out repairs to her boiler and one of his workmen had repaired the window. She said that she didn't know anything of Lewis's habits.

THE FINAL INQUEST

On September 20th 1939 the final inquest was held at Pontypool, this time at Griffithstown Police Station, in relation to the murder of William Alfred Lewis. It was decided by the Coroner not to call for Inspector Rees to attend, as his summary of the case was sufficient in his stead.

'Despite widespread inquiries', said the South Wales Argus 'no tangible clue has been encountered'.

Dr T.J. McAllen once again testified that the wounds on the head of the victim could not have been self-inflicted. Lewis had died from shock and haemorrhage following multiple blows to the head. He had also been suffering from 'myocardial degeneration, due to coronary atheroma.' Dr McAllen was quizzed by Coroner Treasure;

'Had the victim been grasped by the throat?'

'No, I would not say that. He must have been held by a hand pressed down against his cheek bones. He was not grasped over the windpipe.'

'There was no fracture of the skull?'

'No.'

'There were blood splashes on the wall?'

'Yes, they were caused either by the bleeding of the wounds or by the instrument with which they were caused.'

'What kind of instrument do you think was used?'

'It was probably more or less blunt. The wounds were ragged, not sharp, as might have been caused with a knife, or something like that.'

'Did you see bruising on the fingers as if he made attempts to defend himself?

'Somebody must have held him tight before he died.'

'How long had death taken place before you saw him? '

'Between six and twenty four hours before.'

'Could these wounds be self- inflicted?' '

'No, absolutely impossible. There were too many of them in the first place and they were in the wrong places to be self-inflicted'.'

Police Constable James Thomas described what he saw when he arrived at at Plasmont agreeing with Brimble's testimony that he had entered the house by the back door, which was open. He went upstairs to the bedroom and discovered the body though he did not see the injuries as the victim had a pillow over his face.

The Coroner

'From appearances you came to the obvious conclusion that there had been foul play?'

'Yes'.

Lewis Pritchard was asked once more by the Coroner D. J. Treasure to attest to his identification of his uncle's body.

'What was your uncle's temperament? Was he reserved by nature?'

'No, I would not say he was reserved. He was very well-known in the town. He lived on his own, of course, and was inclined to be a little bit eccentric, perhaps.'

'Would that account for him living alone?'

Superintendent Arthur Gover of Abergavenny Police approached the Coroner with a large bundle of documents and a statement. The statement, read in court covered the entire police investigation.

'Some 278 people were interviewed and statements taken and over 400 people were interviewed. This involved a tremendous amount of correspondence and many anonymous letters and cards were received, all of which had to be investigated. Despite all these and the inquiries by Scotland Yard and our own police all over the county, no evidence was forthcoming to show who committed the crime. I am perfectly satisfied and so is Inspector Rees, that every inquiry that could be made has been made. The Chief Constable was also of the same view and on June 26th 1939, it was decided that no further purpose could be served by Inspector Rees and Sergeant Davies and they returned to London. A little inquiry has been made since but with the same negative results'.

Addressing the Jury the Coroner said there was only one possible verdict

'The poor old gentleman was badly battered about, with no opportunity apparently, of defending himself. Not only was he battered about with some blunt instrument, but whoever caused the death evidently meant to make a good job of it, because in addition to the injuries he caused, he made sure Lewis was suffocated by placing a pillow over his face after he rendered Lewis unconscious by the blows which he rained upon him.'

The Coroner paid glowing tributes to the police.

'Their work seems incredible, they had a superhuman task and it is no fault of theirs that this crime has not been solved.'

Without retiring the jury returned a verdict of

'Murder by some person or person's unknown.' The jury added their appreciation of the efforts of the police. Mr Pritchard said that members of the Lewis family were grateful for what had been done. With that the inquest closed.

INSPECTOR REES REVIEWS THE CASE

Chief Inspector Rees, in his summary of the case believed that the murder was committed during a robbery. He cites the opened drawers in the bedroom, however, he admits that it was not established that anything, money or otherwise, was taken. The sisters Miriam and Emily felt that they could account for all the valuables. Money had last been banked on 17th May. Lewis' weekly rent collections averaged around £80 and that amount, with the exception of a few shillings, was found, wrapped in brown paper in the ransacked bedroom. One of the pound notes in the parcel was issued by the Bank of England on 18th May 1939. It was sent in a batch of £2,000 to the National Provincial Bank in Pontypool. The bank manager believed that it would have been in a batch used by local employers for wages – thus Lewis could have collected it on his last rent round on the morning of 22nd May.

Rees said

'It was not clear how the assailant or assailants got admission to the house. There were no marks visible to show that the window found open on the ground floor of the house had in any way been forced and the chances of finding any marks showing that a person had entered by that means were defeated, as the decorator Brimble, painted the whole of that window on 23rd May, 1939, before the crime was discovered. If the thief or thieves got admission to the house by way of the window they may well have left by the kitchen door, leaving it unlocked.Several persons in the town stated that they had seen the deceased between 11 am and 12 noon on 23rd May but if Lewis left his house that morning, the painter Brimble would certainly have seen him. The medical evidence also goes to support the fact that he died on the night of 22nd or early morning of 23rd may 1939. It may well be that upon his return home after seeing his sister and brother-in-law off and having had his tea at 5.15 pm, Lewis consumed the milk which his sister states was remaining after tea, just prior to going to have his gas mask fitted, and if this were so he might well have died about 11 pm on 22nd May 1939. If, on the other hand, he consumed the milk after the gas mask fitting, it naturally follows that he died later than 11 pm, but he might have been attacked at that time and died later, digestion continuing to the time of death.

Inspector Rees goes on to examine the statements made by May and Doreen Drinkwater, Bessie and Doreen West, Hilda Hubbert and Adeline Fenwick all of whom saw the two strangers around the area of Plasmont.

'The women who made these statements are all definite as to their times. It is of course, impossible to fix times to the absolute minute, but they all seem to point to the fact that two strange men were in Conway Road at some time between 10.40 pm and 11 pm on 22nd May.

Philip McDonough passed two men who he knows as workmen from the local ammunition factory, but does not know their names. It has not been established who the two men are who were seen by McDonough, although we kept in constant touch he did not see any person in Pontypool who resembled them during our time there. Frederick Griffiths, a young lad was passing the front gate of Plasmont House about 10.30 pm on 22nd May when he saw two men standing in the gateway. One of the men was on the step, the other behind him. Griffiths gives a vague description of these men and says he would not know them again. Charles Millett saw two men standing talking, about 200 yards from Plasmont House. He was of the opinion that they were men who worked in the local ammunition factory, but could give no further assistance.

Samuel Harris, who lives on the northern side of Plasmont House, was returning home with his wife at about 12.30 am. He describes how suddenly, and without any warning a stranger appeared on the other side of the road. He vaguely describes this man, who wore a belted raincoat, and he says this man was walking in the direction of Wainfelin Road, which is going in the opposite direction to Plasmont House.

The reluctance of people to come forward was a handicap and all the people who have been mentioned as having seen persons in Conway Road on the night of 22nd May were interviewed by the Police, who obtained their names and what they knew only as a result of diligent, house-to-house enquiries and by listening to and sifting local and hotel bar gossip. An appeal was published in the press for persons who might have been in the vicinity on the night of 22nd May, to come forward. Only two persons did so, one being Arthur Henry Brown. He passed Plasmont House at 10 am on 22nd May, but saw nothing suspicious.

The other man who came forward was Francis Edward Taylor, who said that around 7.55 pm on 22nd May when passing Plasmont House he saw two strangers, one standing near the door leading to the back yard, the other about five yards distant. Taylor describes both these men and says he can identify one. Anyone visiting Plasmont House at this time could hardly be regarded with suspicion as a number of people called there in the evenings for the purpose of seeing whether the deceased had a house or houses to let.

An appeal was also made in the Press for the two men who were seen in Conway Road, near Plasmont House, and sat or rested on a window sill nearby, to come forward, but there was no response to this.

There are no grounds to doubt the words of Mrs Hubbert that she was told by Mrs West on the morning of 23rd May that she had seen two men on her window sill the previous night, but Mrs West has been seen by the Police on five or six occasions and denies having told Mrs Hubbert any such thing. The fact that two men did sit or rest against Mrs West's window sill is corroborated by Mrs Drinkwater and her daughter.

On 22nd June 1939 (four weeks after the murder) Mrs May Drinkwater went to Pontypool Police Station with a newspaper extract containing a photograph of Thomas Brimble, the painter who discovered the body. She produced the photograph and made a statement in which she says she definitely identifies Brimble as being one of the two men she saw in Conway Road on the evening of 22nd May 1939.

Mrs Drinkwater was certainly emphatic on this point. Her statement was taken by a local officer, but at the first opportunity I saw her and she gave the impression of being genuine and definite in her belief. I gathered from her, however, that prior to coming to the Police she had conferred with Mrs Maud Barnett, of Plasmont Cottage, to whom she had shown the photograph and vouchsafed her opinion that Brimble was one of the men she saw. Mrs Drinkwater's version of Mrs Barnett's comment when told this was enlightening. Apparently Mrs Barnett said 'That must be him, you tell the Police' and Mrs Drinkwater did so. The photograph she produced appeared in the Argus newspaper on 25th May 1939. Several other photographs of Brimble appeared in other newspapers about that time and a few days afterwards, when he attended the funeral of the victim.

Summing it up, I think that as a result of listening to local gossip, together with the rumours of Brimble's arrest, which were common at that time, Mrs Drinkwater persuaded herself that Brimble was one of the men she saw.

It is known that the deceased contemplated marriage and on or about 12th May 1939, Brimble and he agreed on a price of £36 for decorating the exterior of Plasmont House. There were other small contracts for minor jobs. Brimble accordingly put his men to work there and practically completed the colour washing of the walls and minor jobs, leaving only the window frames to be done. Brimble attended to this personally and was so engaged when the crime was discovered. He had sent his men, with the exception of his brother William, to other work for Lewis a week or so prior to 22nd May.

On Monday 22nd May, Brimble was at Plasmont House about 3.30 pm. He was with the deceased and the Rev Watkins until shortly after 10 pm and his statements as to his calls have been proved absolutely by corroborating statements from Ethel Highnam of Pwllmeurig, Wainfelin Avenue; John Henry Cooper and John Lyndon Cooper of 7 and 9, Chapel Street, Pontnewydd; Sarah Ann Burgham and Joseph Leonard Parker, both of 6, New Street, Pontnewydd; Rosina Jones of 68, Commercial Street, Pontnewydd; Miss Beese of Richmond Road, Pontnewydd and Mrs Jones, Bronglyn Bungalow, Cwmfrwddoer.

At 10.30 pm 22nd May, Brimble was at home and was with his brother and his wife until midnight. He was preparing estimates as a result of the calls he made on that day and did not leave his house again that night.

On Tuesday 23rd May Brimble went to work at Plasmont House alone. He had told his brother on the previous night to go on another job which he wanted rushed though. Brimble worked at Plasmont House until 7.30 pm that day, but before leaving, mentioned to Mrs Maud Barnett that it was strange that Mr Lewis had not been about. Brimble kept some appointments that night and arrived home about 9 pm. He stayed there all night.

The next day, Wednesday 24th May, he went to Plasmont House about 8am. Mr Alfred Barnett of Plasmont Cottage came on to the lawn where Brimble was mixing paint. After a conversation as to whether Mr Lewis had been seen, which has already been referred to, Brimble entered the house and found the body in the circumstances already described.

When the news of the murder became public, rumours immediately spread, associating Brimble with the crime. He was seen and a statement of some length obtained from him. He willingly allowed his finger prints to be taken. His demeanour was that of a man with nothing to fear and he handed his clothes to the Police without demur when requested in order that they might be subjected to examination by Dr Webster, the Pathologist. There are minor discrepancies in his statements, but when challenged on these points, he was quite easily able to explain them.

His version of how he intended to fit a rimlock on the back door of Plasmont House in place of the existing Yale pattern lock, the keys of which Lewis had supposedly mislaid, is quite understandable. He had purchased, on behalf of Lewis, on 22nd May, three rimlocks to fit on doors of properties owned by Lewis. One of these locks only was required and it is in keeping with what we hear of the parsimonious nature of the dead man, to believe that he would use a cheap rimlock on his back door in place of the existing useless Yale lock. rather than purchase a new Yale lock.

Brimble has a concrete alibi. He emphatically denied that he was in Conway Road at the time stated by Mrs Drinkwater and unless the evidence is hopelessly wrong, and all the persons who corroborated his statement are lying, then Thomas Brimble could not have committed the murder.'

It is significant to note that up until the present day, people still believe that Brimble was arrested and *acquitted* of the murder. The above statement by Inspector Rees shows this to be inacurate, Mr Brimble was eliminated as a suspect very early on in the Scotland Yard investigation. He gave statements voluntarily and was never arrested, even as a suspect. Inspector Rees now turns his attention on Maud and Albert Edward Barnett, from Plasmont Cottage. It is notable that on the last page of each of their statements are the words 'written down and read over' by Detective Sergeant Davies.

'I have already mentioned the Barnett's. Albert Edward Barnett is a colliery worker. He is illiterate and lives in poverty. His wife is also illiterate and a garrulous, inquisitive woman.

On the night of 22nd May Barnett was working and did not get home until 11.30 pm, and following this, he states he went to bed and did not leave the house until he went to work the following day. There is a communicating door between Plasmont Cottage and Plasmont House. It has been examined from both sides and has obviously not been opened for many years.

Mrs Barnett, as previously stated, has been in the habit of going into Plasmont House to do housework for the deceased man. She describes the habits of the dead man and states that on the night of the murder, 22nd May, she did not come home until about 9 pm, was in bed at 10.30 pm and heard nothing unusual. She says she usually heard Lewis securing the back door between 10 and 10.30 pm and then goes to bed.

I have already mentioned that the deceased was contemplating marriage, and despite his affliction *(hernia)* and age, there is no doubt, judging by the literature found in the house and the suggestive nature of jokes which he had pencilled on scraps of paper, obviously for the purpose of remembering them, that he was a man amorously inclined. He had four women acquaintances, and three of them at least could justifiably have regarded themselves as the object of his affections. They are, Ethel Parker, Irene Harris and Vera Humphreys.

Miss Ethel Parker of Glencoe, Pontypool is the daughter of a first cousin of the deceased. In 1934 for some while she commenced regularly visiting the deceased at Plasmont House and became very well acquainted with him. His sister, Sarah Anne Lewis, was alive at the time, and before she died, she expressed a wish that Ethel Parker and William Alfred Lewis should marry. The latter was apparently agreeable to this, but Miss Parker declined on the grounds that she did not like Plasmont House. She continued to be very friendly with Mr Lewis and he advised her as to many of her business transactions, for she too, was interested in property.

In her statement to me, Miss Parker speaks of her last visit to Plasmont House and her last talk with Lewis, on Saturday 20th May 1939. She also talks of the dead man's habits and mentions several of his female acquaintances. By her demeanour when she made her statement on 2nd June 1939, Miss Parker was obviously reluctant to be in any way involved in the whole case and we can put this down to the fact that she was jealous of Lewis' other female acquaintances. We know that she quarrelled with the dead man on 20th May and it is believed that this quarrel was over Miss Irene Harris.

In her statement she says she slapped him on the face but before leaving at 8 pm they were quite good friends.

There is little doubt that Miss Parker would have married the deceased had he agreed to have moved from Plasmont House to a modern residence. The deceased was apparently fond of Miss Parker and it may be that he made a show of his affections for Miss Harris in an endeavour to get Miss Parker to marry him. He had proposed marriage to her on several occasions, no doubt being influenced by her financial position.

Annie Irene Harris is 38 years of age, daughter of one time well-to-do people who reside at Maesycwmmer, Goytre, near Pontypool. She suffers from rheumatism and as a result it was necessary on 29th April 1939 for her to go to a nursing home, St Margaret's, Corbett Avenue, Droitwich where she was seen on 6th June 1939 and a statement obtained from her.

Miss Harris is somewhat simple minded, she met Lewis through some business transactions and there is no doubt that she would have contemplated marriage with him if he had been prepared to leave Plasmont House after the marriage. He apparently repeatedly proposed marriage to her but she declined to accept for the reasons stated. Miss Harris was in Droitwich on 22nd May 1939, as will be seen by the statement of Bessie hall.

Vera Humphries, of 25, The Avenue, Griffithstown, was proposed to by Lewis. She is an intelligent woman, secretary to the head of a big estate agency in Pontypool, and despite the fact that she made a joke about the marriage proposal of the dead man, there can be very little doubt that had he been prepared to leave the gloomy Plasmont House, she would have accepted him. She is by far the more personable of the three female friends of the dead man and by far the most intelligent. She stated that she did not wish to make a statement as she had very little to tell. She had not seen the dead man for some weeks prior to his death.

These are three persons who we know were proposed to by the dead man.

There is one other female acquaintance, Edith James of Llancayo, near Usk. She was seen but declined to make a statement, saying she only knew Mr Lewis as a customer on her stall in Pontypool Market, where she sells dairy produce. This is hardly true because from correspondence found in the house we know she had invited the deceased to spend a few days holiday with her. This was in 1938 and she accompanied him to his sister's address at Cardiff on one occasion.

It was stated by a Miss Gwendoline Evelyn Daniel that on 24th May 1939, two described Irishmen came to her shop in Pontypool and made a purchase for which they paid with a one pound note extracted from a large roll of notes. Simultaneously with this information, Inspector John Ridd of the Great Western Railway Police came to the Police Station with a discoloured note tendered as fare to Bristol by one of two Irishmen whose descriptions tallied with that supplied by Miss Daniel. At this juncture of the enquiry it was not known whether or not a number of bank notes had been stolen.

Mr Ridd brought with him Alfred Percy Coles, the clerk who had taken the £1 note. The note was sent to Dr Webster for examination and the discolouration proved to have been caused by damp red dust. The two Irishmen were traced and proved to be two brothers, William and Albert Edward Maggs, who were visiting Bristol, but had stopped at Pontypool to look for work. The money they were showing freely had been earned by them during the time they had been working in Glasgow on a Government Ammunition scheme. They had a complete alibi for their movements on 22nd and 23rd May 1939 and they were not in Pontypool on those dates. It was only after statements had been taken from the man Coles, already mentioned, Albert Perkins, Alfred Sydney Attwood and Lily Horswill that the Maggs brothers were traced to Hanham, near Bristol, where they were interviewed by Detective Constable Griffin of the Gloucestershire Constabulary.

In one other case two coloured men were subject of local rumour as having been seen in the vicinity of Plasmont House on 22nd may 1939. These men were in a motorcar.

It was established by taking statements from William Jack Blake, Emma Rose Blake, Gertrude Lewis and Charles Merchant that these two coloured men were 'quack' doctors from Bridgend, South Wales and that they had left the district before the crime was committed.

A man named Caleb Jones, a local mason, then made a statement as to what he had been told by his friend Percy Parsell, namely that the latter had two lodgers, foremen at the Royal Ordnance Factory at Glascoed, who knew certain things connected with the murder, and suspected some fellow workmen of committing the crime. Apparently these workmen were 'flat broke' one day and on the next day 'had money to burn'. In Caleb Jones' statement there is a suggestion that it would be an easy way to dispose of any incriminating article by dropping it into the concrete at the Ammunition Factory.

Benjamin Percy Parsell, of 64, Wainfelin Avenue, Pontypool, the friend of Caleb Jones was seen but didn't substantiate fully the statement made by Jones. He did have two lodgers, Cecil Haynes and George Hill, of Malvern, who had made the remark, after hearing of the murder 'It's funny if it is those two fellows who were spending all the money.'

The man Cecil Haynes, a foreman joiner at the Royal Ordnance factory, was seen. His home address is, Elm Tree Cottage, Little Malvern and he lodges with Benjamin Percy Parsell during his working days, visiting home at weekends.

Cecil Haynes has a friend named George Edward Hill, who is also a foreman joiner at the Royal Ordnance Factory and lives in Lansdown Villas, Assarts Road, Malvern Wells. He lives at Mr Parsells house when working in Pontypool, and journeys to Malvern during weekends.

Both these men have made statements as to their movements on 22nd and 23rd May 1939. It appears that Haynes frequented a local public house called 'The castle'. One evening, when visiting this hostelry, Haynes met a man named 'Tich' Heys, of Burnley. They left the public house at about 10.15 pm and walked down the town when Heys said 'I know where I can get some money this weekend' and indicating the direction of Plasmont House with his thumb said 'At back.' Heys had previously told Haynes that he had spent time in Parkhurst for robbery.

They then walked back towards Hayne's lodgings. They stopped near a bridge, a few yards away from Plasmont House, and after a few minutes talk, Heys went to his lodgings in Malthouse Lane, on the town side of Plasmont House. Haynes continued to his lodgings at Wainfelin Avenue, which would take him past Plasmont House. Haynes told his friend Hill of the conversation.

The conversation between Haynes and Heys took place a few days before 20th May 1939, and on that later date Haynes and Hill, according to their custom, went home to Malvern. When in that town Haynes, who had to make a call at Malvern Wells Police Station, spoke to Gladys May Hemming, a policeman's wife and told her she would hear of a big robbery at Pontypool. This has been verified by a statement made by Mrs Hemming, wife of Police Constable R.J. Hemming of the Worcester Constabulary.

Haynes and Hill returned from Malvern to the Royal Ordnance Factory, Glascoed, on the early morning of 22nd May 1939 and worked throughout the day. They went to their lodgings at Wainfelin Avenue at 7 pm that day and at 9 pm Haynes left his lodgings to go to the Castle public house in George Street where he saw Charlie Noon, Joe Clarke and Fred Griffin, with others employed at Glascoed works. He left the public house about 10 pm and walked up the road towards his lodgings with another man who he knows only by sight having seen him at the Glascoed Factory and the Castle public house. Haynes left this man walking up Conway Road, while he returned to his lodgings. When he got to the house his friend Hill was there.

Haynes was at work at the Glascoed Factory on 23rd May working from 7.30 am, returning home between 7 and 7.30 pm. He states that Heys was at work daily during that week at Glascoed Factory.

George Edward Hill corroborates the statement of Haynes as to the times they went to work, returned home etc. On the evening of 22nd May, after finishing work at Glascoed Factory at 6.30 pm, he drove Haynes and Heys home with him in the motor car, dropping Heys near the Castle public house. Hill did not leave his lodgings that night.

On Tuesday 23rd Haynes and Hill, after finishing work and having had food at their lodgings went to the Castle public house where they met Heys. They drank together until 10 pm and then went to Turner's Fish and Chip shop in George Street. At the end of the evening they returned to their respective lodgings.

Haynes and Hill agreed to have their fingerprints taken and their clothes were examined for bloodstains, with a negative result. Mrs Grace Margaret Parsell of 64, Wainfelin Avenue corroborates the fact that Haynes left her house at about 9 pm on 22nd May and returned about 10.20 pm; Hill did not leave the house that night. She also says that on the night of 23rd May, they both left the house at 9 pm and returned at 10.30 pm. She mentioned to her lodgers on the night of 24th that a murder had been committed at Plasmont House. She remembers this as they arrived home about 11 pm that night after having sent a message to her about 8.30pm to say they were going to a supper.

Haynes mentions in his statement that he was told of the murder by Mrs Parsell on Tuesday night, but it will be realised that this was before the discovery of the crime and Mrs Parsell is positive that she mentioned it to them on the night that they went to the supper.

A statement was taken from Wilfred Heys, married and residing with his wife at 33, Rectory Road, Burnley. He was also employed at Glascoed and lodged at 4, Malthouse Lane, Pontypool.

On 22nd May he left his lodgings and proceeded to the Glascoed works arriving at the Timekeeper's Office at 7.25 am. He left work at 6.30 pm and returned home in the motor car with Haynes and Hill as previously stated. After having his tea, Heys says he went to the Castle public house about 8.30 pm and later that night had a couple of drinks with 'Jack' Haynes. They left at 10 pm, closing time. He agrees that they parted about 10.30 pm that night. He refers to a man called William Jackson who travelled to work with him. Jackson has been found and corroborates this.

In view of the fact that Heys was alleged to have been in Parkhurst for robbery he was requested to have his finger prints taken, to which he readily agreed. His clothes were also examined but there were no apparent bloodstains thereon. As a result of the finger print examination it was found he has no previous convictions for crime or any offence of violence. He was, however, convicted on one occasion, in Burnley, for drunkenness and is said by the Burnley Police to be of a boastful nature.

All these men (Haynes, Hill, Heys) are heavy drinkers and it is doubtful if they would remember with any degree of certainty from one day to the other who they were with on the previous night or night or the times they left each other.

From the description of Haynes and Heys they may well have been the two men seen by Philip McDonough, if for instance they were half an hour later arriving home than the time given in their statements. The place where the two men were seen by McDonough is the spot where these men would part to go to their respective lodgings.

A man named Charlie Noon of 3, King Street, Pontypool who is also employed at the Glascoed Factory, states he was in the Castle public house on the night of 22nd May and left there shortly before 10 pm.

He then proceeded to a local dance hall, where at 11pm, he left with a lady friend. He saw this friend onto a train for Usk and later, at about 11.50 pm he was in Upper George Street, proceeding towards Conway Road, when he saw a man coming along Upper George Street towards him. This man was dressed in a shirt and trousers. Noon gave a brief description of the man but said he could not identify him again.

Many enquiries were made to establish the identity of the man seen by Noon, but with no success.

John Richard Palmer, of Silverdale, Broadway, Pontypool, made a statement to the effect that about 10.30 pm on 22nd May 1939, he saw two men who he could not describe, pushing a motor cycle up the hill, past the Catholic Church, which is near Plasmont House. Enquiries were made to trace these men but without success.

On 12th June a telephone message was received from Brecon Constabulary, Brynmawr to the effect that two men on a motor cycle had been seen in the district and it was known they were sleeping out, further that they had deposited, at the Hafod Garage, Brynmawr, two haversacks, one containing clothing and the other containing engineers tools.

'I visited the garage and inspected the haversacks and one bore distinctive splashes of blood. The haversacks were taken into Police possession.'

The men had been seen by Acting Police Sergeant Hibbert, of Brecon

As is usual in cases of this description many rumours were going around and many names were mentioned. It was said freely that a man named William Allen, a builder's labourer of 9, Rockfield Terrace, Pontypool, had committed the crime. Allen, who has several convictions recorded against him for crimes of violence, at one time worked for Lewis, there is nothing to show why his name was mentioned.

Enoch Thomas, a coal tipper, of Newport, reported that a man styled 'Tancy' had been in Newport on 25th May 1939, discussing the murder. A person who was present spoke to 'Tancy' who did not answer, drank up his beer and hurriedly left the public house.

The man known as 'Tancy' proved to be Stanley Powell, a man with a criminal record, including crimes of violence. A statement was obtained from this man in which he accounts for his movements at material times. He was at his lodgings, at Amberley House, George Street, Pontypool, after 10 pm on 22nd May 1939, prior to that time being in a local public house.

Many local men with convictions or reputations as violent men were interviewed and asked to account for their movements. A record of all criminals released into the surrounding districts was obtained. This embraced Glamorgan and Breconshire, the adjoining counties and the Forces of these counties were asked to locate and interrogate known criminals in their districts as to their movements at the time of the murder. Many provincial Forces were asked to do likewise, Leeds City being requested to interrogate Alfred Greenhow (aka Guy), CRO No. 9017/21. They apparently could not locate him.

It was tremendously difficult to find many of the persons we required to interview and without the very excellent inside knowledge of the local officers the task of finding persons would have been doubled. In normal times Pontypool has a population of just over 7,000 people. Recently however the Glascoed Ordnance Factory was commenced. The factory situated about five miles from Pontypool, on the Pontypool – Usk road. There are 4,500 men employed there, most of them are strangers to the district, principally Irishmen and Welshmen, and they resided for the major part in Pontypool. In an undertaking of this kind there is constant coming and going of workmen, some only staying for a few days and then leaving. without trace. We were faced with an ever changing population and on many occasions it was necessary to see a dozen or more people before we found the man who we wished to interview. I instance the case of Stewartson as a typical example.

To add a little more to the difficulties, these workmen in most cases stayed only for a short while at any address, sometimes moving without paying their bills. The landlords kept very little in the way of records, therefore it can be readily seen that finding these persons even after an address has been supplied was not easy.

An Inquest was opened on the body of William Alfred Lewis, by D.J. Treasure, Esq., Coroner, with a Jury of seven members, on 25th May 1939 at the Coed-y-gric Institution, Griffithstown. After evidence was given by Lewis A. Pritchard of Cyncoed Road, Cardiff, a solicitor and nephew of the deceased, and brief evidence of the cause of death by Dr McAllen, Police Surgeon of Pontypool., the enquiry was adjourned until 10 am 8th June 1939, on which date, without further evidence being given an adjournment was made to 10am, 20th September 1939. Copies of material statements have been handed to the Coroner.

Many days were spent searching the scene of the crime, the surrounding grounds and railway embankments running at the north side of Plasmont House, but no instrument or other clue could be found to connect any person with this crime. From a bloodstain on the blanket on the bed, together with the nature of the wounds afflicted, there is but little doubt that the instrument used was an iron one, about one inch wide and approximately one foot in length. An appeal was made through the medium of the Press requesting householders to search their gardens with a view to a likely instrument, but although much publicity was given to this appeal by the press, and on the screens of picture palaces, there was no tangible result.

As previously mentioned, in my opinion the motive in this case was robbery, and it is difficult to come to any other conclusion than that the person or persons responsible must have a good knowledge of the habits of the deceased man and the position of the room in which he slept. If, as is supposed the thief or thieves entered by the window which was found open, one would have expected to have found some other rooms in the house ransacked prior to entering the bedroom in which the deceased slept which was upstairs on the opposite side of the house.

It was common knowledge in the town that Lewis was a wealthy man and that he collected rents weekly. This information could easily be gleaned by a stranger and with a short observation the room in which Lewis slept could be established.

On 26th June 1939, the relatives of the deceased offered £1,000 reward[16] through the medium of the Press for any information that would lead to the apprehension and conviction of any person or persons responsible for the death of the deceased. This was given a good deal of

---

[16] In the region of £48,000 in 2012 – www.measuringworth.com

publicity in various papers but up to the moment nothing useful has come to light as a result.

It is unfortunate that neither Mrs West or Mrs Drinkwater could provide a reasonable description of the two men they saw between about 10.40 pm and 11.10 pm on the night of the 22nd May 1939., and who Mrs West saw leaving the back door of Plasmont House, as I feel that if their identity could be established, it might have been the turning point of successfully clearing up this crime.

In conclusion I would like to add that the assistance rendered by the officers of the Monmouthshire Constabulary, through the Chief Constable, made the task of this enquiry much lighter than it would otherwise have been.

I ask that a copy of this report and statements be forwarded to the Chief Constable, Monmouthshire Constabulary, Abergavenny for his information. The original statements are in his possession.

Signed A. Rees Chief Inspector

To A.C.C.

Although up to the present there has been not any success it is quite patent even on reading the report that it is not for the want of effort. I do not think that the matter can yet be regarded as anything like hopeless, in fact Chief Inspector Rees has gone to Cardiff to interview three prisoners regarding some conversations inside the Prison which might have some bearing on the case.

It would be as well to await the rest of these further enquiries before sending the copy report to Chief

Constable, Monmouthshire Constabulary, who can then be informed of the position up to date.

UNSOLVED MURDERS

In 1939, Scotland Yard seemed to have a spate of high-profile unsolved murder cases. This was discussed by the British national newspapers and in America too. 'The 'Morning Avalanche' in Texas picked up the theme August 18th 1939.

'Scotland Yard has so many unsolved murders on its hands, together with the Irish Republican Army terrorist campaign that its famous detectives are working overtime continuously. Normally Scotland Yard can throw a force into any district in the country so that no possible clue is left unexamined, thus following the famous Scotland Yard dictum 'It's thoroughness that does it'.

Murder Cases Defy Scotland Yard

The newspapers however didn't give up the chase. An article on August 1st 1939 in the Daily Mail headed

'Six Words Keep Murders Unsolved'

revealed that perhaps the police knew the identity of a number of murderers in cases which appeared to the public at least, to be unsolved. However, the police said the Mail had been hampered by the legal system. The article stated:

'A six-word alteration in a legal ruling would enable Scotland Yard to write 'solved' to a dozen or more murders and a number of big robberies. At the moment a Judge's ruling is that suspected persons may be questioned only on a statement made of their own free will. An officer cannot ask a suspect to account for his movements and then question him at length on his story. But it is by such methods – 99 per cent methodical inquiry and 1 per cent brilliant intuition – that crimes are solved. The cleverest officers in Scotland Yard have solves cases of murder, robbery and other crimes, but they cannot make an arrest because they are handicapped by the Judge's ruling. This was laid down a few years ago when the method was alleged to have been used by a well-known officer, now retired, when he questioned a girl in a famous case. In the meantime, Scotland Yard, with astute officers, one of the finest crime laboratories in the world at their back, smarts under undeserved criticism of failing to solve cases. In a little more than a year ten murders investigated by Scotland Yard men, are as far as public records are concerned, classed as unsolved. Chief Inspector Rees has been investigating the murder of William Alfred Lewis, wealthy South Wales bachelor.'

The article went on to name another half-dozen 'unsolved' cases.

'In nearly every instance the police officers have a complete report prepared and a case almost ready to go into court. But half a dozen words voiced by a Judge and recorded as a ruling, prevent them from completing their investigations.'

There is no intimation in the Scotland Yard file of William Lewis that the police knew who the murderer or murderers were but this article certainly gives the impression that perhaps for the want of a correct caution they could proceed no further.

'Suspected persons may be questioned only on a statement made of their own free will. An officer cannot ask a suspect to account for his movements and then question him at length on his story.'

During researches, there have been many people in Pontypool keen to share the name of the murderer or murderers with the author. Some suspect's names have been hinted at, the 'two strangers' have been named. Seventy year old gossip has been passed through generations of Pontypool folk, naming the murderer. People born many years after the murder 'know who did it because their grancha told them.' This book seeks through the Scotland Yard files, to give alibis to those wrongly suspected or accused.

But who did kill Dripping Lewis? Can the murderer finally be named after all these years? Yes, the name might already be printed in the pages of this book but the laws of libel forbid the naming of someone who might still be alive. The *Defamation Bill 2012-13* is currently going through the UK parliament as this book draws to a close (September 2012). The Libel Reform Campaign is of interest.[17]

Someone out there knows – *really* knows who did it.

---

[17] www.libelreform.org

APPENDIX

Last Will and Testament of William Alfred Lewis

William Alfred Lewis made his last Will and Testament on August 2nd 1927 to his solicitor Hubert H. Watkins, and had not revised it after his brother Walter died in 1931 or when Sarah Anne died in 1936. As a result, both are featured in the Will along with the sisters who survived him, Miriam and Emily Edith.

Walter and Sarah Anne had been appointed executors and trustees. Under the terms of the Will, Sarah was left a number of properties – 25, Commercial Street (occupied at that time by Eastman's Ltd.), 'Gwynfa', Osbourne Road, 83 and 84, Osbourne Road, 17, 17, 18, 19 Bridge Street in Pontypool. In addition his half share in Jubilee Buildings on Crane Street (aforesaid shop being occupied by Mrs Baker) was left to Sarah.

To Walter 'three shops in George Street occupied by Messrs' Thorne Curtain and Trace and two cottages in the rear thereof, two houses in Clydach Terrace occupied by Messrs' Waters and Parker and my half share in two shops. in George Street adjoining the castle Hotel and two cottages in the rear thereof.'

In this Will, Emily was due to inherit the shop in Cwmffrwdoer (occupied by Lemuel Price) and a cottage, 72, Hanbury Road, Pontnewydd.

Miriam, married to Arthur Pritchard stood to inherit five hundred ordinary shares in Baldwin's Ltd. and three hundred ordinary shares in John Paton and Partridges Jones Ltd. 'I devise and bequeath all the real and personal estate whatsoever and wheresoever of or to which I shall be possessed or entitled at the time of my death or over which I shall have any general power of appointment or disposition by Will (except property otherwise disposed of by this my Will and Codicil hereto) unto my Trustees shall sell, call in and convert into money.

Family Wills

Miriam Lewis died 14th January 1913. Probate was granted to Thomas henry Lewis (butcher's assistant) and Sarah Anne Lewis (spinster) Effects £2449. Resworn £2705

Elizabeth Lewis died 6th November 1925. Probate to Walter Lewis (cattle dealer) and William Alfred Lewis (draper). Effects £5640.

When Frederick John Lewis hanged himself on July 4th 1926 he left £1490 13s 5d. Administration to Walter Lewis (retired cattle dealer).

Walter died on February 7th 1931 leaving £8363 6s 11d to William Alfred Lewis (draper), Sarah Ann Lewis (Spinster) and Miriam Pritchard (wife of Alfred Pritchard).

When Sarah Ann died on October 21st 1936, probate was granted to William Alfred (described as of 'no occupation') and Miriam Pritchard. She left £11023 2s 1d.

Penygarn

The chapel at Penygarn was founded by the Reverend Miles Harry and built in 1727. The date can be seen carved into the lintel of the fireplace on the west wall. The membership was made up of Welsh and English speakers. Its capacity of 50 was soon outgrown as Pontypool expanded and in 1835 services for Welsh speakers were moved to the new Tabernacle in Crane Street. On the demolition of the latter in

1970, its gates were re-erected at Penygarn. English speakers worshipped separately and erected their own chapel also in Crane Street in 1847 (see details below). Penygarn chapel has a large burial ground which falls within the remit of the Friends of Trevethin Church (the ancient parish church) and Penygarn Baptist Chapel, aided by the Gwent Living Churchyards Project. A health & safety survey of the ground has been undertaken and information boards about the chapel and burial ground have been erected. The Lewis Family grave is on the right hand side of the chapel, it is of red granite and the names of Thomas (father), Miriam (mother), Sarah, Elizabeth and Walter can be seen on the memorial. The names of Frederick, William and sisters Miriam and Elizabeth have not been added to the memorial or any memorial near the main vault. However, evidence in the Penygarn Chapel burial book suggests that they are all buried in or around the same plot.

Family Funerals

Miriam Lewis, the matriarch of the Lewis family was buried at Penygarn. A memorial service was conducted at the Chapel by Rev J.D. Rees (Pontrhydryn), the Rev John Evans (late of Tabernacle, Pontypool) and the Rev J. G. Watts (Merchants hill Baptist Church). The cortege consisted of a hearse and seven coaches. First coach – Mr Water Lewis, Mr T.H. Lewis, Mr F. J. Lewis, Mr W.A. Lewis (sons). In the second coach Mr Pritchard (son-in-law), Mr Lloyd (brother), Mr Azariah Lloyd (nephew), Councillor Evans (nephew), Mr Berrow (nephew). Third coach - Mr Tomas Lewis (nephew), Mr T. Jones (cousin), Mr F.O. Lawrence, Mr Tom Parker.

Fourth coach – Major W.H. Pitten J.P., Mr H.H.Pratt (Lloyds bank), Mr David Jones J.P. (Belle Vue), Councillor David Davies J.P. (Sycamore House). Fifth coach – Councillor Edgar Probyn, Councillor W.R. Williams, Councillor Daniel Griffiths, Mr Gittens (representing Messrs Bythway and Sons, solicitors). Sixth coach – Mr Campbell Probyn, Mr Granville Probyn, Mr Cyril Flood, Mr Mellor. Seventh coach – Mr H. H.Haden, Mr Williams, Councillor G. Udell, Mr J. Thomas, Mr J.C. Forrest. Mr Jones (Sheffield) and Mr Jones (Pontnewydd) and Mr Abbot were also among the mourners.

The Bearers were Major W.H. Pitten J.P., Councillor Edgar Probyn, Councillor Daniel Griffiths (Granville House), Mr Knapp (Ash Grove), Mr S. Jenkins (schoolmaster), Mr John Gwatkin, Mr Sydney Fisher, Mr Albert Truman and Mr Dowell and Mr Cook (deacons of Tabernacle Church. Wreathes were sent by the following – Mr Walter Lewis (son), Mr Thomas Lewis (son), Mr Frederick Lewis (son), Mr William Lewis, Cwm, Ebbw Vale (son) Mr and Mrs Pritchard, Great Western Hotel, Cardiff (son-in-law and daughter),Dr and Mrs Wright, London (sister and brother-in-law), Mr and Mrs Lloyd, Grasmere, Frenchay, Bristol (brother and sister-in-law), Mrs Richard Lewis, Wainfelin (sister-in-law), Mr and Mrs Azariah Lloyd, Pontnewydd, (nephew and niece), Mr and Mrs Thomas Lewis, Commercial Street (nephew), Councillor and Mrs Evans, Cardiff (cousin), Mr and Mrs Barrow, Christchurch (niece), Mr and Mrs Jones, Pontnewydd (niece), Mrs David Lewis and sons, Mr John Evans and family, Carmarthen (nephew), Mr and Mrs Tom Jones, Cwmyniscoy (cousin), Mr Bythway 'Glantorvaen, Major W.H.Pitten, Trefloyd, Mr and Mrs Williams (Pontypool Works), Mr and Mrs Campbell Probyn, Mr and Mrs Udell, Commercial Street, Mr F.O.Lawrence, St. Cuthberts, Mr and Mrs O. Lawrence, Blenheim House,

Messrs J. and W. Banner, Caerleon, Mrs Truman and family, Mr and Mrs Boswell and family, Mrs Elizah Littlehales and family, Mrs John Littlehales and Mrs C. Probyn, Mr W.Ingram, Commercial Road, Newport, Staff and Scholars of Pontymoel Infants School, Staff Great Western Hotel, Cardiff.

Walter Lewis. The Pontypool Free Press described the mourners as 'a representative' turn-out for Walter's funeral 'demonstrating the esteem in which the deceased was generally held'. A short service was conducted at Plasmont by the Rev E.W. Pryce Evans , prior to the cortege proceeding to Penygarn Cemetery, where the family vault had been lined with flowers. Mourners present were: Messrs W. A. Lewis (Cwm) brother, A. Pritchard (Cardiff) [Emily's husband]and the Rev W.G.Watkins (Swansea) [Miriam's husband] brothers-in-law; J.H. Lloyd (Birmingham) uncle; L. Pritchard, nephew; T. Lewis, A. Lloyd , W. Lloyd, T .Lloyd, S. Lloyd, l. Lloyd, F. Lloyd, A. McIlrath, and W. Jones – cousins. The bearers were tenants of Walter Lewis, reflecting his standing as a landlord – Messrs. C. Amos, A. Trueman, G.T. Bindon, Mr Clements, R. Williams, W. Parker and W. Lewis.

A profusion of floral tributes not only from family but reflecting Walter's standing in the community covered the vault. The names on the wreathes - sister Sarah Anne; sister Minnie (Miriam), Alf and Lewis, brother Willie; Sister and Brother-in-law Emily and Watty; Marjorie (niece; Uncle and Aunt harry Lloyd (Birmingham); Cousins (Carmarthen); Gretta, Molly, Peggy (Carmarthen); Mr and Mrs Thomas Lewis and family (Penygarn House); Cousin Lorrie and family; Mr and Mrs E. Richards (Garndiffaith); Mrs Parker and family (New Inn); Mrs Berrow and daughter (Christchurch);Cousins Lloyd, Jones and McIlrath (Pontnewydd); Cousins Azariah and son; J. and W. Banner

(Caerleon);, Mrs J. Forest and family; Mr B. Evans and family ('Ardliu'); Messrs Bach and son (Griffithstown); Staff of Great Western Hotel, Cardiff; Women's Guild Mount Calvary, Swansea; Officers and members Calvary, Swansea; Mr and Mrs D. Scott, Conway Road; Mr and Mrs Clement and family ('Avalon'); Mr and Mrs W.G.Mills; Mr Rees Williams and family; Mr and Mrs T.N. Ruther and staff; Minister and members of Crane Street Baptist Church; Mr and Mrs W.A. Parker (8, Penywain,Wainfelin) Messrs Davis Bros.; Mr and Mrs E. Seymour (Greyhound Hotel); Members of the Constitutional Club; Mr W.H.V.Bythway; May ('Plasmont'); Pontypool Rugby Football Club; Mr Charles Bladon and family; Mr and Mrs W. Lewis (Wainfelin); Mr and Mrs W.Court; Mr and Mrs Udell and Mary; Mrs and Mrs James Knapp (Blenheim House, Pontypool); Miss E. Trueman, Molly and Arch; Mr Olivier Lawrence; Mr and Mrs Alan Trueman and Miss B. Trueman. The undertaker was Mr C. C. Pritchard.

The undertaker was Mr C. C. Pritchard.

Sarah Anne Lewis never married and died aged 69, at Plasmont House where she had lived with her maid. She was buried at Penygarn on October 24th 1936.The obituary in the Pontypool Free Press read:

'Miss Lewis was the second daughter of the late Mr and Mrs Thomas Lewis, Mr Lewis being a well-known Eastern Valley business man. Miss Lewis was one of the oldest members of Crane Street Baptist Church, Pontypool.

Services at the house, Penygarn Chapel and at the graveside were conducted by Rev. E.W. Price Evans, M.A., pastor of Crane Street Baptist Church, and the Rev. Richard Rees, pastor of Tabernacle Baptist Church, Pontypool.

The principal mourners were Mr W.A. Lewis, brother, The Rev W.G. Watkins, Swansea, Mr Alfred Pritchard, Cardiff, brothers-in-law; Mr Lewis A. Pritchard, Cardiff, nephew; Messrs Azariah and Thomas Lloyd, Pontnewydd, Councillor A. McIlrath, J.P., Cwmbran, County Councillor Ernest L.Parker, J.P., Croesyceiliog, cousins.

The bearers were Messrs R. Harris, W.H. Thorne (representing Crane Street Church), W.T. Trueman, R.J. Doe, D.C. Udell and J.M. Cope.

Among the general public were Messrs C. Rogers, Secretary of Crane Street Church, Mr W.J. Suter (Roath Furnishings, Pontypool), W.D. North (Boyle and Co. Pontypool) E.S.Probyn, J.P., J.H. Humphreys, A.W. Thomas, W. Gardener, Pontypool. Messrs D. Scott, P. Alsop, F. Newman and T. Truman, tenants of Miss Lewis.

William Alfred Lewis. As well as Lewis' two sisters Miriam and Emily and their respective husbands the small congregation in Crane Street Baptist Church consisted of Mr Lewis Pritchard (nephew), Mr F. Lloyd, Ystrad Mynach (cousin) and Miss Marjorie Lloyd ((niece). The South Wales Argus noted: others present included County Councillor E.L. Parker J.P., Messrs T. Brimble (who made the tragic discovery at Plasmont), A.E. Barnett (Plasmont Cottage), O.J.R. Pruden, Charles Tibbs, Captain J. M. Cope, , Messrs W.H. Griffiths and F.P. Thomas (Secretary and Treasurer respectively of Mount Calvary Baptist Church, Danygraig, Swansea where Rev W.G.Watkins is pastor). Flowers were sent by Minnie and Alf ((To Willie with deep affection),Emily and Watty (to our dearest Willie in heart-broken sorrow), Lewis, nephew, Marjorie, niece, Ethel (In fond memory), Mr O.J. Pruden, Mr and Mrs Dowell, Fowler Street, T. and N. Williams, George Street, Mr W.H.V. Bythway, Mr and Mrs

C. Clements, Directors and Staff, Sandbrook and Dawe Ltd, Mr and Mrs J. Knapp, Mr and Mrs O.C. Hoskins and family, Miss Bessie Truman, Officers and Members of Mount Calvary Sisterhood, C.V. Wood, London Hosiery, D.T. Powell, Tenants of Conway Road, Mr and Mrs Forrester. Messrs C.C. Pritchard were the undertakers.

A relative Henry Lawrence Lloyd from Miriam's side of the family committed suicide. Like many of the Lewis/Lloyd family he was a butcher. He had run a stall at Pontypool Market for 40 years at the time of his death in 1935. The verdict by Coroner D. J. Treasure, (who sat at Lewis' Inquest) gave a narrative verdict of 'Suicide whilst of unsound mind'. The Pontypool Free Press stated 'Pontnewydd Butcher's End – Mentally Unbalanced'. Aged 62 and described as a butcher and cattle dealer.

The Coach Crash

I am indebted to Kathryn Curran – grand daughter of Elwyn Thomas, the driver of the Peakes' coach for this information:

> Elwyn George Thomas Palmer was my grandfather. My mother, Jean, his daughter was 7years old at the time of his death. My grandmother, Violet Ivy Palmer, would not talk about him. She was totally devastated by his death as you might imagine.
>
> My grandfather was teetotal and had signed The Pledge so it's highly unlikely that he would have drunk any alcohol. He was a very religious man who ensured that grace was said before meals. During the week he worked at Filton in Bristol as an aircraft mechanic. He sometimes drove buses for Peakes at the weekend to earn a little extra money. My grandmother told me that they had saved enough money to pay the deposit on a house in

Bristol. She showed me where the house was on a visit to Bristol and said, "That would have been the start of our new life together".

Going back to the bus crash in 1939, I understand that the cause of the crash was brake failure. The bus gained speed as it came down the hill towards the bridge at Ewyas Harold and was going too fast to manoeuvre around the bend onto the bridge. A substantial amount of money was paid by Peake's insurers to be held in trust for the children, Jean Margaret Palmer and Lionel Elwyn George Palmer. I have been told that despite bleeding from an artery himself my grandfather tried to help others who were injured in the crash. I have a death certificate which states that he died from an arterial bleed in the left arm caused by broken glass from the windscreen. Sadly there was no safety glass at that time.'

The Auction

The Auction on 19th and 20th July 1939 was very well attended. Somewhere out there in Pontypool there must remain items bought at the sale. The Italian Brass Bedsteads must have been beautiful, especially as they were considered important enough for Miriam Lewis to leave them to her daughters in her Will. The Large Italian Vase 4ft 6ins high, made in 1752, painted by Giovanni Marconi, where is it now? This is a list of the items auctioned – which includes items of Gent's underwear.

YARD

Lawn Mower, Hand Fork, Clippers and Stone

3 Buckets, Pan, Pot and 2 C.I. Saucepans

Table Dresser and Box

Contents of Outhouse, containing Pair Steps, 2 Tables and Timber

Contents of Shed, containing 2 Counters, Show Case and Timber

Deal Kitchen Table

22 Odd Plates

4 Plates, 4 Saucers, 10 Cups

4 Vases

Bread Dish, Fruit Dish and odd Cheese Stand

6 Plates, 5 saucers, 10 Cups

Knife Box and Contents

Quantity of China

Sprit Lamp and Kettle, Brass Candlestick and Syphon

2 Dishes, Cheese Dish and 2 Teapots

4 Pots and 2 Jugs

4 Plaque Plates

Meat Jack, Tea Box, Lamp and Iron Sundries

Small Bench

Tray of Sundries

Basket of Sundries and Measure

KITCHEN

Quantity of Paints and Oils

4 Brushes

5 Plates, 13 Basins

Meat Dish, Tureen, Hot-water Bottle and Stew Dish

2 Partitions and Screen

Kitchen Shelves

Box and Shelving

6 Brushes

3 Kitchen Chairs
Water Boiler and Fender
3 Kettles and Bakestone Plate
Wall Clock by Evans, Pontypool
Easy Chair and Cushions
3 Tea Urns and Knife and contents
Part Dinner Service, Willow Pattern
Quantity of Glass
Deal Dresser
Scales, Weights, Trays etc.
3 Cocoanut Mattings
Quantity of Pots, Pan with Lid on Wall
Deal Settle
Tea Urn, Meat Covers, Bowls and Tins
Gas Cooker

DINING ROOM
Mahogany Butler's Tray and Stand
Very Fine mahogany 6ft 6 in, Sideboard, 9ft high, Mirrored
Back, 3 Cupboards, 3 Drawers
Plus Sideboard Cloth
Trays, mats and Stands
2 Cruets
2 Cruets
Decanter, 2 Dishes and Biscuit Barrel
White Metal Teapot and Glass Cheese Dish
Tray, 3 Teapots, 2 Water Jugs etc.
2 Large and 1 Small Pictures
Oil Painting
Pair Prints
Pair Oil Paintings by V.Manger 'Sheep Scenes'
Pair Marly Horses Figures, 2 vases and Frames
Marble Clock

Brass Stand, Copper Kettle, B & B Fender and Fire Irons
Pair Easy Chairs in Tapestry and 2 Cushions
2 gent's Silver Watches
Set of 3 Red and Gilt Jugs
Black and Gilt Water Jug, Teapot and Stand
Flower vase, 2 Jugs and Plate
White Metal 3 Teapots and Toast Rack
White Metal 2 Teapots, Sugar Basin and Jug
9-piece Dining Suite
3 Curtains
Georgian Piano by William Stobart and Son, London
Wireless Loud Speaker with cord and plug
Bird in Case
Axminster Carpet 10ft x 12ft
2 Hunting Pictures
Pair Oil Paintings by G.M. Gilbert 'Skating Lady'
Oil Painting by G. Fielding 'Campers Scene'
Oil Painting, believed to be Peter and 2 Angels
Oil Painting 'River Scene'
Mahogany Dining Table extending to 8 ft
Stool and Piston
Jug and 4 Glasses
Part Tea Set
Part Tea Set
Part Tea Set
Part Tea Set
Bottle and 3 Glass Jugs
5 Fruit Dishes
EPNS Fish Set in 2 cases
Flower vase and 4 Gas Shades
10 Glass and Jugs, 5 Sugar Stirrers
2 Vases
10 Wine Glasses

Knife Box and Contents
Bundle of Cutlery
7 Forks
3 Dessert Spoons
6 Knives
Bundle Tea Spoons
2 Soup Ladles
7 Spoons
Quantity Glass and China
2 Glass Stands and 2 Sugar Basins
2 Basins and 2 Jugs
Teapot and 2 Water Jugs
White Metal Stand of 3 Decanters, 2 Cruets, Bottles and 2 Stands
Old Oak Tea Caddy
Loving Cup
Loving Cup
Challenge Cup and Plinth
4 Glass Candlesticks
INTERVAL FOR LUNCH Recommence 2 pm
LAWN
Garden Seat x 3
Lawn Plant Vase
Pair Lawn Plant Vases
4 Plant Vases
Pot Plants
Garden Roller
New Summer House 5ft x 5ft
4 Mats and Umbrella Pipe
HALL
Very Fine Oil Painting on Canvas 7ft x 5ft
Case of various Birds and Stand
Fox in Case

Pair Buffalo Horns
Stag's Head x 2
Pair Fox Heads x 2
Bird in Case
Swan in Case and stand
2 Pairs Horns and Skull
Pair of Deer Horns
Otter in Case
Pair of Birds in Case
Flower vase and Stand
Barometer and Case of Birds
Pair mahogany Hall Chairs
Mahogany Hall Stand
Mahogany Pillar-Legged Table
2 Door Dogs and Scraper
Very Early Grandfather Clock, Brace Face by Webster, Salop 1760
Mahogany Grandfather Clock 8 Day
2 Gents Umbrellas
DRAWING ROOM
6 Pictures
Mirror and Framed Paintings in Glass
Pair Mirrors and Candelabra
3 Vases
4 vases
Birds in Case
Walnut Piano by L & L Hopkinson, London
Piano Stool
Music Stand
Pair Figures, Shade, 3 Jugs and Pot
2 Vases
3 Dishes, 1 Plate, Fruit Dish and Flower Vase
Pheasant on Stand

Large Italian Vase 4ft 6ins high, made in 1752, painted by Giovanni Marconi

Walnut Sideboard 6 ft

Large Mirror

Books and Game Box

4 Glass Pints and Photo Frames

2 Stands, 2 Measures and 2 Candlesticks

Very Fine Clock under case

Gas Fire

Fender, Iron and Dogs

Birds in Case x 2

Easy Chair and 4 Cushions

9 Piece Suite

Carpet on Floor

1st STAIRCASE

Carpet on Stairs and First Landing

14 Stair Rods and Eyes

Grandfather Clock, Brass Face by Griffiths Williams, Newport

SITTING ROOM

5 Pictures

Mahogany Pedestal Table

Occasion Table

Bamboo Table x 2

Bible, Works of John Bunyon, Hymn Book etc

Oil Painting on Canvas by Harris

4 Pictures

4 Pictures

Pair Oil Portraits

5ft Walnut Sideboard

5 Decanters and 3 Jugs

9 Piece Suite

Biscuit Barrel, Flower vase, Decanter, Jug etc

Coal Scuttle x 2
Child's Chair and Table
Overmantle
3 Pair Vases
Birds in case and Clock
Fender, Irons, Dogs and Screen
2 Screens
Pair Smoker's Chairs
Pair Brackets and Heads
Bamboo China Cabinet
Oil Painting by G. Fielding
Ewbank Carpet Sweeper
Round Mahogany Pedestal Table
Walnut 3-corner Whatnot and Tray
Mahogany Flat Piano by John Broadwood, London
2 Plaques, 2 Fans, Ash Trays etc
12 Glasses and 1 Salt Cellar
Teapot on Stand
Stand, Wager Jug *(a puzzle jug)* and 2 Glasses
2 Oil Paintings and 2 Books
Mahogany Couch
3 Cushions
2 Cushions
2 Tea Cosies, Cushion and 2 Foot-rests
Carpet on Floor
2 Skin Rugs
2 Skin Rugs
1 Rug
2 Skin Rugs
2 Carpets
6 Slip Mats
Axminster Carpet
Oil Painting by G. Grant

Oil Painting by J.D. Morris
2 Electric Shades and Bulbs and 1 Glass Shade
2nd STAIRCASE
Carpet on Stairs
Grandfather Clock, Oak case, Brass face 8-day by Head of London
Large Linen Chest
2 Leather Trunks
2 Tin Trunks
2 Tin Trunks
2 Hat Boxes
3 Carpets, 2 Mats etc
Linen Chest and Contents
BATHROOM
Marble-Top Washstand and 3 Mirrors
END OF FIRST DAY'S SALE
1st BEDROOM
Carpet 2 x 2 yards
Carpet on Floor
2 Basket Chairs
Smoker's Chair
Linen Basket, Basket and loose Cover inside and 2 Chairs
Commode and spare China
Pair Bowling Woods
2 Suitcases, Table and Music Board
Safe by Withers – and stand
Overmantle
Pair Pictures
Framed Mirror, 4 Frames and Small Clock
Pair Glass Candlesticks
Part Trinket Set and Water Bottle
Part Set Toilet Ware
4ft 6ins Brass bedstead and 4ft Spring Mattress

4ft Walnut Bedroom Suite, Wardrobe, Was Stand, Dressing Table, 3 Chairs and Towel Rail

2nd BEDROOM

3FT 6 IN Satin Walnut Bedroom Suite of Wardrobe, Wash Stand, Dressing Table and Pedestal

Commode and Box

5 Pictures, Mat and Pole

6 Candlesticks

4 Glass Candlesticks

Carpet on Floor

TOP LANDING

Lino on Floor

3rd BEDROOM

9 Pictures

4 Bedroom Chairs

Overmantle

Swing Mirror

Bamboo Stand, Towel Rail and Fender

Case of Spoons, 2 Brushes etc.

Odd Trinket Ware

Part Set of Ware and Curtain Rings and Pole

Mahogany Bedstead

Mahogany Chest of Drawers

Mahogany Bedroom Suite

Box Mattress in two

Carpet on Floor

4th BEDROOM

4 Pictures

Fire Screen

3ft Mahogany Bedstead and Spring

All Brass Italian Bedstead

Box Mattress

Medicine Chest and Small Glass case

Mahogany Bow-Fronted Chest of Drawers
Mahogany bedroom Suite – Wardrobe, Wash Stand, Dressing
Table and Pedestal
Fender, Irons and Coalbox
Pair Dogs, 3 Vases etc
Overmantle
Feather Bed
Feather Bolster and Pillow
Feather Bed
5 Bedroom Chairs and Towel rail
Carpet on Floor
5th BEDROOM
10 Pictures
Wash Stand and Table
Armchair, Night Commode
Easy Chairand Bedroom Chair
Part Set of Toilet Ware
Part Trinket Set, Clock, Flower vase etc.
Gilt Overmantle
2 Small Tables and 2 Small Chairs
Chest of Drawers
All Brass Italian Bedstead
New gent's Suit Grey
New gent's Suit Blue
Gent's Blue Coat and Trousers and Black War Coat
Black Suit
2 Gent's Overcoats
1 Gent's Overcoat
2 Raincoats
1 gent's Tweed Overcoat
Pair gent's Brown Shoes size 7 – Practically New
Pair gent's Black Boots size 7 and Stockings
New Bowler Hat size 7

2 New Gent's Shirts, Spare Collars and Ties
3 New Gent's Vests
New pair of Gent's Pyjamas and case
2 White Linen and 2 Coloured Tablecloths
12 serviettes
6 Pillow Cases
8 Pillow Cases
8 Pillow Cases
6 Towels
10 Serviettes
Odd Linen
Odd Linen
Coloured Blanket
2 Quilts
2 Quilts
2 Sheets and Blanket
3 New Ladies' Vests
2 Tablecloths
7 Pairs Gent's Pants
2 Tablecloths
2 Linen Tablecloths
4 Sheets
Odd Linen etc.
Quilt
6 Curtains, Rings and Pole
2 red Plush Curtains
Eiderdown
Quilt
Eiderdown
Travelling Rug
Bundle of Straw Mats

Research

The majority of information in this book has been created from the Metropolitan Police file at the National Archives, Kew, London. Local newspapers include The South Wales Argus, The Pontypool Free Press, The Western Mail. Further afield the Daily Mail and The Times and other national papers. The failure by Scotland Yard to find a number of murderers throughout Britain was also discussed in the American press.

Scotland Yard dealt with my query for further information under a Freedom of Information Request Reference No: 2011080003311.

I was impressed, the query was answered expediently. Herewith the response:
'I write in connection with your request for information received by the Metropolitan Police Service (MP.S.) on 19/08/2011. I note you seek access to the following information:

Further to your enquiry, please allow me to confirm that the Metropolitan Police Service is required, under the Public Records Acts 1958 and 1967, to justify to the Lord Chancellor any records retained that are over 30 years old. Consequently any records that the Metropolitan Police may have had about William Alfred Lewis will now have been transferred to The National Archives. I note you refer to "Mepo". "Mepo" is the short form of Metropolitan Police used by The National Archives when it accepts a piece of the MP.S. files for its custodianship. Consequently, and without having personally seen the piece to which you refer, Mepo 3/809, MP.S. records seem transferred in their entirety on schedule. I have personally checked - there are no apparent remaining records about William Alfred Lewis held by the MPS.

Superintendent Frederick Rupert Cherrill's record of service shows no information. Similarly, Superintendent Richard Ivor Rees' record shows no information about this case.'

Acknowledgements

Writing a book might seem like a solitary occupation but far from it. Many people have contributed – some I had not met at the beginning of the writing process.

Great thanks must go to Susan Woolford, my Editor and Bernard Pearson, proof-reader. To Will Cross, my writing partner and publisher and my fellow writers at the NYO for their friendship. To David Brown, Richard Guppy, David Hughes, Malcolm Taylor and Michael Taylor for information and photographs. Kathryn Curran (granddaughter of Elwyn Palmer), Anne Vinnecome (Blackwood Branch Gwent Family History Society's trips to The National Archives). Mary Mahabir, Peter Sweeting and all the volunteers at Pontypool Museum. Newport Reference Library Staff.

Tom Dart – my husband has been a great help, thanks for encouragement, and the film 'Who Killed Dripping Lewis'.

Apologies if names and places are incorrect. The 'Welsh speaking' policemen from Scotland Yard struggled with the local names. I have recorded them as they were written in the statements.

Books of Interest

Some of these books are now out of print – check
www.bookfinder.com
Pontypool and Usk Japan Ware by Reginald Nichols
Pontypool Remembered – a Pictorial Collection - Bryan
Roden –
Pictorial Memories of Old Pontypool Barlow et al –
Pontypool's Past – in Pictures and Pontypool's Heritage
Crane, Derrrick and Donovan
Tales of Torfaen - W.G.Lloyd
A Living in Torfaen – edited by Sue Pickavance See you in
the park in August – Village Publishing
Talywain at war – Ken Clark

Websites of interest

Gwent Family History Society http://www.gwentfhs.info/
The visits to the National Archives at Kew, London arranged
by the GFHS are invaluable for researchers
Reminiscences of Old Pontypool
http://oldpontypool.wordpress.com/
Pontypool Past and Present - http://www.carwyn.co/home1/ld
Pontypool Museum - http://www.pontypoolmuseum.org.uk/

Written in conjunction with the Pontypool Townscape
Community Project and Torfaen Museum Trust, discovering
the hidden treasures of forgotten Pontypool.

Index of People and Places

Chapel Lane No 8 188
Chapel Lane Pontypool No 11 188
Chapel Lane Pontypool No 28 188
Chapel Street 111
Chapel Street No7Pontnewydd 225
Chapel street No9 Pontnewydd 225
Chapel Yard, High Street,
Pontypool 188
Charles Fox Ltd 11
Charles St Griffithstown No 26 137
Cherrill , Chief Detective-
Inspector 21, 22,30, 178, 179, 180,181
Christie, John Reginald Halliday 180, 181
City Lodge 172
City Rd London 214
Clarence Corner 91
Clarence Hotel 52, 104,107, 111,145,147, 165
Clarence Street (Pontypool) 14, 42,114
Clarence Street station 162
Clarewarn Street, New Inn No 12 113
Clark, Richard 5
Clarke Joe 145, 234
Claughan, James 157
Clements, Christopher 202
Clifton Place, Pontypool No2 188
Clydach Place No 36 212
Clydach Terrace 245
Clydach Terrace 34 202
Clydach Terrace No30 211
Co operative Stores, Commercial
Rd, Pontypool 72

Coed Cae Cottages, Llanhilleth Old Church	139
Coedcae Place No15	188
Coedcae, Pontypool	188
Coed-y-cric Mortuary (institution), Griffithstown	23, 24,29, 239
Coles Alfred Percy	137, 231
Coles Brothers Builders	62, 112
College Rd No 46	125
College Rd Penygarn No 19	153
College Rd Penygarn No 46	120
College Rd Pontypool No 30	86
Collins Clifford James (Pontnewydd)	120, 121
Comley, Dora Elsie	57, 58
Commercial Rd No25	245
Commercial Street Pontnewydd, No 58	114
Commercial Street, Pontypool	40, 52, 214
Commercial Street. Pontypool No23	72
Comrades Club, Market Street	127
Concannon, Mrs	132
Concannon, Nicholas John	131, 132
Conway Rd (Pontypool)	15, 31,34,38, 46, 62,63,106,112,116,117, 118, 120 121-123, 125, 128, 146, 148-150, 173, 222- 224, 227, 234, 236
Conway Rd No 18	122
Conway Rd No 2	201

Crumlin Rd	141
Crumlin Street, Pontypool, No 45	188
Crump, Mr L	190
Curtis, Ida	166
Cwm, (Ebbw Vale)	8, 27, 41, 98, 160
Cwmavon	14
Cwmbran,	9, 99, 113, 171
Cwmffrdoer	245
Cwmynyscoy	101, 103, 106, 115, 166, 238
Cwmyravon	14
Cyncoed Rd, Cardiff	27, 49, 239
Daily Mail	197, 242
Daniel, Gwendoline, Evelyn	136, 230, 231
Daniel's Grocers (Pontypool)	8, 59
Daniels, Mrs	108
Danter, Percy	175
Dany craig Rd Baptists church Swansea	41
Dany craig Rd St Thomas's Swansea	41, 51
Danygraig Rd, Swansea No 66	53,
Dartmoor Prison, Princetown	70
David St, Ebbw Vale No11	58
Davidson, Police Sergeant William	34, 38, 121,122, 128, 185, 186
Davies Mr F. H	186
Davies, Gladys May	167
Davies, Homfray Mr	183
Davies, Mrs R	212
Davies, Nellie	57
Davies, Sergeant D.G	21, 23, 24, 49, 59, 74, 82, 83, 127,

Lightfoot and Co Ebbw Vale works	132
Lime Street London	131
Lion Cross	101
Little Crown, Pontnewydd	163, 164
Littlehales	39
Liverpool	131, 132
Llanarth Street, Pontymister	38
Llancayo	86, 230
Llanfrechfa	39, 141
Llangua Bridge	193
Llanhilleth	150
Llanhilleth Petty Sessions	57
Llanhilleth Railway Station	151
Llanover	141
Llantarnum Railway Statio	172
Llanyravon Farm	172
Llanyravon Mill	172
Llwydd Afon	128
Lodge, Jack	165
London	13,138, 191
Long Row Upper Race Pontypool No 2	188
Loveday Harold	188
Lovejoy, Molly (New Inn)	10
Lower Bridge Street No 18	216, 245
Lower Bridge Street	209
Lower Bridge Street, No16	213, 216
Lower Bridge Street, No18	213, 245
Lower Park Terrace	91
Lucas, Chief Constable, Major	12, 22,23,24,27,30,33,44,180

About the Author

Monty Dart is a writer, archivist and researcher. She was educated in Army Schools in Hong Kong, Germany and Wales. She is a researcher for HTV and BBC Wales and BBC radio on local subjects. She is the co-author (with William Cross) of 'A Beautiful Nuisance: The Life and Death of Hon. Gwyneth Ericka Morgan', published by Book Midden Publishing in 2012.

This book is published by William P Cross
Bookmidden Publishing
58 Sutton Road
Newport
Gwent
South Wales
NP19 7JF
United Kingdom

Other Titles from Book Midden Publishing

The Life and Secrets of Almina Carnarvon : A Candid Biography of Almina, 5th Countess of Carnarvon. 3rd Edition . ISBN 9781905914081

Lady Carnarvon's Nursing Homes: Nursing the Privileged in Wartime and Peace. ISBN 9781905914036

The Dustbin Case : Dennistoun versus Dennistoun ISBN 9781905914043

Lordy! Tutankhamun's Patron As A Young Man. ISBN 9781905914050

A Beautiful Nuisance by Monty Dart and William Cross. ISBN 9781905914104

Daphne's Story : The Long Journey from the Red Brick Building by Daphne Condon. ISBN 9781905914128

Steaming Light : by Bernard Pearson. ISBN 9781905914135

The Dancing Countess of Carnarvon: Tilly Losch & Her Husbands. By William Cross ISBN 9781905914098 [To be published 2013]

The Court Martial of Evan, Viscount Tredegar by Monty Dart and William Cross. ISBN 9781905914142 [To be published 10 December 2012]
Contact Book Midden by e-mail williecross@aol.com